Xiushi:
The Story of Lacquer

www.royalcollins.com

GREAT CHINESE INVENTIONS

Xiushi:
The Story of Lacquer

Edited by

Hua Jueming and Feng Lisheng

By Chang Bei

Translated by

Chen Wei and Pan Mengjie
(Jiangnan University)

RC

Books Beyond Boundaries

ROYAL COLLINS

Great Chinese Inventions:
Xiushi: The Story of Lacquer

Edited by Hua Jueming and Feng Lisheng
By Chang Bei
Translated by Chen Wei and Pan Mengjie (Jiangnan University)

Project Coordinator: Zhang Shaowen and Wang Xiaoyuan

First published in 2025 by Royal Collins Publishing Group Inc.
Groupe Publication Royal Collins Inc.
550-555 boul. René-Lévesque O Montréal (Québec) H2Z1B1 Canada

10 9 8 7 6 5 4 3 2 1

ISBN: 978-1-4878-1284-3

To find out more about our publications,
please visit www.royalcollins.com.

Contents

Preface

The "Four Great Inventions" of China have attracted significant attention from the Chinese people due to their profound impact on the course of modern world history. The term "Four Great Inventions" is widely known, but it originated from Western scholars. While this term holds classical significance, it carries a specific background and meaning. However, it fails to comprehensively reflect the significant inventions and technological cultural traditions of China. Throughout its five-thousand-year history of civilization, China's major inventions far exceed these four great inventions. Since the 20th century, especially in recent decades, China's science and technology have undergone rapid development, playing an increasingly important role in social and economic development. The question of what great inventions and creations exist in Chinese history has become a matter of concern not only for the academic community but also for the public. To answer this question truthfully, objectively, and scientifically, further exploration and sorting are needed based on the study of the history of science and technology in China. This involves selecting major inventions that are original, distinct in character, and have made outstanding contributions and significant impacts on both Chinese and world civilizations and discussing their background and evolutionary processes. To this end, we invited experts in the history of science and related fields to compile the book *Thirty Great Inventions of China*, which was published in May 2017. The book received praise from academia and readers, gaining widespread attention. It was awarded the 13th Wenjin Book Award and the National Excellent Popular Science Works Award by the Ministry of Science and Technology in 2018. It was also selected as one of the "Good Books of China" for 2017 and one of the "40 Most Influential Popular Science Books in China in 40 Years of Reform and Opening Up."

To further promote the research on the history of inventions in China and disseminate knowledge of Chinese science and technology culture, we have organized and compiled the Great Chinese Inventions series based on the book *Thirty Great Inventions of China*. The aim is to provide a more comprehensive and detailed exposition of the significance of major technological inventions in China, to understand their origins and developments, and to enable readers to better comprehend and appreciate the historical and modern value of important ancient Chinese technological inventions and creations. Each book in this series is relatively concise, focusing on knowledge dissemination with rich illustrations, aiming to allow readers to obtain relevant information and knowledge about each invention from the narratives of historians of science and technology in a relatively short period of time.

China boasts a profound history and culture, with the Chinese nation having made numerous great inventions and creations that not only propelled the advancement of Chinese civilization but also exerted significant influence on the progress of world civilization. Every Chinese individual should strive to understand history as accurately as possible. Chinese affairs should be clarified by the Chinese themselves, and Chinese people should have a say in matters of invention and creation. This series of books aims to embody the concept of cultural consciousness and comprehensively summarize the significant contributions of the Chinese nation to human technological civilization as much as possible. In the selection of great inventions, adjustments and expansions have been made, expanding the original thirty inventions to more than forty items, particularly adding significant inventions of modern and contemporary China. This series of books examines Chinese great inventions from both cultural tradition and a global perspective. For instance, Chinese characters and traditional Chinese cooking techniques were previously less regarded as major inventions. Still, they serve as important symbols of Chinese civilization and hold significant positions in Chinese cultural and technological traditions, qualifying as great Chinese inventions. Particularly, Chinese characters, as tools for recording information and expressing thoughts for Chinese people, remain vibrant to this day. They not only play an irreplaceable role in the formation, dissemination, and inheritance of Chinese culture but also have had a significant influence on neighboring countries and regions such as Japan, Korea, and Vietnam. Traditional Chinese cooking techniques have played a crucial role in improving the quality of people's lives and enhancing physical health. With the strengthening of China's comprehensive national strength and international influence, Chinese cooking techniques have spread to various parts of the world and are playing an increasingly important role. Traditional Chinese medicine also embodies some pioneering achievements in modern science and technology, such as the practice of variolation, which is a pioneering immunological achievement with global impact.

We also pay attention to significant inventions in modern and contemporary China. For example, Tu Youyou, representing a group of Chinese scientists, extracted artemisinin, a highly effective and low-toxicity antimalarial drug, based on the inheritance of traditional clinical experience in Chinese medicine and the application of modern scientific methods. After its clinical application, artemisinin has saved the lives of thousands of patients, making a tremendous contribution to human health. Rice is one of the world's major food crops, serving as the staple food for about half the global population. The super hybrid rice cultivation technology invented by Yuan Longping is considered a world-class original and significant invention. Hanzi laser typesetting technology, founded by Wang Xuan, is a great invention in the history of modern printing technology in China. It has played an important role in promoting the dissemination of science and culture. Cultural consciousness is a challenging process. On one hand, we need to understand our technological and cultural traditions to enhance cultural identity and confidence. On the other hand, we need to update and transform our cultural traditions and technology, integrating traditional techniques with modern and foreign technologies and enabling modern technology to take root and develop vigorously in China.

Invention and discovery are inherent drivers of the development of human social civilization. Ancient Chinese science and technology have achieved remarkable success, with our ancestors making significant contributions to the progress of world civilization. Over the past century, China has undergone drastic social changes and cultural transformations, so it is understandable that there haven't been many great inventions and creations during this time. While cherishing and valuing our national cultural traditions and historical experiences, we should also take the initiative in cultural transformation and technological development, continuously enhancing our capacity for independent innovation and making greater contributions to the development of human technology and civilization. Looking at the long-term trend of historical development, Chinese science and technology have entered a new period of accelerated development. The innovation consciousness and capability of the Chinese people have been activated, and we can expect more and more original inventions and creations in the future. The prosperity of Chinese science and technology is something to look forward to.

The question of how many great inventions there have been in Chinese history is subjective, and opinions or disputes are inevitable. We hope that the publication of this series of books will attract more attention and participation from experts and readers, stimulating further discussion and exchanges and contributing to the improvement of related research. We also welcome corrections and feedback from colleagues in the academic community and readers on our work.

Hua Jueming and Feng Lisheng

July 28, 2021

What Is *Xiushi*?

The term "髹饰" (*xiushi*) has been alive for over two thousand years in the history of Chinese civilization. As a creative craftsmanship, it is closely related to people's lives. The term "髹" (xiū) (ancient characters include "髤" and "髹") refers to the action of using a brush with a wooden handle to dip in lacquer and apply it to objects. It encompasses the surface coating of all objects and gradually evolved into the phono-semantic character "髹." "饰" (shì) means decoration. The compound term "髹饰" points to decorative painting with artistic designs. *Xiushi Lu* (*Record of Xiushi*) includes the application of natural lacquer to tools and the decoration of various artistic techniques such as painting, carving, filling, covering, polishing, hooking, pasting, sculpting, inlaying, embedding, and more into the category of *xiushi*. Workers may not necessarily use brushes; some use knives, while others use brushes. By now, readers generally understand that *xiushi* has been widely seen in people's lives throughout history, transforming craftsmanship into an artistic activity. *Xiushi* primarily refers to the craftsmanship of manufacturing lacquerware.

So, what is lacquerware? Lacquerware is a handmade craftsmanship that involves applying natural lacquer and decorating it using various artistic techniques such as painting, carving, filling, covering, polishing, hooking, sculpting, inlaying, pasting, and embedding. In the history of world civilization, there is ongoing debate about which ancient civilization invented various craftsmanship such as stone tool making, pottery firing, and metal casting. However, it is widely acknowledged worldwide that the ancient Chinese people were the first to use lacquer and pioneered the craftsmanship of *xiushi*. Lacquerware, like Chinese ceramics and silk, enjoys a highly esteemed reputation globally. In modern times, the art of lacquer rooted in traditional craftsmanship of *xiushi*—including lacquerware, lacquer painting, lacquer sculpture, and more—is collectively referred to as "lacquer art." This book tells stories from the history of the craftsmanship *xiushi*.

CHAPTER I

Lacquer Discovered

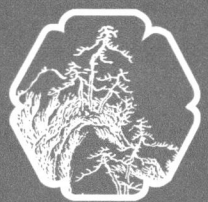

As early as the early Neolithic period, Chinese ancestors discovered that lacquer tree sap had strong adhesive properties (Figure 1.1). It could be used for bonding and reinforcement of wooden tools and implements. It left behind a dense, waterproof, durable, and glossy protective film when applied to wooden or ceramic objects. Wooden and ceramic items no longer leaked, making them easier to clean and extending their lifespan. An example is the Lacquered Wooden Bow (Figure 1.2) unearthed from the Kuahuqiao site in Xiaoshan District, Hangzhou, Zhejiang, dating back approximately 8,000 years. Measuring 121 centimeters, the bow was coated with natural lacquer on mulberry wood. Similarly, artifacts such as lacquered

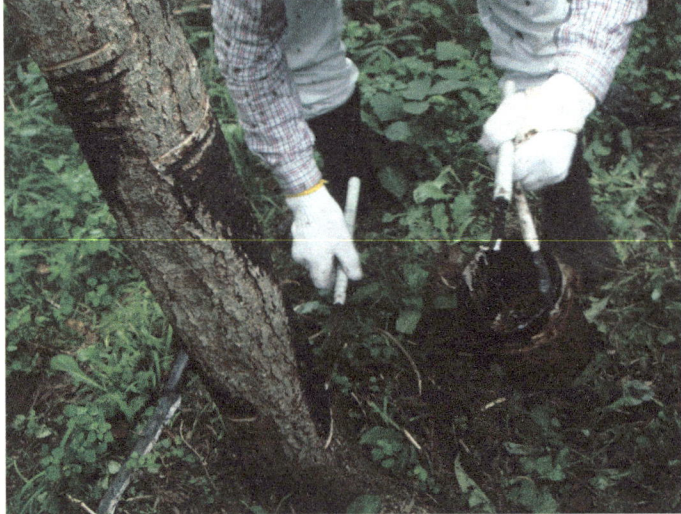

Figure 1.1 The collection of lacquer tree sap in the deep mountain forest, provided by Yu Zheng

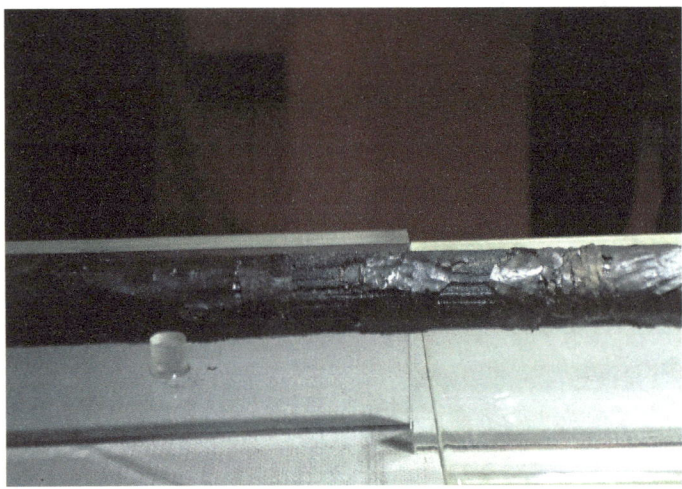

Figure 1.2 [Neolithic] Lacquered Wooden Bow, photographed by the author at the Kuahuqiao Site Museum in Xiaoshan, Hangzhou, Zhejiang

wooden bowls, bamboo-wrapped lacquered wooden buckets, lacquered wooden vessels with painted butterfly patterns, and black lacquered wooden cylinders were unearthed from the Hemudu site in Yuyao, Zhejiang, dating back around 7,000 years. It is evident that as early as the early Neolithic period, the ancestors downstream of the Yangtze River discovered natural lacquer and began the craftsmanship of applying natural lacquer to objects.

The discovery of natural lacquer initially involved simple coating on wooden and ceramic objects. "Yao abdicated in favor of Shun, who, upon acceptance, crafted a utensil. He felled mountain trees, processed them into shape, underwent cutting, sawing, and refining, and then applied flowing lacquer and ink on them. It was sent to the palace for use as a utensil. However, the feudal lords deemed it extravagant, and thirteen countries opposed it. Later, Shun abdicated in favor of Yu, who crafted a sacrificial vessel. The exterior was dyed with ink, and the interior was painted vermilion ... This was even more extravagant, leading to the opposition of thirty-three countries." (*Han Feizi · Ten Faults*) Archaeological evidence shows that the ancient ancestors discovered the use of crushed black magnetite (Fe_3O_4) and red hematite (Fe_2O_3) mixed with lacquer during the remote ages. Therefore, during the time of Shun, utensils appeared black, while during the time of Yu, sacrificial vessels appeared in both vermilion and black. Why would rudimentary lacquered objects provoke complaints? Because the material life of prehistoric ancestors was extremely impoverished, as seen in the time of Yao when "not trimming the thatched roof covering during construction, nor cutting down the wood used for building house beams" (*Han Feizi · Five Pests*), and in the time of Yu when "using the plow and hoe as farming tools, personally leading the way in cultivating for the people, with thighs lacking muscles, and shins not growing hair" (*Han Feizi · Five Pests*), clay was abundant, and the pottery-making process was simple, while lacquer, resembling drops of gold, involved a complex lacquering process. The use of lacquered objects was naturally considered extravagant. The practice of using raw lacquer for simple coatings on utensils persisted until the Warring States period (Figure 1.3) and even continued in certain ethnic minority areas.

Based on the material properties of natural lacquer tree sap, Chinese ancestors designated lacquer tree sap as "漆" (qī). Its structure includes the character for "wood" above, indicating it comes from the lacquer tree, with a left-slant and right-downward stroke, resembling the incision on a lacquer tree, and the radical for "water" below. *Shuowen Jiezi* (*Explaining Simple and Analyzing Compound Characters*) states: "桼, wood sap, can be used for lacquering objects, pictograph; 桼 is like water droplets

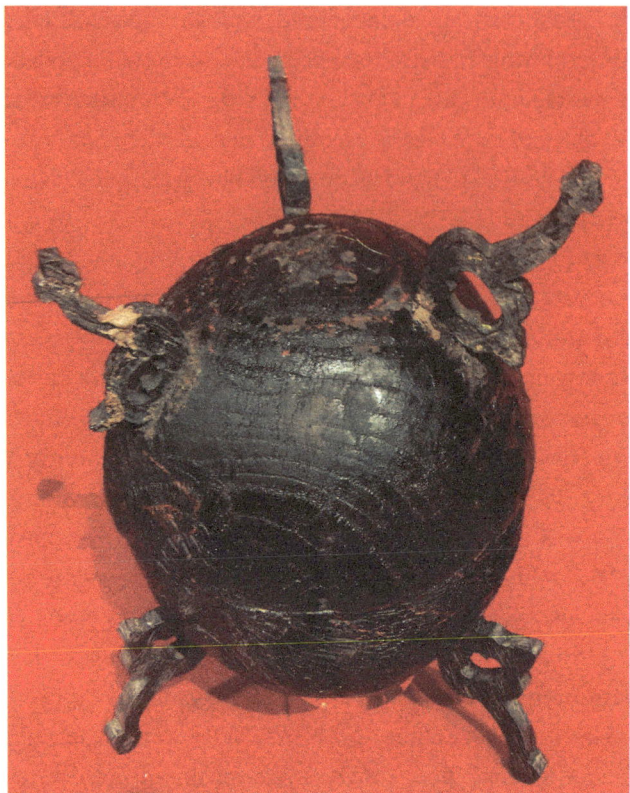

Figure 1.3 [Warring States] Wooden Combs Coated with Raw
Lacquer, photographed by the author at the "Exhibition of Chu
Tomb Cultural Relics at Jiuliandun in Zaoyang, Hubei" in 2011

falling down."[1] It can be seen that "桼," as a pictographic character, represents the
tree sap flowing down from a lacquer tree. In the continuous evolution of Chinese
characters, "桼" acquired the "氵" radical and became a phono-semantic character "
漆" (qī). However, its designation as the specific term for natural lacquer tree sap did
not change, and it is affectionately referred to by the Chinese as "国漆" (guó qī) or "大
漆" (dà qī). In the industrial age, chemical coatings have impacted natural lacquer, but
the aesthetic difference between their coatings and those of natural lacquer is stark.
Those familiar with lacquerware can easily distinguish between chemical coatings
and natural lacquer.

---

1. [Han] Xu Shen, *Shuowen Jiezi* (*Explaining Simple and Analyzing Compound Characters*)
   (Zhonghua Book Company, 1963), 128.

The tree sap extracted from the lacquer tree is called "raw lacquer," which has a high water content and contains impurities. Its molecular structure is loose, has high viscosity and quick drying, and cannot be applied thickly. The coating is rough and lacking in leveling and gloss. Lacquer workers describe raw lacquer as "only scraping, not brushing." As a result, the ancient people invented methods such as sun-drying and boiling to refine raw lacquer into refined lacquer (Figure 1.4). This was done to slow down its drying properties and achieve a smooth and leveled coating. Subsequently, they discovered that incorporating refined drying plant oils, such

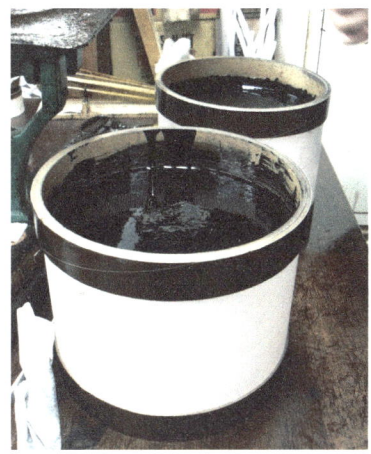

Figure 1.4 Refined lacquer, photographed by the author

as boiled tung oil, into the lacquer improved the brightness of the coating. When did the ancient people start refining lacquer? It is known from historical records that terms like "明膏" (bright paste), "膏漆" (paste lacquer), "合光" (combine brightness), and "晒光漆" (sun-dried bright lacquer) were recorded as late as the Ming Dynasty. From the analysis of the wooden artifacts in the Qin and Han periods that used refined lacquer coatings, it is evident that lacquer refining activities existed during the Qin and Han periods. Applying raw lacquer coating does not require a shaded room, while applying refined lacquer coating requires a shaded room, and the need for shaded rooms in the lacquering process is mentioned in *Shiji · Huaji Liezhuan* (*Records of the Grand Historian · Biographies of Humorous Characters*), where You Zhan talks about the difficulty of providing shaded rooms.[2] The refining of drying plant oils by the ancient people likely followed the refinement of raw lacquer. Records

---

2. *Shiji · Huaji Liezhuan (Records of the Grand Historian · Biographies of Humorous Characters)*, vol. 10 (Zhonghua Book Company, 1982, 3203. "The Second Emperor (of Qin Dynasty) wanted to lacquer the city again. You Zhan said, 'Good ... Although lacquering the city causes distress and expenses for the people, it is excellent! Lacquered walls are smooth, and enemies cannot climb. If you want to do it, it's easy to lacquer but difficult to create shaded chambers.' So, the Second Emperor laughed at this and stopped his plan." This passage describes Hu Hai's intention to lacquer the entire city wall. You Zhan initially praises the idea, pointing out that lacquered walls would prevent enemies from climbing. However, he cleverly raises the issue of creating shaded chambers within the lacquered walls, making the plan impractical. The story unintentionally records a historical fact: refined lacquer had been developed during the time of the Second Emperor of the Qin Dynasty. Unlike natural lacquer used for coating, refined lacquer requires the addition of shaded chambers to facilitate the drying of the coating.

in the book *Mingyi Bielu* (*Separate Record of Famous Physicians*) by Tao Hongjing from the Qi and Liang dynasties state, "Use the seeds of perilla to make oil, fry it daily; this is what is used for oil-paper and mixed lacquer today." Additionally, the Northern Qi Dynasty's *Yanshi Jiaxun* (*Yan Family Instructions*) has a sentence, "Fry walnut oil and refine tin into silver."[3] Lacquer coatings with added oil were used in the Warring States period, resulting in a glossy surface (Figure 1.5).

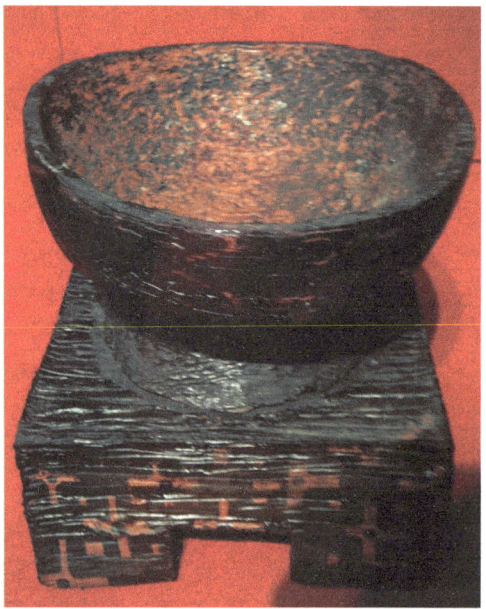

Figure 1.5 [Warring States] The lacquer-coated wooden tray with oil blending radiates a glossy shine, photographed by the author at the "Exhibition of Chu Tomb Cultural Relics at Jiuliandun in Zaoyang, Hubei" in 2011

---

3. The first part is from the revised edition of *Zhiwuming Shitukao Changbian* (*Illustrated Study of Plant Names and Realities*) by Wu Qijun from the Qing Dynasty (The Commercial Press, 1959), 676. The second part is from *Shengshi Dishier* (*Thrift: Chapter Twelve*), vol. 5 of *Yanshi Jiaxun* (*Yan Family Instructions*) by Yan Zhitui from Northern Qi, bk. 1121 of *Xuxiu Siku Quanshu* (*Continuation of the Complete Library in Four Branches*) (Shanghai Classics Publishing House, 2002), 643.

CHAPTER II

Lacquer Garden of Zhuangzi

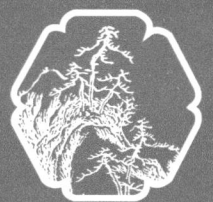

Once the bonding ability, protective function, and decorative effects of natural lacquer were discovered by our ancestors, lacquer became an indispensable material in the daily lives of ancient Chinese people. In the self-sufficient agricultural society of China that lasted for thousands of years, whether it was clothing, food, shelter, transportation, weddings, funerals, or other aspects such as bridal sedan chairs and burial coffins, musical instruments, weapons, utensils, and furniture, none of them could do without *xiushi*. With the increasing demand for lacquer tree sap, wild lacquer trees evolved into cultivated varieties. During the Spring and Autumn period, *Shangshu · Yugong* (*Book of Documents · Biography of Yugong*) recorded the tribute of lacquer silk from Yanzhou and the tribute of lacquer, cypress, and hemp from Yuzhou.[1] In *Shijing · Tangfeng* (*Book of Songs · Tang Feng*), a verse says, "There are lacquer trees on the mountain and chestnut trees by the water. You have wine and food; why not play the zither every day?" This vividly records that in the socio-economic structure of a small agricultural society, as long as people planted enough lacquer trees and grains, they could live carefree lives. In the Spring and Autumn period, the classic work *Kaogong Ji* (*Record of Crafts*) documented various craftsmen, such as woodworkers and metalworkers. Still, it did not specifically list lacquer workers as a distinct profession. This is not because the ancestors of the Zhou Dynasty did not value the craftsmanship of *xiushi*; on the contrary, due to the widespread use of *xiushi* in tools made of wood, bamboo, leather, and other materials, *xiushi* was considered a fundamental skill that all craftsmen must master. Therefore, it was not listed as a separate profession. In the opening of *Kaogong Ji*, about one-third of the text is dedicated to the detailed description of the construction of "carriages," highlighting the Confucian concept of ritual governance in the Eastern Zhou period. The term *xiushi* first appeared in the records of the chariot system in the *Zhouli* (*Rites of Zhou*).[2] The luxuriousness of the "carriages" of various vassals in the Eastern Zhou period is evident from the chariot unearthed from the Ma family mound in Gansu Province dating back to the Warring States period.

Due to the significant role of natural lacquer in the economic life of the ancient people, officials were appointed to manage lacquer gardens throughout various

---

1. Zang Kehe, *Shangshu Wenzizu Jiaogu* (*An Exegesis of the Texts of the Book of Documents*) (Shanghai Education Press, 1999), 103, 113.

2. The term "髹饰" is found in the *Zhouli · Chunguan · Mangche* (*The Rites of Zhou · Spring Official · Mang Chariot*). Quoted from *Zhouli Zhushu* (*Commentaries and Annotations on the Rites of Zhou*), bk. 90 of *Wenyuange Siku Quanshu* (*Complete Library in Four Branches of Literature from the Wenyuange*) (Commercial Press, Taiwan, 1986), 504.

dynasties. During the Warring States period, Zhuangzi is said to have served as an official in a lacquer garden.[3] Legend has it that King Wei of Chu once offered a generous reward to invite Zhuangzi to be his prime minister. However, Zhuangzi, in response to the messenger, said, "You quickly leave, don't defile me. I would rather wander and enjoy myself in filth than be constrained by those who govern a country." (*Records of the Grand Historian · Biography of Laozi and Han Fei*) He preferred to "freely roam in thought to the early stages of the formation of things" in the lacquer garden (*Zhuangzi · Outer Chapters · Tian Zifang*), engaging in free philosophical contemplation. Zhuangzi's story of defiantly rejecting the offer from kings and finding solace in the lacquer garden became legendary, and he became a founding figure of Daoist philosophy. The term "lacquer garden" subsequently became a symbol of the reclusive sentiments of literati. During the Western Han Dynasty, the economic status of lacquer trees was further elevated. "Shandong was rich in fish, salt, lacquer, silk, and various forms of entertainment," a record stating, "In the region of Chenxia, there were about 666,670 square meters of lacquer trees ... Those engaged in the lacquer industry were equivalent to the ranks of thousand-holding marquises ... Lacquered wooden articles numbered a thousand pieces ... Lacquer production amounted to about 6,250 kilograms. Such wealth levels even surpassed those of households with a thousand chariots."[4] Individuals who planted about 666,670 square meters of lacquer trees and harvested about 6,250 kilograms of lacquer sap were wealthier than marquises, equivalent to possessing a military force of a thousand chariots. In the Eastern Jin Dynasty, Guo Pu wrote the poem *Youxianshi* (*Wandering among the Immortals*), praising "the proud official in the lacquer garden." During the Tang Dynasty, Wang Wei secluded himself in Wangchuan of Lantian. In his renowned poetry collection *Wangchuan Ji* (*The Collection of Wangchuan*), there is a poem titled *Qiyuan* (*The Lacquer Garden*), "Ancient people weren't all proud officials, they too faced worldly affairs. I've been given a humble position by chance; quietly among a few trees, I muse." Since then, poets of various dynasties have praised the lacquer garden, and painters throughout the ages depicted it. In the Song Dynasty, Zhu Xi wrote *Yun Gu Er Shi Liu Yong* (*Twenty-Six Songs of the Cloud Valley*), and

---

3. [Han] Sima Qian, *Shiji · Laozi Hanfei Liezhuan* (*Records of the Grand Historian · Biographies of Laozi and Han Fei*), vol. 7 (Zhonghua Book Company, 1982), 2143. The name of the place "漆园" (Lacquer Garden) is mentioned in different contexts in the *Dictionary of Ancient and Modern Place Names*. Zhuangzi, who was from the Song State, worked at a "漆园," which should be in one of the three locations, northeast of Shangqiu County in Henan.

4. [Han] Sima Qian, *Shiji · Huozhi Liezhuan* (*Records of the Grand Historian · Records of Merchants*), vol. 10 (Zhonghua Book Company, 1982), 3253, 3272, 3274.

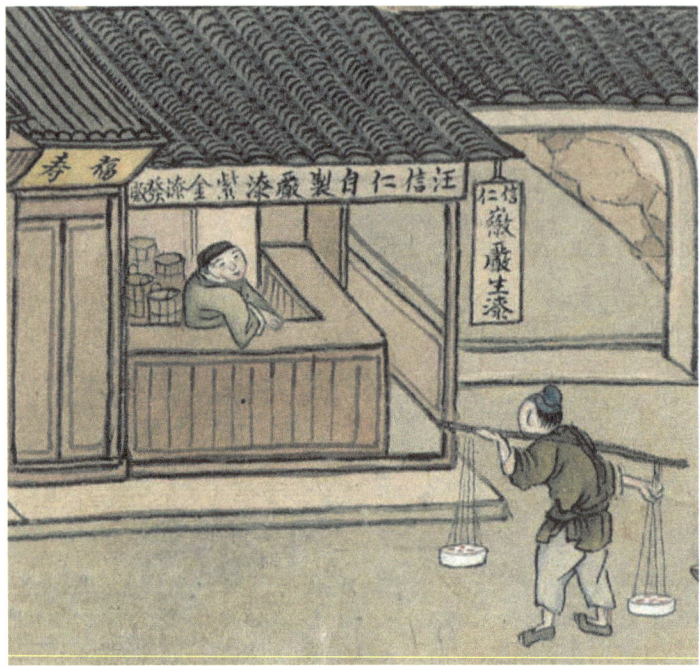

Figure 2.1 Store selling Yansheng Lacquer as depicted in the painting by Qiu Ying from the Ming Dynasty, provided by Gao Zuoxian

in its twenty-first poem, *Qiyuan* (*The Lacquer Garden*), he expressed, "Heard of the immortal of South China, once served as an official in the lacquer garden. Should have realized how to cut away worries, yet in the end, it all vanished into emptiness." All these reflect the reminiscence of Zhuangzi and the yearning for seclusion. During the Ming and Qing dynasties, the literati immersed in the climax of popular culture did not forget to sing praises for the lacquer garden. The eminent collector Xiang Yuanbian called himself "a proud official of the lacquer garden." The painter Qiu Ying, who resided in his residence, also greatly admired the lacquer garden. He painted the storefront of Yansheng Lacquer,[5] shown in Figure 2.1. He depicted *Wangchuan Tu* (*Wangchuan Picture*) in Figure 2.2, where the Lacquer Garden, protected by a railing, stands out prominently. Qiu Ying's attention to the lacquer garden and the lacquer economy is not only due to his professional habits developed from being "initially a lacquer worker, also engaged in the colorful painting of buildings" (Zhang Chao, *Yuchu Xinzhi*, vol. 8), but also to cater to the preferences of the literati in the Ming Dynasty, who embraced refinement in the mundane, and the citizens who blended the mundane with sophistication.

---

5. Yansheng Lacquer refers to good raw lacquer that has been purified by removing impurities and filtering.

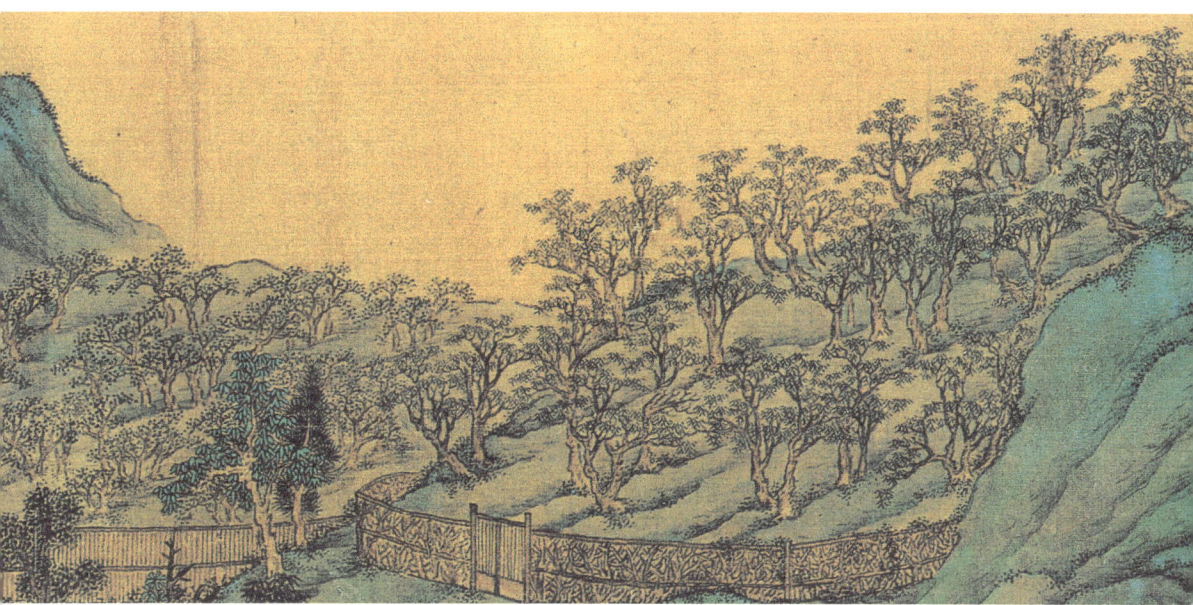

Figure 2.2 Lacquer garden depicted in Qiu Ying's *Wangchuan Tu* (*Wangchuan Picture*) from the Ming Dynasty, provided by Gao Zuoxian

CHAPTER III

Everything Can Be Lacquered

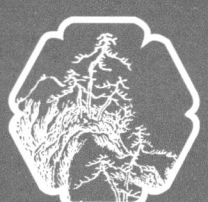

The Warring States, Qin, and Han periods marked the first peak of *xiushi* craftsmanship in China. During the Warring States period, the state of Chu, located in the middle and lower reaches of the Yangtze River, was rich in wood and lacquer production. The humid and hot climate was conducive to the drying of lacquer, leading to a particularly advanced development of *xiushi* craftsmanship. Numerous lacquered artifacts were unearthed in locations such as Jiuliandun in Zaoyang City, Baoshan in Jingmen City, Wangshan and Tianxingguan Chu tombs in Jiangling County of Jingzhou City, as well as in Changsha, Hunan, and Xinyang, Henan. If lacquered artifacts during this period tended to emphasize practicality, Chu's lacquered items notably manifested a sacrificial atmosphere and aesthetic function. Many Chu tombs yielded lacquered items like the Tiger-Seat Bird-Stand Drum (Figure 3.1), where the drum stand features a phoenix with wings

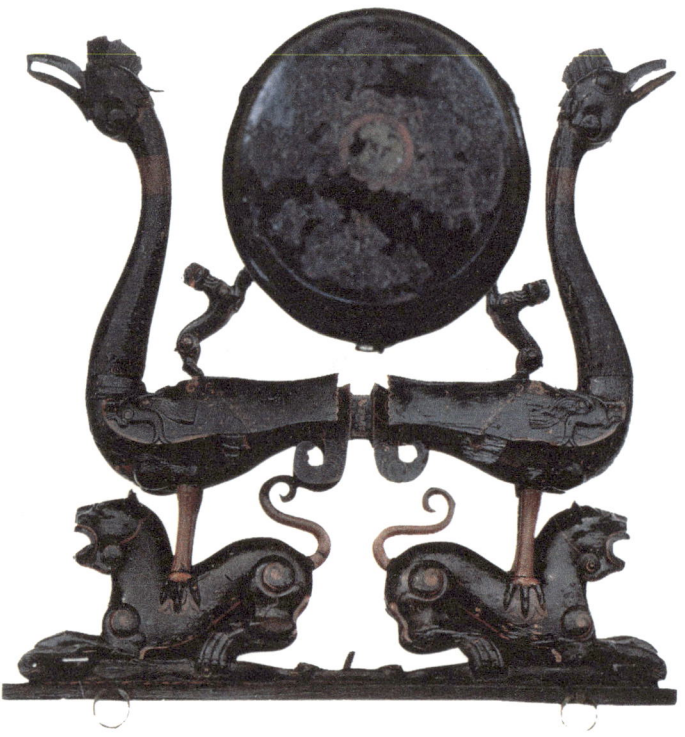

Figure 3.1 [Warring States] Lacquered Tiger-Seat Bird-Stand Drum, unearthed from the Chu Tomb in Jiangling, selected from the book *Chutu Baoshui Zhumu Qiqi Tuoshui Baohu Jishu* (*Dehydration Protection Techniques for Excavated Saturated Bamboo, Wood, and Lacquer Objects*) by Chen Zhongxing, Cheng Lizhen, and Li Lan

and a tiger as the base. The tiger is sturdy and burdened, while the phoenix is tall and majestic, singing with a high pitch. This illustrates the Chu people's reverence for the phoenix and the symbolic significance of the phoenix as a totem. In 1978, the tomb of Marquis Yi of Zeng in Sui County, Hubei, unearthed a total of 124 lacquered musical instruments and bases, including *sheng* (a Chinese mouth-blown free reed instrument), drum, *qin* (a seven-stringed Chinese musical instrument of the zither family), *se* (a Chinese plucked zither similar to the guzheng but with a larger resonator), pan flute, bamboo flute, *bianzhong* (an ancient Chinese musical instrument consisting of a set of bronze bells played melodically) frame, and *bianqing* (an ancient Chinese musical instrument consisting of a set of stone chimes played melodically) frame. These items could furnish a large ancient music hall, serving as a concentrated expression of Chu's sacrificial traditions. In 2002, the Chu tomb in Jiuliandun, Zaoyang City, Hubei, yielded nearly a thousand lacquered artifacts, surpassing the cumulative total of lacquered items unearthed in the Jingchu region before that. In this collection of lacquered wooden artifacts, we can observe the ancestral exploration from using raw lacquer coating (such as lacquered wooden dun and lacquered wooden square mirror) to employing lacquer mixed with oil (as seen in lacquered wooden gui and lacquered wooden square box), and further to using polished lacquer coating (as seen in lacquered wooden reclining deer and lacquered wooden dragon-snake pedestal bean). Additionally, the artifacts exhibit the use of copper buttons and decoration with gilded and silvered pieces (Figure 3.2). In 2000, the No. 2 tomb of Chu State at Tianxingguan in Jiangling revealed a new peak in the craftsmanship of lacquered wooden artifacts. For instance, a lacquered wooden wine vessel in the shape of a pig was unearthed (Figure 3.3). Inside the box

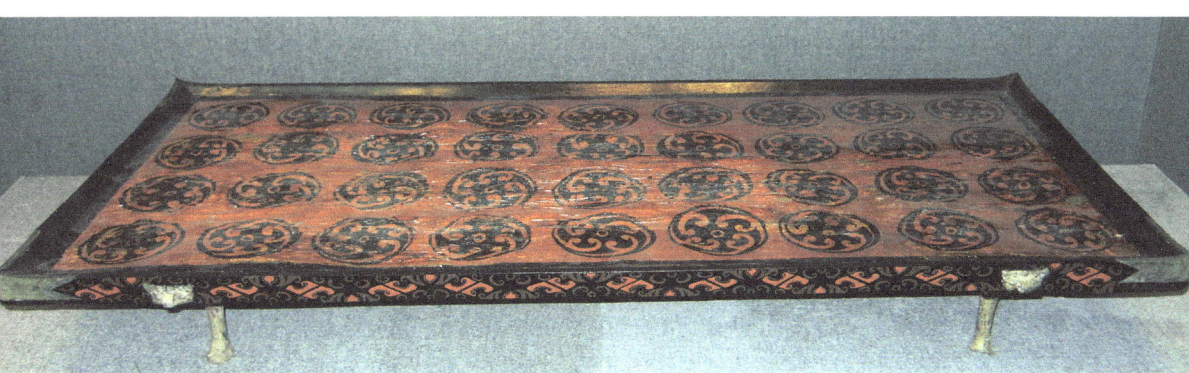

Figure 3.2 [Warring States] Painted Bronze Button with Lacquered Wood Design, photographed by the author at the "Exhibition of Chu Tomb Cultural Relics at Jiuliandun in Zaoyang, Hubei"

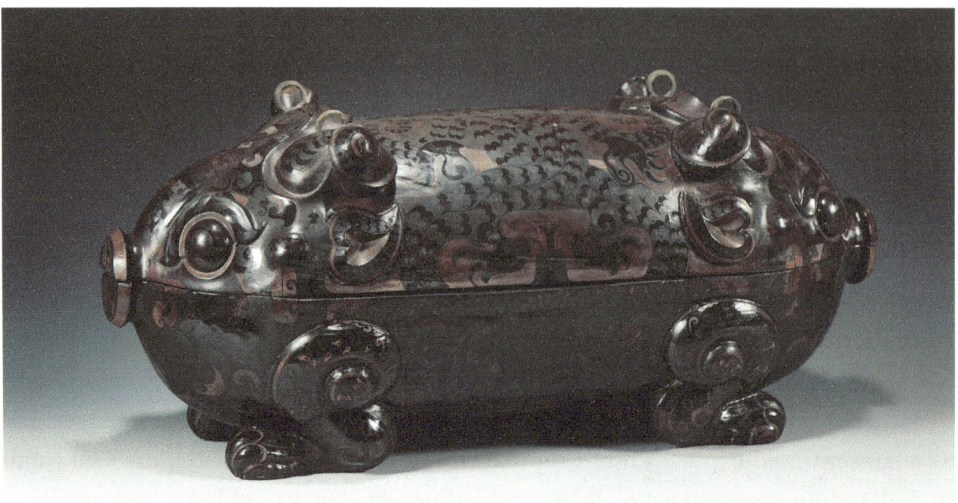

Figure 3.3 [Warring States] Pig-Shaped Lacquered Wooden Liquor Container, unearthed from the No. 2 Tomb at Tianxingguan, provided by Liu Lu of the Jingzhou Museum

are cups with attached ears, and the pig-shaped carving exudes vitality. The outer walls are covered with a rough red lacquer layer adorned with hidden flower dragon patterns. The formation of hidden flowers suggests that after the polished lacquer flower painting had dried, it underwent a grinding process. On top of the hidden flowers are bright and shiny flowers painted in black lacquer. The dragon pattern depicts scales, and outside the dragon, there are cloud patterns, clearly requiring the use of finely filtered polished lacquer. Next to the mouths of the twin pigs, there are four grape-sized cheek flesh areas, each with three or four grouped figures dressed in clothing. The meticulous grinding, delicate polishing, and exquisite depiction of these details are all truly astonishing. The lacquered sculptures unearthed from this tomb, such as the painted standing feathered figure, the phoenix-shaped lotus bean, and the black lacquer table with a dragon head, are all carved with vibrant energy. The artistic expressions in Chu's lacquer-decorated items are filled with imaginative ideas and romantic flavors, becoming the most powerful expression of life's rhythm in the history of Chinese *xiushi* craftsmanship. From using raw lacquer coating to mastering lacquer mixed with oil and polished lacquer coating techniques, constant exploration in craftsmanship led to the invention of new techniques such as incising, metal buttons, and gilded and silvered pieces, thereby initiating the heyday of *xiushi* craftsmanship in the Han Dynasty. From this point onward, an era primarily focused on lacquering for sacrificial rites concluded, and an era centered around lacquering for daily use emerged. Polished lacquer coating became the primary *xiushi* technique for Han Dynasty lacquerware, with painting, incising, metal buttons, and gilded and silvered decorations becoming the main forms of embellishment. Almost every type of item, including furniture, cooking utensils, tableware, weapons, musical instruments, stationery, toys, funeral objects, and transportation tools, underwent lacquering during the Han Dynasty. Lacquered items made of materials such as wood, leather, bamboo, rattan, and fabric, appreciated for their lightweight, beauty, and durability, became widespread in the daily lives of the aristocracy.

In 1972, multiple lacquered coffins were unearthed from the No. 1 Tomb of Han State in Mawangdui, Changsha, Hunan. Except for the outer coffin with a plain black lacquer surface, the three inner lacquered coffins were adorned with captivating paintings using oil paint. The outer coffin, measuring 256 centimeters in length, featured vivid depictions of feathered figures and mythical creatures painted with various colors such as red, white, yellow, black, gold, green, and gray. These figures raced and chased amidst the clouds, where the cloud patterns resembled hanging cliffs and cascading waterfalls at times and tumultuous waves at others. The brush strokes, at times slow, caused the paint to gather like powder heaps, while swift strokes resulted in the paint extending beyond the borders. The feathered figures and mythical creatures displayed various activities—running, chasing, descending with waterfall-like clouds, ascending with surging waves, holding bamboo poles horizontally as if taming sea monsters, sitting thoughtfully with hands on knees—portraying a myriad of postures, all vibrant and lifelike. The lacquer paintings on the black lacquered wooden coffin from the Mawangdui tomb (Figure 3.4) conveyed the vigorous life force of the people during the Han Dynasty, reflecting the expansive spirit of Han Dynasty painting. The middle-lacquered coffin, adorned with vermilion lacquer, featured various paintings in multiple colors, including green, pink-brown, reddish-brown, and white. The lid depicted dragons and tigers traversing; the headboard portrayed mountain peaks with deer; the footboard displayed twin dragons penetrating walls; the left side panel illustrated tigers, phoenixes, and strongmen climbing and stepping on the colossal body of a dragon; the right-side panel depicted cloud patterns, and the edges featured geometric patterns, creating a harmonious and bright color scheme. The inner lacquered coffin, also in vermilion lacquer, had bird feathers attached in a diamond pattern, surrounded by brown velvet with pasted flower branch patterns. In 2009, the tomb of Liu Fei, the King of Jiangdu in Dayun Mountain, Xuyi, revealed a "gold and jade inlaid black lacquered wooden coffin" (Figure 3.5). The coffin body and lid were bordered with copper buttons, adorned with 30 copper hanging loops, and embellished with ten pieces of jade discs, *bi* discs, and *hu* discs. The inner wall was

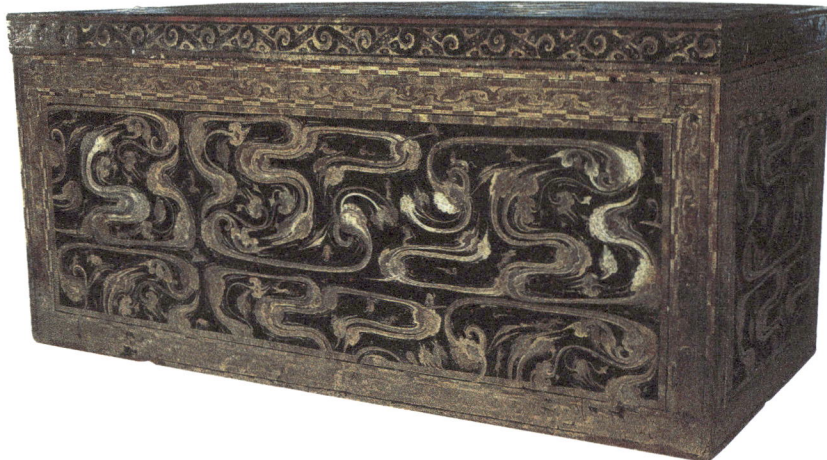

Figure 3.4 [Western Han] Lacquered Wooden Coffin with Painted Decoration, unearthed from the No. 1 Tomb of Han State in Mawangdui, selected from the book of Wang Shixiang, *Zhongguo Gudai Qiqi* (*Ancient Chinese Lacquerware*)

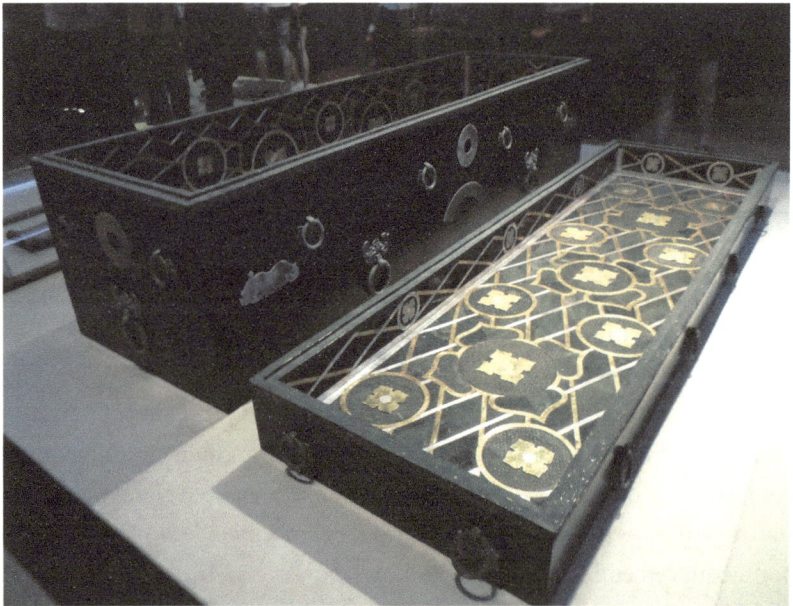

Figure 3.5 [Western Han] Black Lacquered Wooden Coffin with Inlaid Gold and Jade (replica), unearthed from the tomb of Liu Fei on Dayun Mountain, photographed by the author at the Nanjing Museum

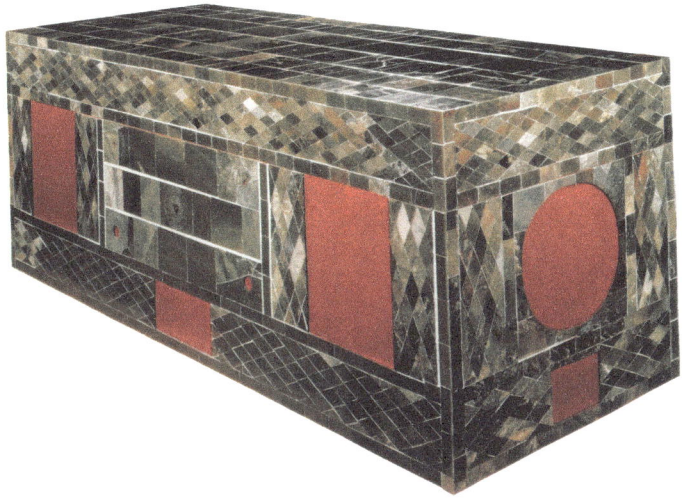

Figure 3.6 [Western Han] Lacquered Wooden Coffin with Jade Inlay (replica), unearthed from the tomb of Liu Wu on Shizishan, selected from the book *Shizishan Chuwangling* (*The Tomb of Emperor Chu in Shizishan*), complied by Han Cultural Scenic Area of Xuzhou and Han Terracotta Warriors Museum of the Mausoleum of Emperor Chu in Xuzhou

covered with gold and silver pieces arranged in diagonal grid patterns and various-sized persimmon patterns, exhibiting exquisite luxury beyond compare. Another discovery in the tomb of Liu Wu, a royal member and Chu Emperor, in Shizishan, Xuzhou, during the Western Han period was a "lacquered wooden coffin with jade inlay" (Figure 3.6) featuring more than 2000 geometrically shaped jade pieces.[1]

It is noteworthy that lacquered wooden items in the early Han period were not referred to as "lacquerware." The burial register of Mawangdui Han tomb designated them as "wood items with lacquer,"[2] and in *Hanshu · Huozhi Zhuan* (*Book of Han · Records of Merchants*), they were noted as "a thousand pieces of wooden items with lacquer." During the Western Han period, official lacquerware workshops (Figure 3.7) were established in cities like Chengdu and Guanghan. *Hanshu · Gongyu Zhuan* (*Book of Han · Biography of Gongyu*) quotes Ruchun from the Three Kingdoms period,

1. The Archaeological Excavation Team of the Tomb of Emperor Chu in Shizishan, "Brief Report on the Excavation of the Tomb of Emperor Chu in Shizishan, Xuzhou," *Cultural Relics*, no. 8 (1998); Han Cultural Scenic Area of Xuzhou and Han Terracotta Warriors Museum of the Mausoleum of Emperor Chu in Xuzhou, eds., *Shizishan Chuwangling* (*The Tomb of Emperor Chu in Shizishan*) (Nanjing Publishing House, 2011).
2. [Han] Sima Qian, *Shiji · Huozhi Liezhuan* (*Records of the Grand Historian · Records of Merchants*), vol. 10 (Zhonghua Book Company, 1982), 3274.

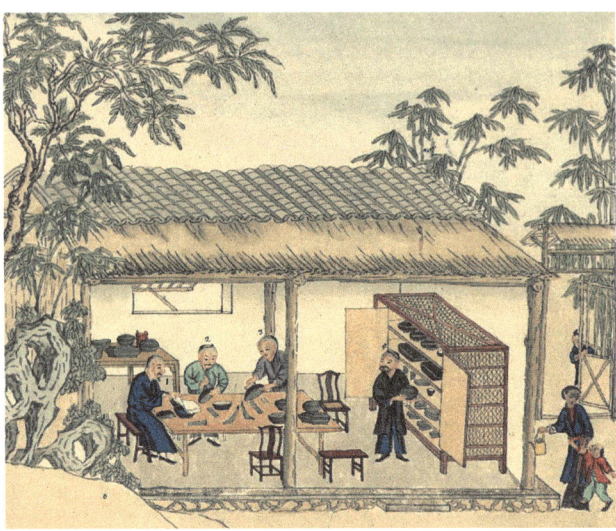

Figure 3.7 Handicraft workshop for manufacturing lacquerware, selected from *Zhonguo Zhiqi Tupu* (*Illustrated Atlas of Lacquer Making in China*)

stating, "*Dili Zhi* (*Geography Record*) mentions that Huai and Shu commanderies, Chengdu, and Guanghan all have official workshops. The official workshops are in charge of making lacquerware."[3] At this point, the name "lacquerware" begins to appear. The official workshops were known for creating lavish lacquerware, with descriptions such as "the rich had silver-mouthed and yellow-eared vessels, gold leopards and jade bells; the average had jade-threaded vessels and gold-inlaid Shu cups" and "a single cup required the labor of a hundred people, and a screen could involve the efforts of ten thousand people."[4] In AD 106, Emperor He passed away, and Empress Dowager Deng issued an order stating, "The buttons and knives from Shu and Han commanderies are no longer needed. Only thirty-nine types of paintings will be retained. Additionally, items such as woven fabrics, embroidered silk, ice-textured fabrics, gold and silver, pearls and jade, rhinoceros' horn and elephant ivory, tortoiseshell, and carved and perforated ornaments will all be discontinued."[5] With this decree, the system of official workshops producing lacquerware came to an end.

---

3. [Han] Ban Gu, *Hanshu · Gongyu Zhuan* (*Book of Han · Biography of Gongyu*), vol. 10 (Zhonghua Book Company, 1962), 3071.

4. [Han] Huan Kuan, *Yantie Lun · Sanbuzu* (*Discourses on Salt and Iron, Section Twenty-Nine · The Inadequacy of Granaries*), bk. 695 of *Wenyuange Siku Quanshu* (*Complete Library in Four Branches of Literature from the Wenyuange*) (Commercial Press, Taiwan, 1986), 577, 582.

5. [Southern Song] Fan Ye, *Houhanshu · Huanghouji* (*Book of Later Han · Records of Empresses*), vol. 2 (Zhonghua Book Company, 1982), 422.

The lacquerware of the Han Dynasty has been unearthed in various regions, including Hunan, Sichuan, Jiangsu, Guangdong, Guangxi, Guizhou, Anhui, Zhejiang, and even Inner Mongolia, Xinjiang, and overseas. In the 1930s, numerous lacquered items with long inscriptions were excavated from Han tombs in Lelang, Korea (which was part of the Chinese territory during the Han Dynasty). Examples include the "Divine Dragon and Tiger Portrait Lacquer Plate," with an inscription on the back carving that reads, "In the twelfth year of Yongping, Lu of Shu Commandery, a skilled artisan, made this for the benefit of his descendants." The inscription is in the Han script and details the lacquer plate's origin, manufacturing process, and purpose. "Shu Commandery" refers to the production location within the present-day Sichuan Province. The inscription highlights the use of lacquer-coated fabric as the base, the application of three layers of gray lacquer on the base, the price of the lacquer plate, the artisan Lu who created it, and the intended purpose of passing it down through generations. In 1958, a lacquered ear cup with an even longer inscription was unearthed from a Han tomb in Pingba, Qingzhen, Guizhou. The inscription reads, "In AD 3, the craftsmen of Guanghan Commandery crafted carriages and painted them with feathers on yellow ears. Each has a capacity of one *sheng* and sixteen *yue* (about 210 ml). The craftsmen were the plain worker, Chang; the lacquerer, Long; the carpenter, Sun; the worker of copper ears with yellow coating, Hui; the painter; the feather worker, Ping; the clear worker, Kuang; and the maker, Zhongzao. The overseer was Historian Yu, the commander was Zhangyin, the assistant prefect was Feng, the assistant official was Lin, and the chief official was Tan."[6] "Guanghan Commandery" refers to the place of origin in present-day Sichuan Province. "Crafted by commandery" means the production supervised by the government workshop. "Carriages" refers to carriages used exclusively by the imperial family or as gifts from the imperial family. The inscription provides details about the creation of the cup, mentioning the year, the commandery of origin (Guanghan, located in present-day Sichuan), the official workshop, the capacity of the cup, and the names of the craftsmen and supervisors involved. This lacquered ear cup required the collaborative effort of eight craftsmen, along with five individuals managing the workshop. The extensive inscription reflects the significant effort put into lacquerware production during the Han Dynasty. Notably, the lacquer plate from Lelang was likely an item of the noble, indicating the owner's surname but not the craftsman's surname, specifying the price but lacking the term "carriages." In contrast, the lacquered ear cup from

---

6. The Museum of Guizhou Provincial, "Excavation Report of Han Tombs in Pingba, Qingzhen, Guizhou," *Archaeology Journal*, no. 1 (1959).

Qingzhen was a custom-made item for the imperial family and local rewards. Similar long-inscription lacquered items have been found in Han tombs in Hanjiang District (Figure 3.8), Yangzhou, indicating the widespread distribution of the Han Dynasty lacquerware.

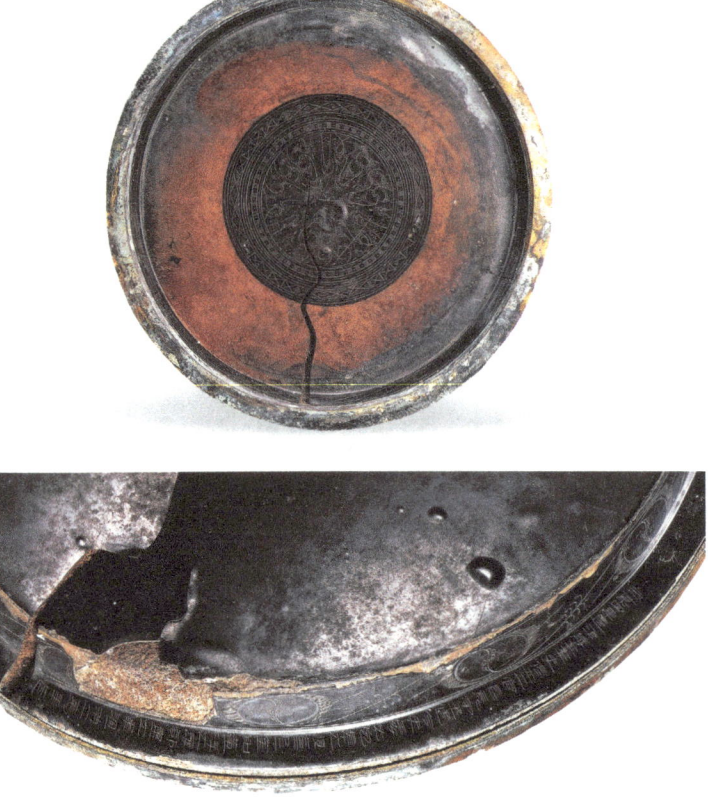

Figure 3.8 [Han] Golden Bronze Button with a long inscription engraved on a lacquered plate, mentioning "the fourth year of Yuankang in Guanghan...," unearthed from Yangshou Township, Hanjiang District, Yangzhou City, selected from the book *Han Guanglingguo Qiqi* (*Han Lacquerware from the Kingdom of Guangling*), compiled by the Yangzhou Museum

CHAPTER IV

Flowing *Yushang* along the Winding Water

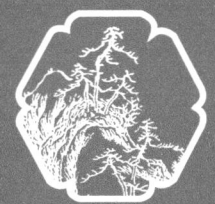

I n the Qin and Han dynasties, most "lacquered wooden items" had a glossy surface formed by lacquer coating. The coating often contained lacquer seeds, and it had not undergone grinding, let alone polishing. After the lacquer coating on the utensils dries, polishing is conducted to effectively remove any glossiness and paint seeds, making the surface smooth and shiny.

The invention of the technique of polishing lacquerware came during the Eastern Jin period when lacquer chests, lacquer boxes, lacquer tables, and other everyday items transitioned from royal and aristocratic circles into the lives of literati, popularizing the use of polished lacquer coating. In the Eastern Jin period, *Nüshi Zhentu* (*Admonitions of the Instructress to the Court Ladies*) of Gu Kaizhi depicted several lacquerware items (Figure 4.1). It is noteworthy that *Bijing* (*The Principles of Penmanship*) of Wang Xizhi mentioned that "some people have left behind green deep-lacquered bamboo tubes and perforated tubes" (Figure 4.2).[1] *Yuanjia Qiju Zhu* (*The Annals of the Emperor's Reign*) of the Southern Song Dynasty mentioned that in the sixteenth year of the Yuanjia era (AD 439), Liu Zhen, an official, reported, "It is rumored that the former governor of Guangchuan, Wei Lang, made twenty-three silver-coated lacquer screens in Guangzhou, as well as one green deep-lacquered screen."[2] For those familiar with lacquerware, it is known that only by polishing the lacquered surface after it has dried and then re-polishing it can the lacquer achieve a clear and translucent appearance akin to being submerged in water. Wang Xizhi's praise for a gift of green deep-lacquered bamboo pen holders indicates that the Eastern Jin period was a fashionable era for the craft of polishing lacquered items after they had dried.

羽觞 (*yushang*) is a drinking vessel shaped like a halved eggshell with wings on both sides resembling ears; hence, it is also known as an "ear cup." In the Warring States period, the *Chuci* (*The Songs of Chu*) contains the line, "The nectar only fills a few *yushang*," and a large number of lacquered *yushang* have been unearthed from Han tombs (Figure 4.3), with over a hundred *yushang* found in the No. 3 Han tomb of the Mawangdui site in Changsha. During the Eastern Jin period, lacquered

---

1. [Jin] Wang Xizhi mentioned in his *Bijing* (*The Principles of Penmanship*) that "some people have left behind green deep-lacquered bamboo tubes and perforated tubes." Refer to the collection *Wuchao Xiaoshuo Daguan · Weijin Xiaoshuo* (*Anthology of Novels from Five Dynasties · Wei-Jin Novels*), vol. 3, collected in Nanjing Library, printed edition from the 15th year of the Republic of China (Shanghai Literature and Art Publishing House, 1991), 298.
2. [Tang] Xu Jian, *Pingfeng Disan* (*Third Section of the Folding Screen*), vol. 25 of *Chuxue Ji* (*Record of Initial Learning*), bk. 890 of *Wenyuange Siku Quanshu* (*Complete Library in Four Branches of Literature from the Wenyuange*) (Commercial Press, Taiwan, 1986), 397.

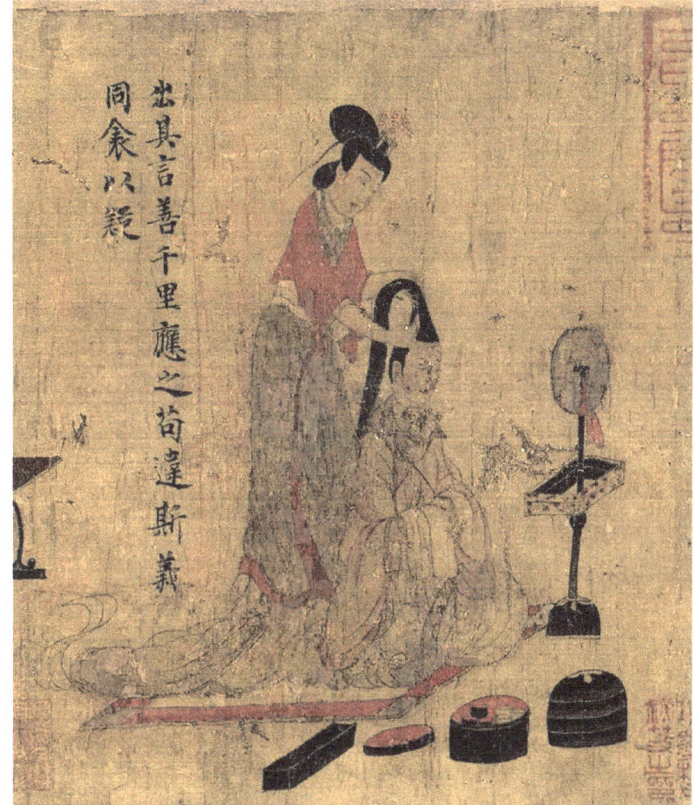

Figure 4.1 [Eastern Jin] *Nüshi Zhentu* (*Admonitions of the Instructress to the Court Ladies*) of Gu Kaizhi depicts several lacquerware, selected from *Zhongguo Meishu Quanji* (*The Complete Collection of Chinese Art*)

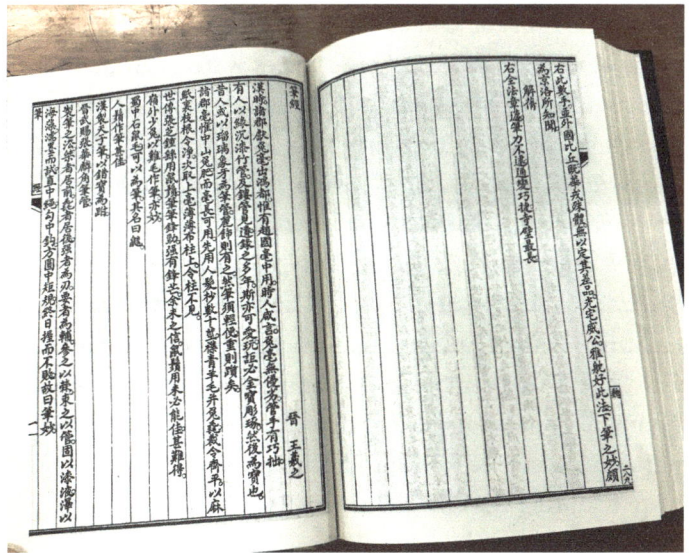

Figure 4.2 [Eastern Jin] *Bijing* (*The Principles of Penmanship*) of Wang Xizhi first mentions "green deep lacquer," printed from the Stele Edition of Sweeping Leaves Mountain House

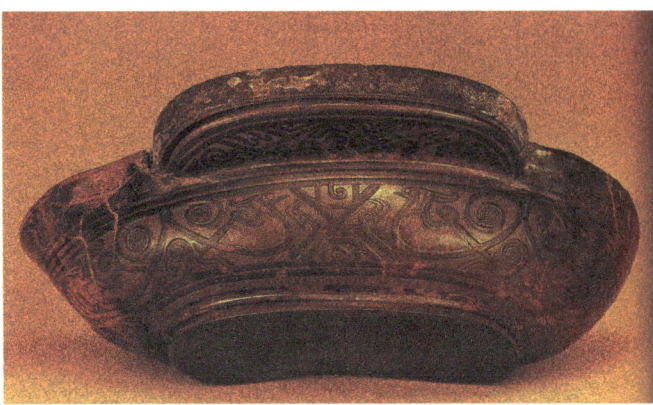

Figure 4.3 [Han] Lacquered *Yushang* Vessel, selected from the compilation *Haiwai Yizhen* (*Overseas Treasures*) by the National Palace Museum in Taipei

lacquered *yushang* vessels filled with fine wine gently into the meandering water. As the vessels drifted along, stopping in front of someone, that person would then have to drink the wine and compose poetry. This is the origin of "flowing *yushang* along the winding water." The *yushang* used for "flowing *yushang*" must not be made of bronze; instead, it must be crafted from lacquered linen fabric. The material is both sturdy and lightweight, resistant to water. Like a small boat drifting with the waves, the cleverly designed *yushang*, with its double "ears," serves as a balance, experiencing minimal resistance and providing significant buoyancy. Even with slight ripples on the water's surface, the lacquered *yushang* would not tip over.

Another historical fact reflecting the influence of literati on southern lacquerware is that the focus of the paintings on lacquerware shifted from the worship of deities during the Han and Qin dynasties to a focus on human subjects. Over 60 lacquerware items of more than ten different types were excavated from the tomb of Zhu Ran in Dongwu, Anhui Ma'anshan. These items depicted historical stories such as *Baili Xi Hui Guqi Tu* (*Baili Xi Meeting his Former Wife*), *Boyu Beiqin Tu* (*Boyu Mourning His Relatives*), and *Jizha Guajian Tu* (*Jizha Hanging His Sword*), as well as scenes from real life like *Guizu Shenghuo Tu* (*Noble Life*), *Tongzi Duigun Tu* (*A Child Facing a Stick*), *Tongzi Xiyu Tu* (*A Child Playing with Fish*), *Shoulie Tu* (*Hunting*), and *Shuzhuang Tu* (*Dressing Up*). Unlike the mysterious and romantic style of the lacquer paintings in the Chu and Han dynasties, these lacquer paintings adopted a realistic artistic style to promote loyalty, filial piety, and righteousness. Although originating from Shu Commandery, they depicted stories from the Wu State, indicating that they were custom-made for Zhu Ran from Dongwu in Shu Commandery. The lacquered plate featuring the *Jizha Guajian Tu* is housed in the Anhui Provincial Institute of Cultural Relics and Archaeology, while the lacquer plate featuring *Guizu Shenghuo*

Tu is kept in the Ma'anshan Museum (Figure 4.4), both designated as cultural relics that cannot be taken out of the country by the National Cultural Heritage Administration. The Southern artistic style spread to the North. Sima Chu, belonging to the royal family of Eastern Jin, fled north due to the change of Southern regimes. Lacquer screens depicting *Xiaozi Lienü Tu* (*Filial Son and Virtuous Women*) (Figure 4.5) were unearthed from the tomb of his son Sima Jinlong. The original sketches came from the South, and the artistic style resembled the *Lienü Renzhi Tu* (*Virtuous Women of Mercy and Wisdom*) by Gu Kaizhi of Eastern Jin. These screens are also designated as cultural relics that cannot be taken out of the country by the National Cultural Heritage Administration. It's noteworthy that the lacquer screen depicting *Xiaozi Lienü Tu* includes both lacquer painting and oil painting, with refined drying vegetable oil containing the drying agent litharge. This allowed for vivid and varied

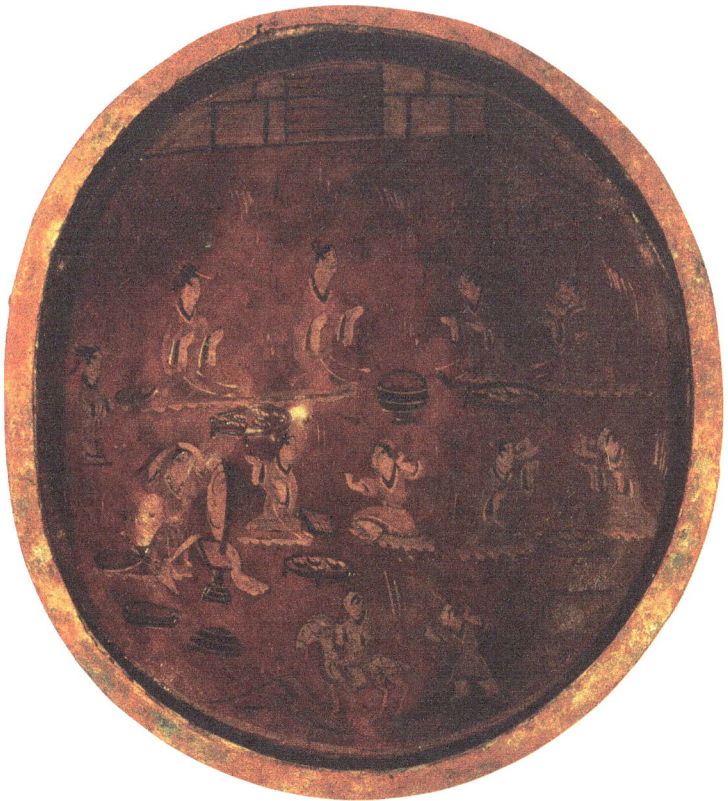

Figure 4.4 [Eastern Wu] Lacquer Plate of *Guizu Shenghuo Tu* (*Noble Life*), unearthed from the tomb of Zhu Ran in Ma'anshan, Anhui Province, held at the Ma'anshan Museum, photo provided by Chen Huafeng

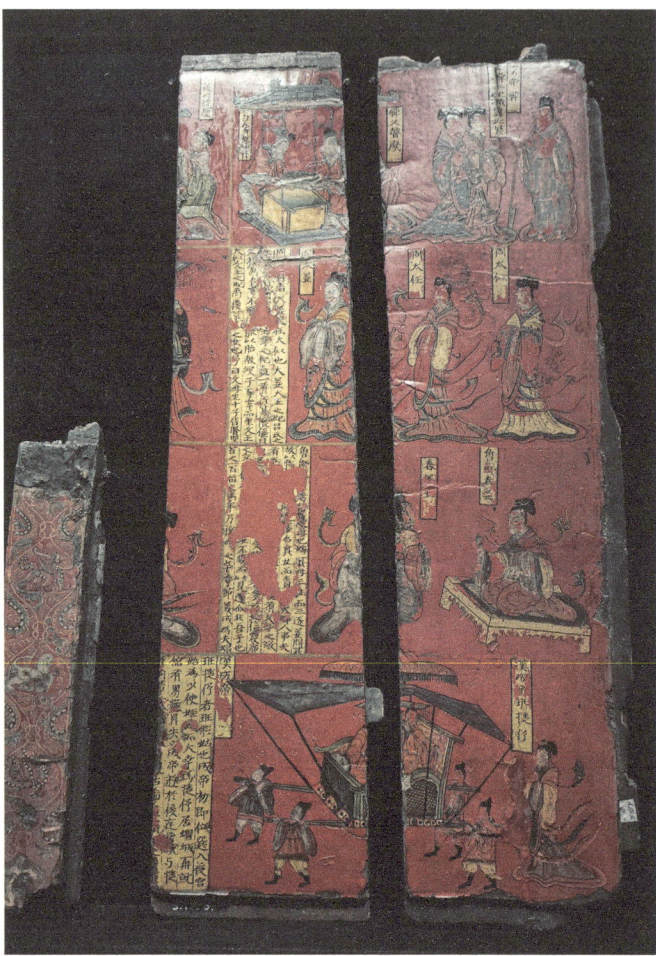

Figure 4.5 [Northern Wei] Oil Painted *Xiaozi Lienü Tu* (*Filial Son and Virtuous Women*), unearthed from the tomb of Sima Jinlong in Datong, Shanxi Province, held at the Shanxi Museum, photographed at the exhibition of "King of Langya—From Eastern Jin to Northern Wei"

colors, aligning with historical records mentioning "the mention of litharge lacquer painting by Cao Wei,"[3] providing mutual confirmation. The scarcity of surviving authentic paintings on silk or paper from the lacquerware of the Three Kingdoms, the Two Jin Dynasties, and the Southern and Northern Dynasties makes them extremely precious.

The story of "flowing *yushang* along the winding water" told by the literati in Shanyin has become a timeless masterpiece. Throughout the ages, literati and non-

---

3. Zheng Shixu, "Qiqi Kao (Study on Lacquerware)," in *Hanyu Yanjiu, Qiqi Kao, Tonggu Kaolue, and Guxiu Kao* (*Research on Han Jade, Study on Lacquerware, Brief Study of Bronze Drums, Study of Guxiu*) (Jiangsu Gongyang Ancient Books Engraving Society, 1991), 18.

literati alike have emulated and appreciated it as an elegant tradition. Emperor Yang of Sui built the Flowing Yusheng Palace, "where he created a nine-curved lacquer channel, water was drawn into the channel from the Guangyuan Palace, and Emperor Yang would often enjoy the flowing toasts there" (*Taiping Yulan · Dwelling Section Three*). This records the emperor indulging in refined pleasures. The poem *Liren Xing* (*A Song for a Beautiful Woman*) by Du Fu records, "On the third day of the third month, the weather is fresh, and by the waterside of Chang'an, there are many beautiful women." This describes the imperial family participating in the *xiuxi*. Li Bai's verse, "feathers fly, toasts are raised, and we get drunk under the moon" (*Preface to the Spring Night Banquet at the Peach Blossom Garden with My Younger Brother*), depicts literati gathering for an elegant event. Even in the first year (1662) and the third year (1664) of the Kangxi era in the Qing Dynasty, the leading figure in the poetry world, Wang Shizhen (styled Yuyang Shanren), initiated the "Hongqiao *xiuxi*" in Yangzhou twice. Lu Yayu, an imperial salt commissioner in the Lianghuai regions, continued the tradition of "Hongqiao *xiuxi*," compiling a poetry collection spanning over 300 volumes. Today, within the Zuiweng Pavilion in Chuzhou, Anhui, there exists a nine-curved lacquer channel resembling an earthworm lying on the ground, which is humorously criticized by literati as "so elegant that it seems common."

CHAPTER V

Lacquer Portrait of Jianzhen

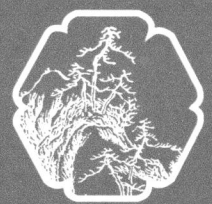

C hina's lacquerware experienced its prosperity for a short period before facing the challenge of porcelain. Porcelain, being convenient in raw materials, relatively simple in craftsmanship, and having a lower price, quickly replaced lacquerware in daily utensils during the Eastern Wu, Jin, Southern and Northern Dynasties, as blue porcelain rapidly developed. Faced with the challenge of porcelain, lacquerware craftsmanship had to innovate, create new varieties, and strive for excellence in the direction of artistry. The ingenious skills of Chinese craftsmen allowed lacquerware craftsmanship to successfully break through, with the Tang and Song dynasties witnessing the most innovations and achievements in lacquerware craftsmanship. The outstanding achievements of Tang Dynasty lacquerware craftsmanship mainly lie in the widespread influence of the technique of *jiazhu* lacquer carving and the invention of the inlaying craft.

Speaking of *jiazhu* lacquer carving, we must trace its origins to the Eastern Jin Dynasty. During the Eastern Jin Dynasty, Buddhism spread rapidly in China. People often had to carry Buddha statues in processions at grand Buddhist events. Buddha statues made of lacquer-coated hemp fabric were sturdy and lightweight, giving rise to the popularity of "traveling statues" crafted in this way. Chinese literature refers to the craft of creating lacquer-coated hemp fabric sculptures as *jiazhu*.[1] Historical records mention that during the Eastern Jin Dynasty, Dai Kui "built the Zhaoyin Temple and personally made five *jiazhu* lacquer statues."[2] At that time, under Hualugang in Jiankang (modern-day Nanjing), there was the Waguan Temple, where Dai Kui[3] crafted five-layered *jiazhu* lacquer Buddha statues. These, along with the bronze statues made by Dai Yong,[4] the wall paintings by the painter Gu Kaizhi for the Waguan Temple, and the jade Buddha presented by the Lion Country, were collectively known as the "Three Wonders of Waguan Temple."[5] During the Southern Liang Dynasty, Waguan Temple still preserved "the five statues made by Dai Andao and the gold

1. Shi Huilin, *Yinyi* (*Phonosemantics*), "Beautifully made with *jiazhu*, using lacquer and cloth to create an empty shell." Quoted from Zheng Shixu, "Qiqi Kao (Study on Lacquerware)," in *Hanyu Yanjiu, Qiqi Kao, Tonggu Kaolue, and Guxiu Kao* (*Research on Han Jade, Study on Lacquerware, Brief Study of Bronze Drums, Study of Guxiu*) (Jiangsu Gongyang Ancient Books Engraving Society, 1991), 22.

2. [Tang] Faling, vol. 3 of *Bianzheng Lun* (*Debate on Rectification*), bk. 62 of *Zhonghua Dacangjing* (*Chinese Tripitaka*) (Zhonghua Book Company, 1993), 495.

3. Dai Kui: Also known as Andao, a sculptor from the Eastern Jin Dynasty.

4. Dai Yong: Son of Dai Kui.

5. Zhou Xunchu, *Zhongguo Diyu Wenhua Tonglan: Jiangsu Juan* (*Overview of Regional Cultures in China: Jiangsu Volume*) (Zhonghua Book Company, 2013), 344.

statue approximately 20 meters tall made by Dai Yong."[6] In the Wu Zhou period, the artisan Xue Huaiyi "built a merit hall of a thousand square feet north of the Mingtang, with a large statue standing nine hundred feet high, nose like a thousand-bushel boat, accommodating dozens of people sitting together, made of lacquer-coated *jiazhu*" ([Tang] Zhang Zhuo, *Comprehensive Mirror for Aid in Government*). This indicates the scale of statue-making in early Tang. The peak of manufacturing lacquer Buddha statues continued until the Huichang era of the Tang Dynasty.[7]

In the first year of the Tianbao era in the Tang Dynasty (AD 742), Japanese monks Yoei and Fusho traveled to Jiangdu (modern-day Yangzhou) to request the transmission of Buddhist teachings from the eminent monk Jianzhen, who resided at the Dayun Temple. Jianzhen readily agreed. In the second year of Tianbao (AD 743), Jianzhen, "accompanied by seventeen individuals including monks such as Xiangyan, Daoxing, Deqing, Yoei, Fusho, Situo, and others, along with craftsmen skilled in jade carving, painting, Buddha sculpture, carving and engraving, casting, calligraphy, embroidery, literary composition, and stone inscription, totaling eighty-five artisans, embarked on a boat"[8] from Jiangdu to the Yangzi ferry in an initial attempt to travel to Japan, which unfortunately ended in failure. Jianzhen brought along thirty lacquer trays and fifty mother-of-pearl scripture cases on the second and fifth attempts. In the twelfth year of Tianbao (AD 753), in October, despite being blind, Jianzhen, at the age of sixty-five, successfully made his sixth journey to Nara, Japan. The group he took to Japan was, in fact, a large cultural mission. Accompanying him were skilled individuals in construction, sculpture, and painting, such as Yijing, Fajin, Situo, Tanjing, Anrubao, Junfali, and others. Yijing was the monk of the Xingyun Temple in Jiangdu before the journey, Fajin was the monk of the Baita Temple in Jiangdu, Anrubao was from the Hu nationality, and Junfali was from the Kunlun nationality. The Toshodai-ji Temple in Nara, designed by Jianzhen's disciple Anrubao, was established in the third year of the Tenpyo-hoji era in Japan (AD 759) and has been recognized as a UNESCO World Heritage Site. The temple's main hall is designated as a National Treasure in Japan.

---

6. [Liang] Shi Huijiao, "Shihuili," in vol. 13 of *Gaoseng Zhuan* (*Biography of Eminent Monks*), bk. 61 of *Zhonghua Dacangjing* (*Chinese Tripitaka*), ed. Chinese Tripitaka Bureau (Zhonghua Book Company, 1993), 451.

7. During the Huichang era, the imperial court conducted a large-scale destruction of Buddha statues due to monks privately storing weapons, known as the Huichang Persecution of Buddhism.

8. Oumi no Mifune, *Tangdaheshang Dongzheng Zhuan* (*The Biography of Tang Taizong's Eastern Campaign*) (Zhonghua Book Company, 1979), 51.

After Jianzhen fell ill from accumulated fatigue, his disciples used the technique of *jiazhu* to create a seated statue for him. "In the spring of the seventh year of the Tenpyo-hoji era, Jianzhen's disciple, Monk Renji, dreamt that the beams of the lecture hall collapsed. Upon waking, he was shocked and frightened, realizing it was a sign of Jianzhen's passing. He then led the disciples to mold an image based on the shadow of Jianzhen."[9] This seated statue of Jianzhen with *Jiazhu* Lacquer Craft (Figure 5.1) stands 80.1 centimeters in height, with a proportionate volume resembling a real person. It vividly depicts Jianzhen draped in a kasaya, eyes closed, lips smiling, seated in the lotus position, with hands folded on his knees, exhibiting the dignified, resolute, serene demeanor of a venerable monk. The statue captures the profound

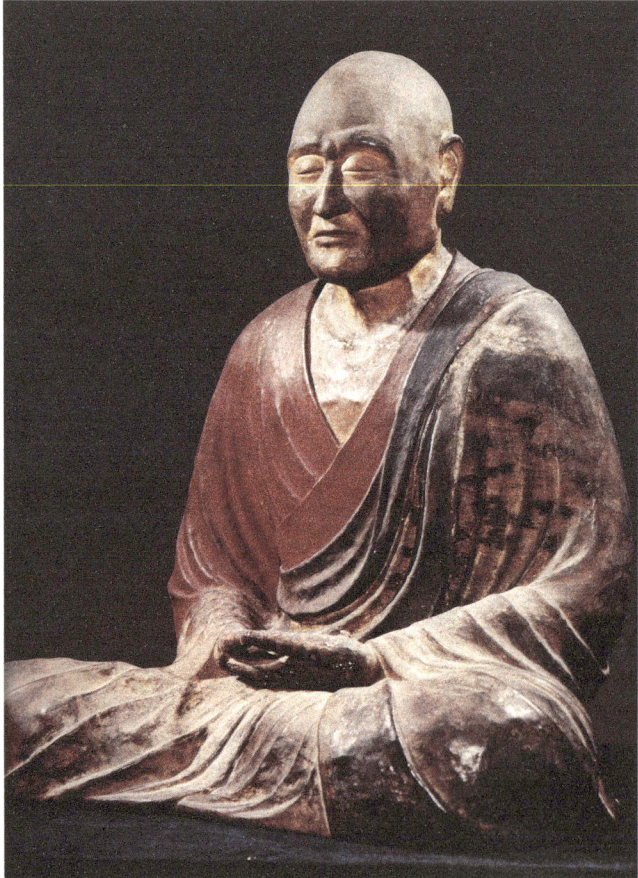

Figure 5.1 [Tenpyō] The Seated Statue of Jianzhen with *Jiazhu* Lacquer Craft, selected from the Japanese edition of *Tang Zhaotisi* (*Toshodai-ji Temple*)

9. Oumi no Mifune, *Tangdaheshang Dongzheng Zhuan* (*The Biography of Tang Taizong's Eastern Campaign*) (Zhonghua Book Company, 1979), 96.

mental state of entering meditation, transcending the ordinary, making it a precious artistic masterpiece in the history of medieval art and Chinese lacquer craftsmanship. The statue was damaged in a fire in 1833 but was restored in 1939 and is enshrined in the Goeido Hall of the Toshodai-ji Temple in Nara.

In the Golden Hall of Toshodai-ji Temple, three lacquered Buddha statues, crafted under the guidance of Jianzhen during the Tenpyō era, are preserved intact and recognized as national treasures in Japan. The Rushana Buddha Seated Statue with an integrated base stands nearly 3.5 meters tall. It is constructed with a bamboo core covered in thirteen layers of fabric and lacquer, supported by an internal wooden frame. Flanking the Rushana Buddha Seated Statue on both sides are the Thousand-Armed Avalokiteshvara Bodhisattva Standing Statue, standing at a height of 5.36 meters, and the Medicine Buddha Tathagata Standing Statue, both created using the technique of wood-core dry lacquer (Figure 5.2).[10] After the Tenpyō era, two sculpting techniques, dry lacquer and wood-core dry lacquer, became popular in Japan. Many ancient dry lacquer Buddha statues, including those created with the technique of wood-core dry lacquer, are housed in various temples in Nara, the Kōfuku-ji National Treasure Hall, and the Tokyo National Museum. According to the book *Riben Siyu Ji Baozang* (*Temples and Treasures of Japan*), the art of dry lacquer sculpting in Japan originated from Chinese monks who accompanied Jianzhen on his eastward journey.[11] If you have visited Japan and witnessed the influence of Chinese culture during the Asuka period, seen the lacquered Buddha statues from the Tenpyō era in Toshodai-ji Temple, and observed the significant advancements in lacquer Buddha statue craftsmanship in Japan after the Tenpyō era, you would understand why the Japanese hold Saint Prince Shotoku and Jianzhen in such high regard, considering them as great contributors to Japanese culture.

After the Huichang Persecution of Buddhism, the indigenous Chinese technique of *jiazhu* lacquer sculpting fell into silence. During the Yuan Dynasty, Kublai Khan appointed Phagpa as the state preceptor, adopting Lamaism as the state religion. With

---

10. The base of the Rushana Buddha seated statue mentions the names of the authors as "Mononobe no Hirotari," "Nuribe no Miyatsuko Maro," and "Novice Jingfu." See *Tang Zhaotisi* (*Toshodai-ji Temple*) and *Tang Zhaotisi Jianli Yuanqi* (*Origin of the Establishment of Toshodai-ji Temple*). *Tang Zhaotisi Yuanqi Lueji* (*Brief Collection of the Origin about Toshodai-ji Temple*) and *Qiansui Zhuanji* (*Biography of a Thousand Years*) record that Chinese monks such as Yijing and Situo participated in the creation of the Rushana Buddha.

11. Zheng Shixu, "Qiqi Kao (Study on Lacquerware)," in *Hanyu Yanjiu, Qiqi Kao, Tonggu Kaolue, and Guxiu Kao* (*Research on Han Jade, Study on Lacquerware, Brief Study of Bronze Drums, Study of Guxiu*) (Jiangsu Gongyang Ancient Books Engraving Society, 1991), 27.

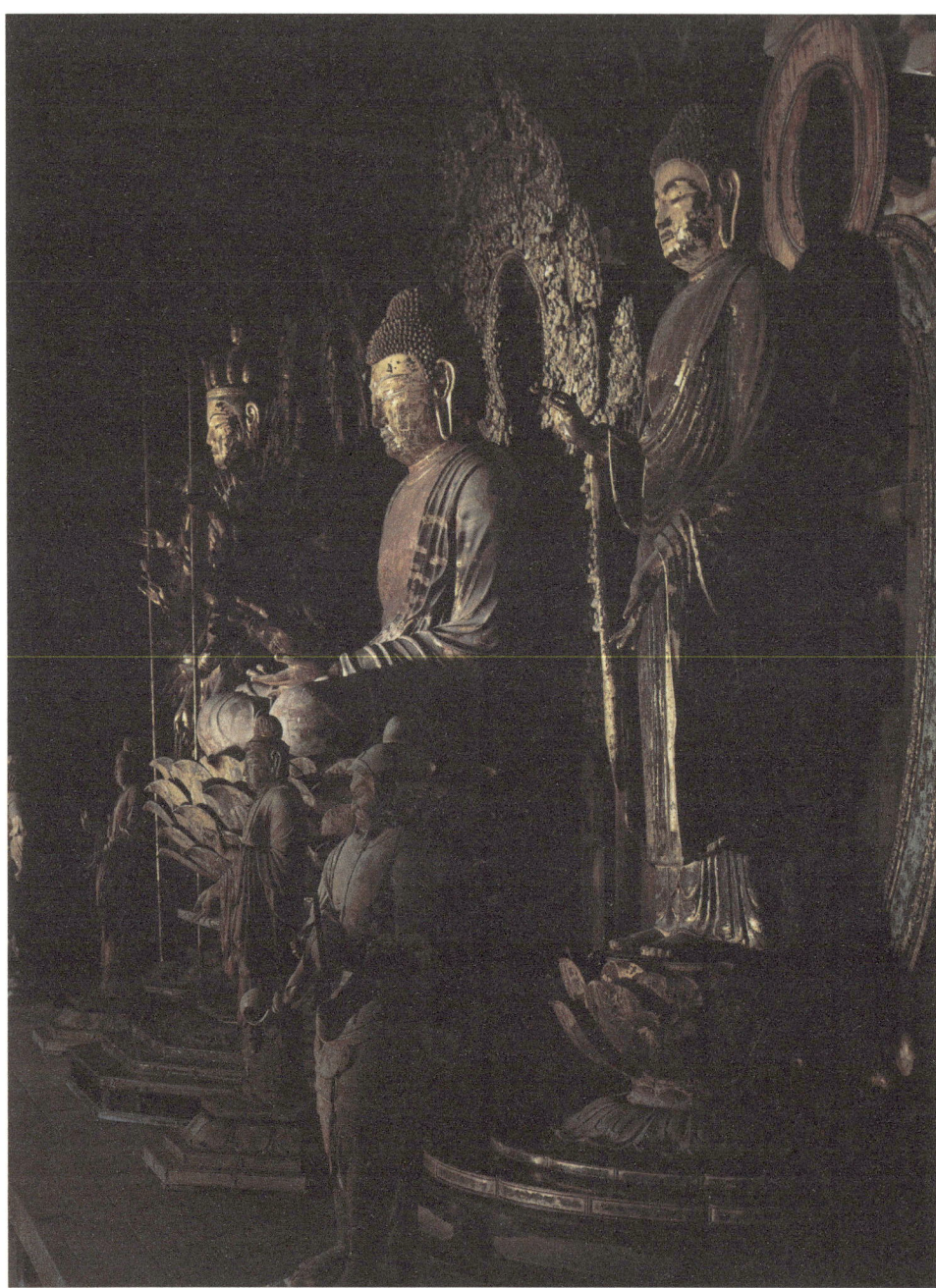

Figure 5.2 [Tenpyō] The Rushana Buddha Seated Statue, the Thousand-Armed Avalokiteshvara Bodhisattva Standing Statue, and the Medicine Buddha Tathagata Standing Statue, selected from the Japanese edition of *Tang Zhaotisi* (*Toshodai-ji Temple*)

Lamaism spreading from Mongolia and Tibet into northern and southern China, it gained popularity nationwide. Lamaism, with its emphasis on esoteric transmission, led to the widespread dissemination of Tibetan-style architecture, painting, and sculpture throughout the country. Aniko, a Nepalese, held the position of overseer in charge of various craftsmen in the Yuan Dynasty's Imperial Workshop, receiving a silver medal and tiger symbol of authority. He played a pivotal role in establishing a new style that combined Han and Tibetan elements in the Buddhist statues, known as the "Western Paradise Brahmanic Appearance." Aniko also took Liu Yuan, a Han Chinese, as his disciple. When Liu Yuan crafted lacquered Buddha statues, he employed techniques known as "tuanhuan" and "tuohuo,"[12] and "the statues were highly praised for their exquisite craftsmanship and profound spirituality."[13] The Beijing Palace Museum once housed 20 statues of Yuan Dynasty lacquered Arhats from Dadu, which are now relocated to the White Horse Temple in Luoyang (Figure 5.3). Additionally, the front hall of the Dabei Temple in the Eight Great Sites on the Western Hills of Beijing preserves 18 Yuan Dynasty lacquered statues created by Liu Yuan.

During the Yuan Dynasty, the lacquer Buddha statue manufacturing technique was referred to as "tuohuo." In the *Qingdai Jiangzuo Zeli* (*Qing Dynasty Artisanal Practices*), the manufacturing technique for lacquer Buddha statues is described as "tuosha" and "baosha," corresponding to Japan's "*tuohuo* dry lacquer" and "*muxin* dry lacquer," respectively. The technique of "tuosha" involves creating a Buddha statue framework by wrapping iron wire around wooden poles or stalks. Clay is then molded into a rough form, air-dried, and coated with soapy water as a releasing agent. Pieces of hemp cloth are applied to the clay, adhering to its contours. The cloth is layered and allowed to air-dry at each step, and the seams are refined to create a complete shell for the Buddha statue. Using diluted lacquer, attach pieces of cloth onto the clay mold, pressing them onto the mold's surface. Layer the cloth, allowing it to dry in the shade between each layer. Trim and refine the seams, forming a complete fabric-molded shell of the Buddha image. Break the clay mold to reveal the fabric-molded shell of the Buddha image. The technique of "baosha" involves carving a wooden core for the Buddha statue, polishing it, applying raw lacquer as a base, and pasting hemp cloth over its entire surface. After both techniques are completed, layers of

---

12. [Yuan] Yu Ji, *Liu Zheng Fengsu Ji* (*Record of Liu Zhengfeng's Sculpture*), vol. 7 of *Daoyuan Xuegu Lu* (*Daoyuan's Ancient Studies*), bk. 2 of *Yu Ji Quance* (*Complete Works of Yu Ji*) (Tianjin Ancient Books Publishing House, 2007), 741.

13. [Ming] Song Lian, *Yuanshi Liezhuan Dijiusi · Liu Yuan Zhuan* (*History of the Yuan Dynasty · Biography of Liu Yuan*), vol. 15 (Zhonghua Book Company, 1976), 4546.

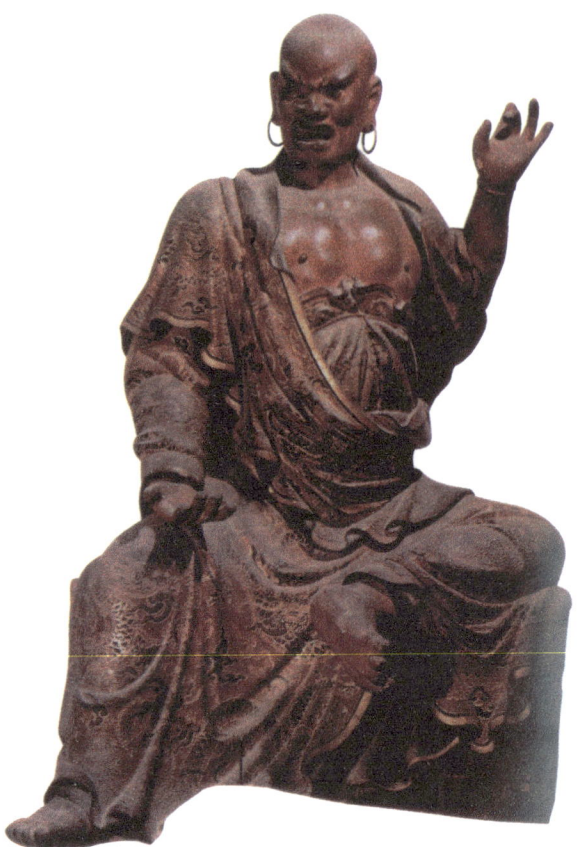

Figure 5.3 [Yuan] Painted Wooden Arhat Statue, original
collection of the Beijing Palace Museum, selected from *Zhongguo
Yishu Tongshi* (*General History of Chinese Art*)

gray lacquer are applied gradually, followed by sanding, drying, rough lacquering, drying again, sanding, and finally, painting with colored lacquer or gilding. The lacquered Arhats at the Bishan Temple on Wutai Mountain in Shanxi, located on both sides of the ordination hall, were created using the technique of "tuosha" by lacquer craftsmen in Suzhou in the seventh year of Shunzhi (1650). The five hundred Arhats at the Biyun Temple in Beijing were made using the "baosha," technique with wooden core lacquer statues.

CHAPTER VI

"Kara-Nuri" Transmitted from Tang Dynasty

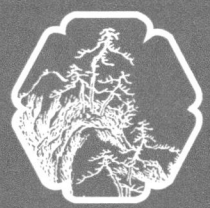

I n the traditional Chinese *xiushi* craftsmanship, there is a category documented as "tianqian" (filling and inlaying), described as "its variety is inexhaustible" (*Xiushi Lu*, written by Huang Cheng and annotated by Yang Ming). The common essence of *tianqian* is to create raised patterns with thick lacquer on the lacquer base or cut materials such as gold, silver, and mother-of-pearl into patterns, affix them onto the lacquer base, cover the entire surface with lacquer, let it dry, and then reveal the patterns by grinding, achieving a polished appearance. The maturity of the grinding and polishing process is a prerequisite for the emergence of the *xiushi* technique of *tianqian*. The evolution of this technique progressed from simple grinding to incorporating decorative materials into grey lacquer for grinding and, eventually, applying materials onto the lacquer base before lacquering and grinding to reveal intricate patterns beneath the lacquer. This craftsmanship developed gradually, advancing from basic to sophisticated levels. During the Tang Dynasty, lacquer artisans innovated a series of *tianqian* techniques such as final gold carving, gold and silver relief, mother-of-pearl relief, rhinoceros-hide texture, and *xipi*.

During the Tang Dynasty, people would calcine deer antlers into blocks, crush them into powder, and call it "deer antler frost." This deer antler frost was mixed into grey lacquer to decorate the *qin* (a traditional Chinese musical instrument). After waiting for it to dry and solidify, it was ground to reveal intricate patterns and achieve a polished appearance. The molecular structure of deer antlers contains numerous micropores that lacquer can penetrate, forming a strong bond between the lacquer and the grey base. This process also enhances the transparency of the *qin*, and, when the deer antler frost is ground and polished, it creates yellow-brown halo patterns or sparkling dots, adding a visually appealing touch. The Palace Museum in Beijing houses 46 ancient *qins* from different dynasties, including four from the Tang Dynasty. Nine Heavens Circlet-Adorned *Qin* is made from cut paulownia wood with a sturdy design. The deep purple and vermilion lacquer on the *qin*'s surface exhibits beautiful patterns resembling the abdominal muscles of a snake. The *qin*'s frets are inlaid with mother-of-pearl, and it is said to be crafted by the renowned Sichuan artisan Lei Wei. Another Tang Dynasty *qin*, "Legacy *Qin* of Great Sage" (Figure 6.1), is also made from cut paulownia wood and features a simple design. The black and reddish-brown lacquer surfaces exhibit exquisite snake belly patterns, with golden inlays for the frets. The dragon pool inside the *qin* has the inscription "Year of Bing Shen of the Zhide Reign" (AD 756), and a poem is carved next to the dragon pool in elegant clerical script, "Giant ravines greet autumn, the cold river stamps the moon. Myriad sounds linger, and the solitary paulownia splits with a rustle."

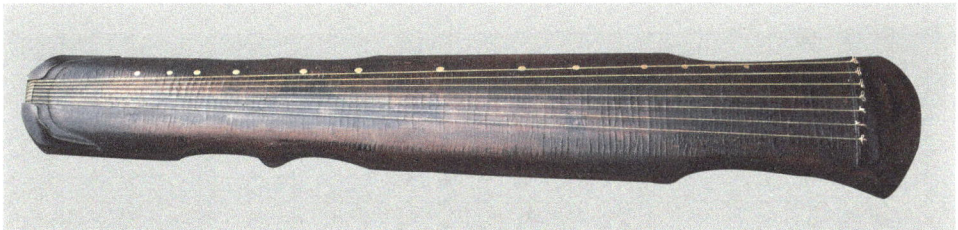

Figure 6.1 [Tang] Legacy *Qin* of Great Sage, collection of the Palace Museum in Beijing, selected from *Zhongguo Lidai Yishu* (*Chinese Art and Craftsmanship through the Ages*) compiled by Li Zhongyue et al.

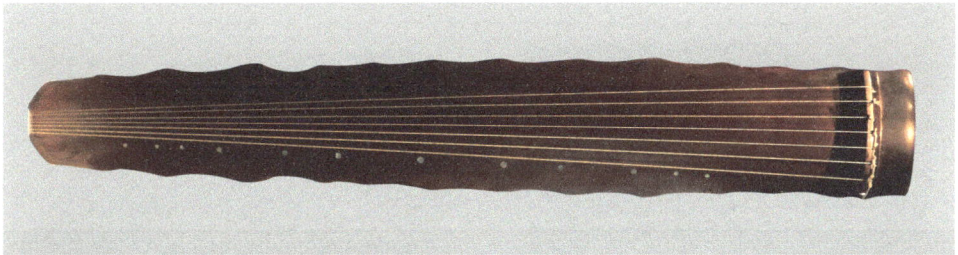

Figure 6.2 [Tang] Luoxia-Style Colorful Phoenix Singing *Qin*, photographed by the author at the Zhejiang Provincial Museum

The Zhejiang Provincial Museum has over 30 ancient *qin*s in its collection, including five from the Tang Dynasty. "Luoxia-Style Colorful Phoenix Singing *Qin*" (Figure 6.2) is one of them, with an inscription inside the dragon pool stating: "crafted by Lei Wei in the 2nd year of the Kaiyuan era of the Great Tang." The achievements of *qin* decoration in the Tang Dynasty owe much to the discovery of deer antler frost and the mastery of the grinding, polishing, and light-reflection techniques by the Tang Dynasty lacquer artisans.

The initial stage of the sprinkled gold technique originated in the Tang Dynasty in China. The Shōsōin Treasure House at Tōdai-ji Temple in Nara, Japan, houses a Gold and Silver Inlaid Large Sword (Figure 6.3) from the Tang Dynasty. The patterns on the scabbard are created using the sprinkled gold technique, where gold filings are sprinkled, and then transparent lacquer is applied, followed by grinding and polishing. The term "final gold carving" is recorded in AD 756 in *Dongdasi Xianwuzhang* (*Offerings Record of the Tōdai-ji Temple*). During the Nara period, Japanese lacquer artisans studied the Chinese "final gold carving" technique, using gold powder to create "flat dusting patterns." An example is the "seaweed-patterned painted robe box"

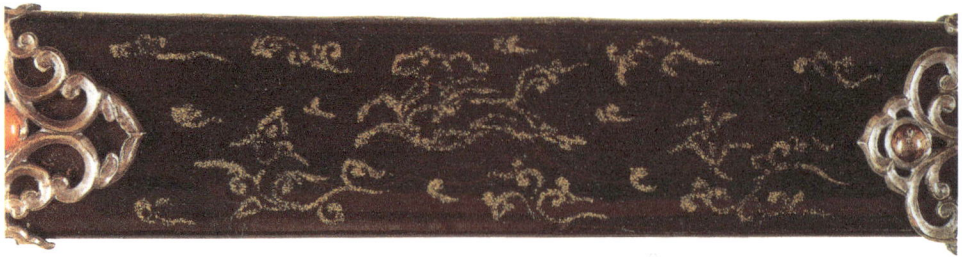

Figure 6.3 [Tang] Gold and Silver Inlaid Large Sword, selected from *The Fine Arts of Japan 11: Decorative Techniques of the Treasures of the Shōsōin* by Nishikawa Akihiko

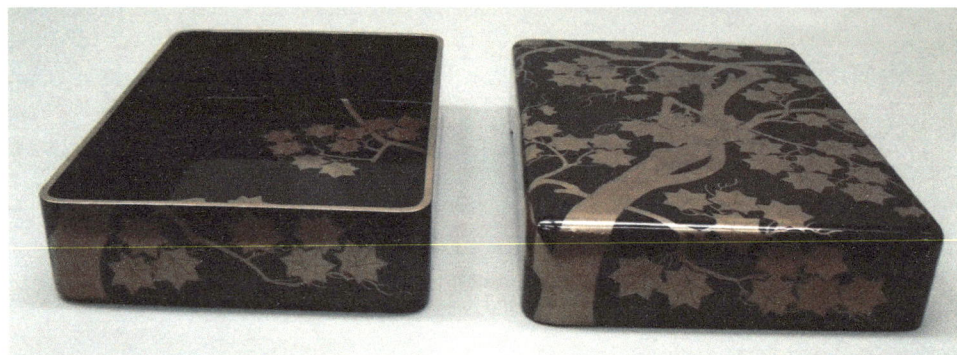

Figure 6.4 [Edo] Maple *Maki-e* Manuscript, National Treasure by Gen Koyo-sai, photographed by the author at the Tokyo National Museum

used by the master Kūkai upon his return from the Tang Dynasty, now designated a national treasure and housed in the Tokyo National Museum. Subsequently, Japanese lacquer artisans continuously innovated, forming a decorative technique system known as *maki-e* characterized by the sprinkling of various gold and silver powders, lacquer application, drying, grinding, and polishing (Figure 6.4). The Japanese academic community recognizes that the precursor of the technique of *maki-e* was the final gold carving that was transmitted during the Tang Dynasty.

The term "xipi" refers to the technique of dipping hands or tools in thick lacquer, creating fine raised protrusions on the lacquer base, filling it with colored lacquer, allowing it to dry, and then grinding to reveal the pattern and achieving a polished effect. Similar to the technique of "xipi," there are other inlay techniques that also reveal patterned images through grinding, such as *zhangxiu* and *qiwen tianqi*. The difference lies in *zhangxiu*, which uses materials to create concave patterns on the lacquer base, while *qiwen tianqi* uses a brush to create intricate patterns on the lacquer base. However, the subsequent steps of filling with lacquer, allowing it to dry, and then grinding to reveal and polish the pattern are the same for both techniques.

There is currently a trend: people like to attribute every invention in Chinese craftsmanship to earlier times, as if the longer the history is claimed, the stronger the confidence. Some individuals like to advance the craft of *tianqian* to the Qin and Han periods. As the author sees it, human inventions and creations are gradual, with each generation contributing to innovation and creation. This continuous process ensures that craftsmanship remains vibrant and enduring. When tracing the origins of craft inventions, there must be existing physical artifacts accompanied by documented records, combined with a comprehensive examination of the overall background of craftsmanship and even culture at that time. Various types of inlay lacquerware, such as deer antler ash lacquer *qin*, final gold carving lacquerware, gold and silver relief lacquerware, and inlaid shell lacquerware, became popular during the Tang Dynasty because they shared a common craftsmanship principle-raising patterns on the lacquer base before embedding them with lacquer and then grinding to reveal. This indicates that the craft of *tianqian* matured during the Tang Dynasty. Literary records mentioning *xipi* can be found no earlier than the Song Dynasty in works like *Yinhua Lu* (*Record of Words Based on Their Context*) by Zeng Sanpin and the encyclopedia *Taiping Guangji* (*Extensive Records of the Taiping Era*) in the Song Dynasty. Surviving artifacts of *xipi* lacquerware are scarce in the Song Dynasty, with most concentrated in the Ming and Qing dynasties (Figures 6.5, 6.6).

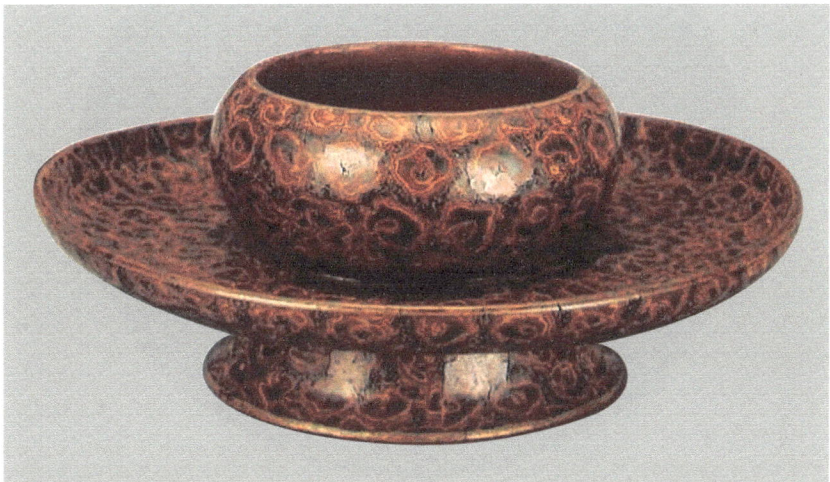

Figure 6.5 [Southern Song] Saucer with *Xipi,* selected from the compilation *Songyuan De Mei* (*Beauty of the Song and Yuan Dynasties*) by the Nezu Museum

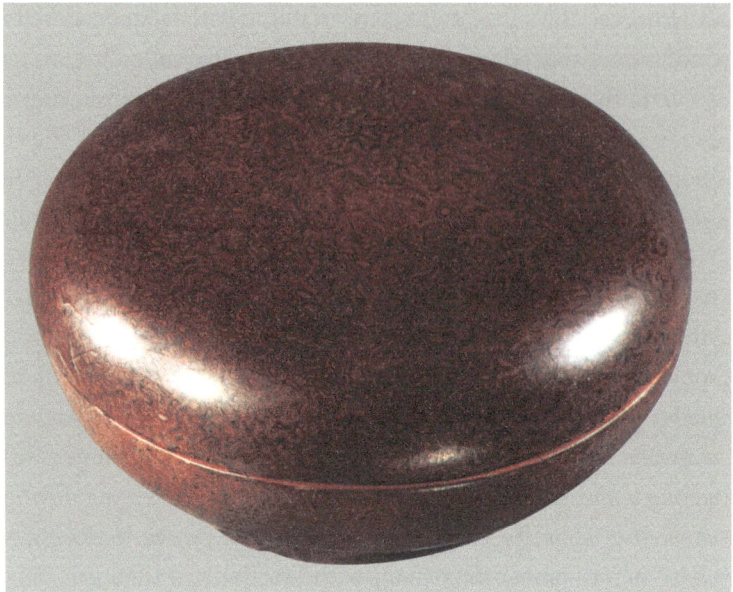

Figure 6.6 [Ming] Round Lacquer Box with *Xipi*, selected from the English edition of *Zhongguo Gudai Qiqi* (*Ancient Chinese Lacquerware*)

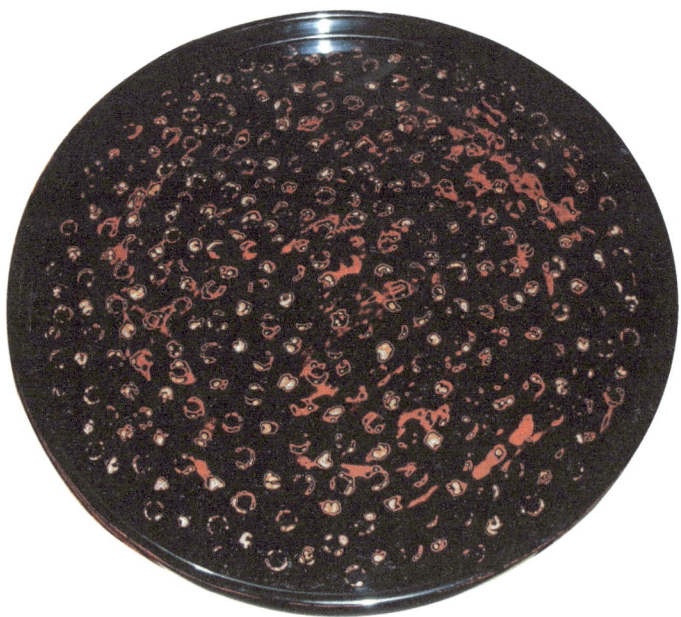

Figure 6.7 [Contemporary] Lacquer Tray with *Wakasa-Nuri*, photographed by the author in Kiso, Japan.

The inlay crafts such as *xipi, zhangxiu,* and *qiwen tianqi* were already transmitted to Japan during the Tang Dynasty. Japanese lacquer craftsmen refer to the inlay technique of raising patterns with lacquer and then grinding to reveal a natural texture as "kara-nuri" (唐涂, táng tú), and the name itself indicates that this craft originated from the Tang Dynasty. Today, "kara-nuri" has various variations in Japan, and Japanese lacquer craftsmen assign names to different patterns, such as "wakasa-nuri" (Figure 6.7), "isokusa-nuri," "tsuishu-nuri," "damask-nuri," "suna-nuri," "momiji-nuri," "matsukawa-nuri," and "aotake-nuri."[1] The roots of these patterns can be traced back to the Tang Dynasty, particularly from the techniques of *xipi* and *zhangxiu.*

---

1. Wakasa-nuri (若狭涂): Wakasa-nuri is a type of Japanese lacquerware that originated in the Wakasa region of Japan. It is known for its use of gold and silver powders to create intricate designs, often featuring landscapes, birds, flowers, and other natural motifs. Isokusa-nuri (矶草塗): Isokusa-nuri refers to lacquerware decorated with a design that resembles seaside plants or seaweed, often found along the coast (矶, iso). This style typically features delicate, flowing patterns that evoke a sense of the ocean. Tsuishu-nuri (堆朱涂): Tsuishu-nuri is a technique used in Japanese lacquerware where multiple layers of cinnabar lacquer are applied and then carved to reveal underlying layers, creating a raised design. This technique results in a rich, three-dimensional effect. Damask-nuri (绫纹涂): Damask-nuri lacquerware features intricate patterns that resemble damask fabric. The patterns are created using various techniques such as painting, inlaying, and carving, resulting in a luxurious and elegant finish. Suna-nuri (砂子涂): Suna-nuri, or sand lacquerware, is a style of Japanese lacquerware where fine sand or powder is sprinkled onto wet lacquer to create a textured surface. The lacquer is then polished to reveal the pattern, resulting in a unique and tactile finish. Momiji-nuri (红叶涂): Momiji-nuri, or red leaf lacquerware, features designs inspired by maple leaves, particularly their vibrant red color in autumn. This style often includes intricate patterns of maple leaves or branches, creating a beautiful and seasonal motif. Matsukawa-nuri (松皮涂): Matsukawa-nuri, or pine bark lacquerware, is characterized by its texture, which resembles the bark of a pine tree. This effect is achieved by applying layers of lacquer mixed with fine sawdust or other materials to create a rough, natural-looking surface. Aotake-nuri (青竹涂): Aotake-nuri, or green bamboo lacquerware, features designs inspired by bamboo, a symbol of longevity and resilience in Japanese culture. This style often includes delicate bamboo leaf patterns or the natural texture of bamboo stalks, creating a fresh and elegant aesthetic.

CHAPTER VII

Rebellion against Ming Emperor

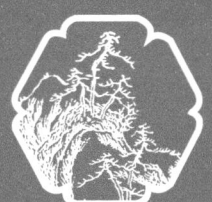

I n the craftsmanship of *tianqian* invented by the people in the Tang Dynasty, the technique of "gold and silver *pingtuo*" (金银平脱) is most relevant to the fate of the royal family. "平" (ping) refers to the gold and silver pattern being level with the lacquer surface, and "脱" (tuo), synonymous with "托" (tuo), refers to lifting the pattern out of the lacquer surface. The process involves attaching intricately carved gold and silver patterns onto the lacquer base, covering them entirely with light-reflecting lacquer to embed the gold and silver pieces. After the lacquer dries and hardens, the patterns are revealed through polishing, making the gold and silver pieces level with the lacquer surface and enhancing the gloss. Due to the high cost of gold and silver and the slow drying of lacquer under the pieces, creating gold and silver *pingtuo* lacquerware is a laborious and costly endeavor.

During the reign of Emperor Tang Xuanzong Li Longji, the country was so prosperous that it was described in the poetry of Du Fu as "remembering the flourishing days of Kaiyuan, even small towns had myriad households. With flowing oil from rice and white millet, both public and private granaries were abundant" (Du Fu, *Two Recollections*). Enamored with his favorite concubine, Yang Yuhuan, The emperor spent his days indulging in song and dance and extravagant spending. At that time, the foreigner An Lushan excelled in the "Huxuan Dance," gaining favor from Emperor Xuanzong and his beloved concubine. Historical records mention that the emperor ordered the construction of a lavish residence for An Lushan in Qiren Fang, sparing no expense and making it extraordinarily magnificent. Two large beds with silver *pingtuo* sandalwood and a gold and silver *pingtuo* screen were used to furnish his residence. Emperor Xuanzong and Yang Yuhuan also gifted many gold and silver *pingtuo* lacquerware items to An Lushan, including chopsticks, plates, dishes, wine cups, vases, boxes, bowls, and more. The emperor remarked that An Lushan had large eye sockets, and he didn't want to be laughed at by him. An Lushan reciprocated with gifts, including a gold and silver *pingtuo* Hu bed.[1] The creation of these gold and silver *pingtuo* lacquerware items consumed significant resources during the prosperous Tang era, becoming one of the factors contributing to the An Lushan Rebellion. As the turmoil of the An Lushan Rebellion continued, Emperor Suzong issued an order to "prohibit pearls, jade, precious ornaments, *pingtuo*, gold paste, and embroidery" (*New Book of Tang · Annals of Emperor Suzong*). The popularity of gold and silver *pingtuo* lacquerware coincided with the prosperity of the Tang Dynasty but eventually came to an end with the decline of the late Tang period.

---

1. Hu bed: A type of lightweight, foldable seat with four legs. Initially used by nomadic peoples.

During the Tang Dynasty, gold and silver *pingtuo* lacquerware is most abundantly preserved in the Shōsōin Treasure House of Todai-ji Temple in Nara, Japan. Examples include the "Gold and Silver *Pingtuo* Lacquerware *Qin*," "Basketry-Skin Silver *Pingtuo* Lacquerware Hu Vase," "Silver *Pingtuo* Octagonal Diamond-Pattern Lacquer Mirror Box" (Figure 7.1), "Gold and Silver *Pingtuo* Lacquerware Flower and Bird-Pattern Octagonal Copper Mirror," "Gold and Silver *Pingtuo* Lacquerware Leather Box," "Silver *Pingtuo* Lacquerware Box," and more. The Nelson-Atkins Museum of Art in the United States holds a Tang Dynasty "Gold and Silver *Pingtuo* Lacquerware Box," and the British Museum has a Tang Dynasty "Silver *Pingtuo* Silver-Tissue Lacquer Bowl." In the storage of the Tokyo National Museum, the author came across a lacquer craftsman from the Edo period in Japan who replicated a Tang Dynasty "Leather-Skin Silver *Pingtuo* Lacquer Sutra Box" (Figure 7.2).

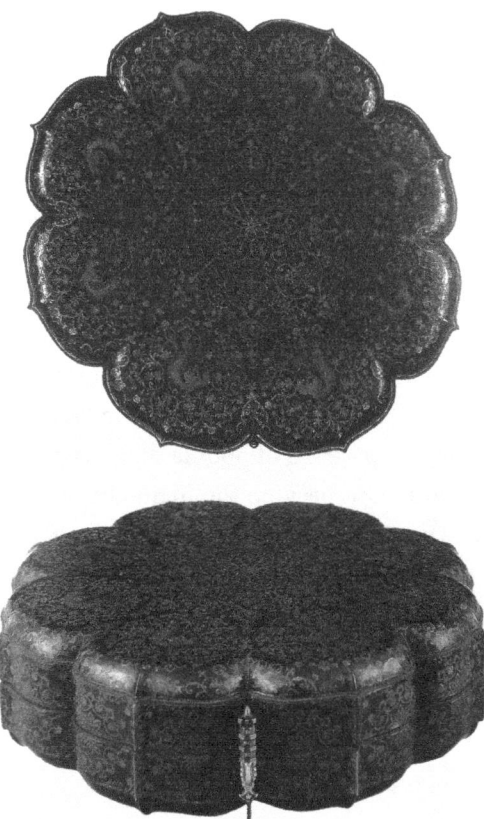

Figure 7.1 [Tang] Silver *Pingtuo* Octagonal Diamond-Pattern Lacquer Mirror Box, housed in the Shōsōin Treasure House of the Tōdai-ji Temple in Nara, Japan, selected from *Zhongguo Meishu Quanji: Qiqi Jiaju* (*The Complete Collection of Chinese Art: Lacquerware and Furniture*) by Chen Zhenyu et al.

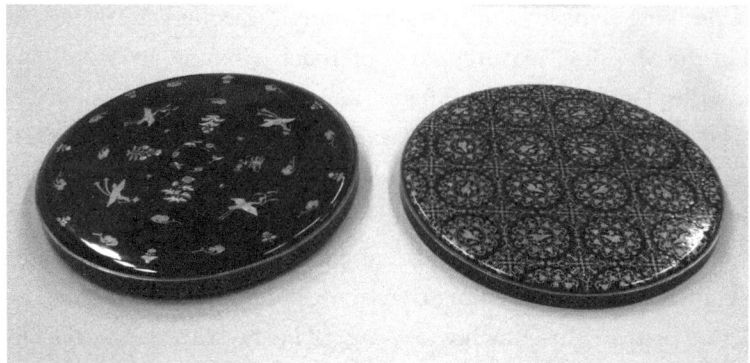

Figure 7.2 [Edo] Leather-Skin Silver *Pingtuo* Lacquer Sutra Box, replicated
based on an original early Tang piece, photographed by the author in the
storage room of the Tokyo National Museum

From October to November 2019, the Nara National Museum held the "71st Exhibition of Shōsōin Treasure House," during which the Tang Dynasty "Gold and Silver *Pingtuo* Lacquerware *Qin*" (Figure 7.3) was displayed for the first time. The *qin* has a length of 114.5 centimeters, a width of 16 centimeters at the head, and 13 centimeters at the tail. Within the square area at the head, three tall figures playing musical instruments are *pingtuo* in gold, surrounded by lush grass and singing birds. Outside the square area, six figures, including two Hu people (Central Asian nomadic people), are *pingtuo* in gold, playing musical instruments. The gold *pingtuo* is crafted into thirteen frets, while the silver *pingtuo* features floral and water wave patterns. On the back of the head, within the square area, there is an inscription in silver *pingtuo* with four lines and 32 characters in regular script, and around the Dragon Pond, there are silver *pingtuo* patterns of double dragons and flowers. The Phoenix Pond features inscriptions "Yihai,[2] the first year" and "Made in the spring season," surrounded by silver *pingtuo* patterns of double dragons and flowers. This Gold and Silver *Pingtuo* Lacquerware *Qin* became the highlight of the "71st Exhibition of Shōsōin Treasure House." During the exhibition period, the glass case was surrounded by visitors who came from around the world to admire it.

Domestic examples of gold and silver *pingtuo* craftsmanship are mainly found in copper mirrors with gold and silver *pingtuo* backs. For instance, the Shaanxi History Museum houses the "Gold and Silver *Pingtuo* Heavenly Horse and Phoenix Mirror" and the "Gold Flower Lacquer-Backed Copper Mirror." In Henan, an

---

2. Yihai: The era name could refer to either the 23rd year of the Kaiyuan era (AD 735) or the 11th year of the Zhenyuan era (AD 795), and there is still no definitive conclusion.

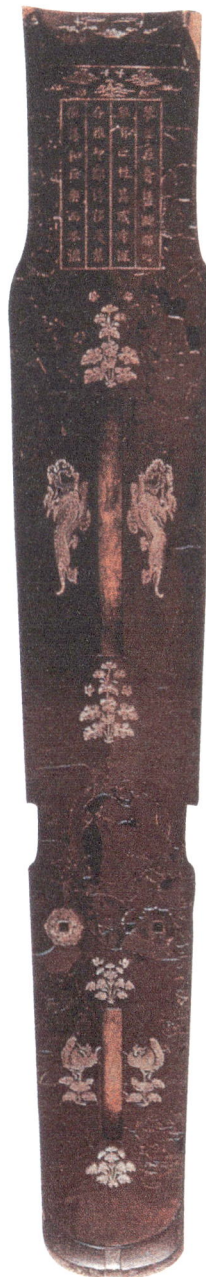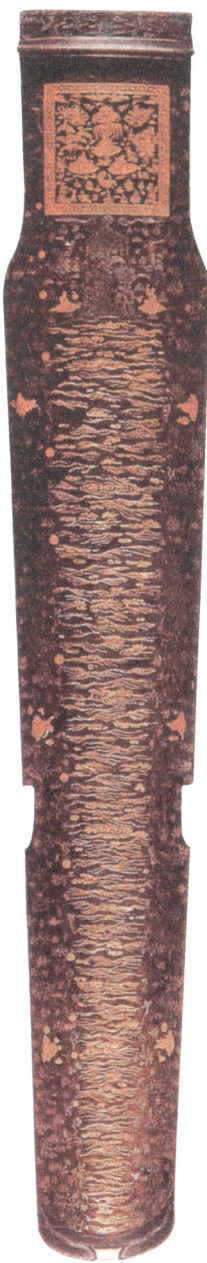

Figure 7.3 [Tang] Gold and Silver *Pingtuo* Lacquerware *Qin*, housed in the Shōsōin Treasure House of the Tōdai-ji Temple in Nara, Japan, selected from *Zhongguo Meishu Shi* (*History of Chinese Art*), edited by Wang Chaowen and Deng Fuxing

excavated mirror from Zhengzhou features a "Gold and Silver *Pingtuo* Figure with Wings, Flying Phoenix, and Flower and Bird Patterns in Sunflower Shape." Another mirror from Guanlin in Luoyang, Henan, exhibits "Gold and Silver *Pingtuo* Mirror with Phoenix, Flower, and Bird Patterns." In Xi'an, Shaanxi, a tomb from the Tang Dynasty yielded the "Silver *Pingtuo* Precious Appearance Flower Copper Mirror," among others. From the underground palace of the Famen Temple in Fufeng, Xi'an, there emerged a late Tang Dynasty "Secret-Color Porcelain-Bodied Silver *Pingtuo* Bowl with Peony Patterns in Lacquer." While copper mirrors and porcelain bowls may not be considered lacquerware, several precious artifacts with silver *pingtuo* remnants of lacquer were unearthed from the royal tomb of Bohai Kingdom in Jilin Province.

Some scholars trace the origin of the gold and silver *pingtuo* technique back to the Han Dynasty. On lacquerware from the late Western Han to the early Eastern Han, one can often find bird and animal patterns made of thin gold and silver sheets attached to the lacquer surface, followed by painted embellishments. I have personally examined several pieces of Han Dynasty lacquerware with gold and silver inlays (Figure 7.4) in the storage of the Yangzhou Museum. The lacquer surface retains the original gloss from the lacquer coating without undergoing polishing to reveal the patterns. It is evident that the gold and silver sheets were applied while the lacquer was still wet. Since there was no subsequent polishing, it cannot be accurately termed "gold and silver *pingtuo*." Ancient texts from the Han Dynasty also never mention the phrase "gold and silver *pingtuo*." *Book of Han · Biography of Gongyu* records "cups and cases adorned with intricate patterns in gold and silver."

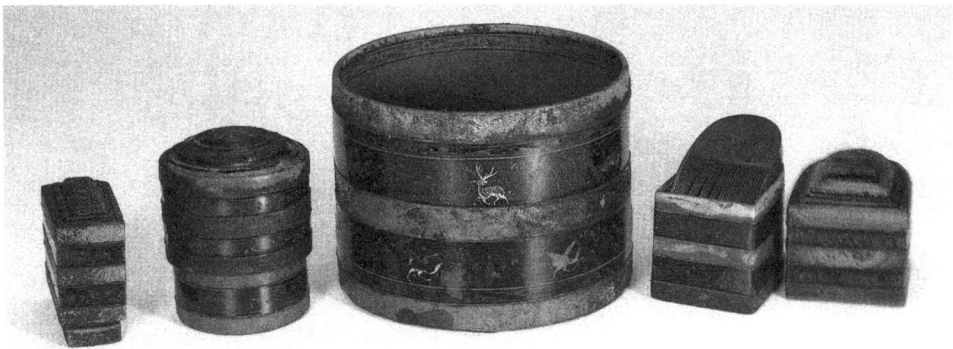

Figure 7.4 [Han] Silver-Buttoned, Gold-Plated, Silver-Inlaid, Painted Lacquer Casket, unearthed from the Han tombs at the Huchang site in Yangzhou, selected from *Zhongguo Wenhua Huabao* (*Chinese Culture Illustrated*)

Building on the metal button craft from the Han Dynasty, people in the Wei and Jin dynasties further developed the silver decorative bands or silver ornaments on lacquerware into intricate patterns, a technique documented as "silver inlay with engraved bands." This technique is mentioned in *Weiwu Shang Zawu Shu* (*Miscellaneous Memorials from the Weiwu Period*).[3] It represents an organized progression from the silver button craft of the Han Dynasty to the application of gold and silver sheets. Archaeological reports mention the discovery of "Silver *Pingtuo* Book Boxes" and "Silver *Pingtuo* Treasure Containers" in the tomb of Wang Jian from the Five Dynasties in Chengdu, Sichuan. In 1984, the author visually inspected replicas of these two items in the Wang Jian Tomb Museum, and the engraved silver patterns on the replicas did not protrude above the lacquer surface in a *pingtuo* manner; instead, they exhibited the technique of "silver inlay with engraved bands." However, the current exhibits at the museum present replicas as silver *pingtuo* items. Additionally, during the "Golden Prosperity Clan—Inner Mongolia Museum Liao Dynasty Cultural Relics Exhibition" held at the National Palace Museum in Taipei, the author encountered a "Goose-Shaped Lacquer Box" (Figure 7.5) excavated from a Liao Dynasty tomb in the Tu'erqi Mountain of Inner Mongolia. The exhibition catalog classified its craftsmanship as "silver *pingtuo*." The author personally examined this lacquer box, which had silver patterns engraved on the lid and silver bands buttoned along the edges. The silver patterns protruded above the lacquer surface without undergoing polishing, making it distinctly not a "silver *pingtuo*" lacquerware but rather a "silver inlay with engraved bands" lacquerware. Another lacquer box from the same tomb, dating to the Liao Dynasty, labeled as "inlaid with precious gems, gilded, and silver-wrapped lacquer box," was also created using the "silver inlay with engraved bands" technique. Citing an authenticated item, the "Wooden Silver-Wrapped Lacquer Jar" displayed in the Yuan Dynasty Great Ming Hall is described as "wrapped in silver bands" and stands about 5.67 meters tall.[4] This artifact is not only documented as the largest ancient lacquer jar but also the largest silver-inlaid lacquerware with carved silver rims documented from ancient times.

---

3. [Song] Cheng Dachang, *Weiwu Shang Zawu Shu* (*Miscellaneous Memorials from the Weiwu Period*), vol. 9 of *Yanfanlu* (*A Record of Washing Away of Wrongs*), bk. 852 of *Wenyuange Siku Quanshu* (*Complete Library in Four Branches of Literature from the Wenyuange*) (Commercial Press, Taiwan, 1986), 148.

4. [Yuan] Tao Zongyi, vol. 21 of *Chuogeng Lu* (*A Record of Abandoning Farming*), bk. 1040 of *Wenyuange Siku Quanshu* (*Complete Library in Four Branches of Literature from the Wenyuange*) (Commercial Press, Taiwan, 1986), 637.

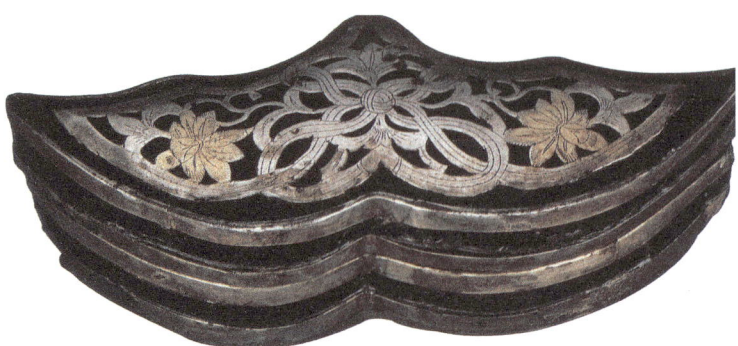

Figure 7.5 [Liao] Goose-Shaped Lacquer Box, unearthed from the Tuerji Mountain tomb in Inner Mongolia, selected from Golden Prosperity Clan— Inner Mongolia Museum Liao Dynasty Cultural Relics Exhibition

In modern China, the gold and silver *pingtuo* technique has evolved into tin *pingtuo*, known as "taihua" in Fuzhou. It is further categorized into "taibaihua," "taicai," and "taitian." An example is the "Lacquer Vase with *Taicai Baihua*" (Figure 7.6), which was crafted by lacquer artisans in Fuzhou. In this process, tin pieces are embedded in the lacquer base, carved and engraved to create silver lines, filled with colored lacquer, and left to dry. Subsequently, the tin lines are polished to reveal the lacquer surface. In Chengdu, lacquer artisans use a similar technique on carved tin pieces, covering them with transparent lacquer, referred to as "Inlaid Tin Silk Shine" and "Silver Plate Carving Covered with Lacquer."

This section discusses the evolution of gold and silver *pingtuo* lacquerware from the Tang Dynasty to its predecessors—Han Dynasty lacquerware with affixed gold and silver foil, Wei-Jin lacquerware with silver filigree bands, and its successors— contemporary lacquerware with tin *pingtuo*. The purpose is to allow readers to distinguish between various types of lacquerwares. Han Dynasty lacquerware with affixed gold and silver foil did not involve polishing to reveal the lacquer surface. The key process in Tang Dynasty gold and silver *pingtuo* lacquerware is polishing to bring out the lacquer surface. In Wei-Jin lacquerware with silver filigree bands, the raised silver filigree and silver bands are unrelated to polishing. In contrast, in the Tang Dynasty gold and silver *pingtuo* lacquerware, polishing is crucial to achieving a smooth surface between gold and silver pieces and the lacquer. In the Tang Dynasty gold and silver *pingtuo* lacquerware, the embedded elements are gold and silver pieces, while in contemporary tin *pingtuo* lacquerware, affordable tin pieces are embedded. Inventions and innovations occur with each era, reflecting the true nature of history.

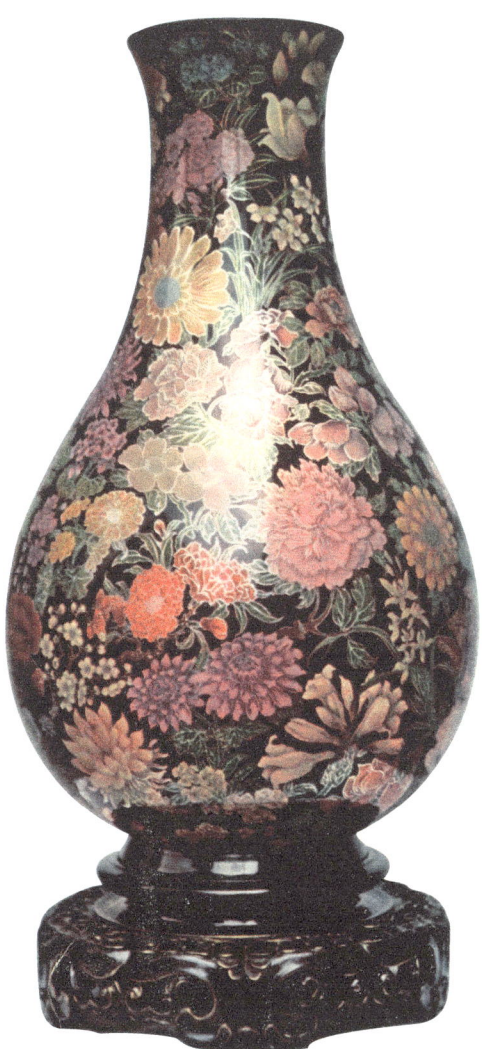

Figure 7.6 [Modern] Lacquer Vase with *Taicai Baihua*, selected from *Zhongguo Gongyi Meishu* (*Chinese Arts and Crafts*), edited by the Editorial Committee of Chinese Arts and Crafts

CHAPTER VIII

Gaozong Destroys Artifacts

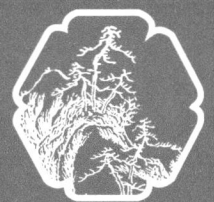

I n the technique of *tianqian* invented by the Tang people, the inlaying of mother-of-pearl was developed by the Song people into two types: thick inlaying of mother-of-pearl and thin inlaying of mother-of-pearl. *Xiushi Lu* refers to it as "one named *zhanqian*, one named *xianbang*, one named *kanluo*, namely, filling with mother-of-pearl." The basic process of thick inlaying of mother-of-pearl is as follows: the patterns carved from conch shell pieces are pasted onto the lacquer body, covered with grey lacquer, carved with patterns, coated with lacquer, and after drying, the patterns are revealed by polishing the lacquer surface. In the hollow of the outer tower of Feiying Pagoda in Huzhou, Zhejiang Province, a "Lacquered Sutra Box with Inlaid Mother-of-Pearl" (Figure 8.1) from the Wuyue Kingdom was discovered. The bottom board's outer wall bears the inscription in vermilion lacquer, "... Guangshun first year (AD 951) October ..." for a total of 47 characters. Although it has been disassembled, it is the earliest extant inlaid mother-of-pearl lacquerware in China. In the brick niche of the central pagoda of Ruiguang Pagoda in Suzhou, a "Lacquered Sutra Box with Inlaid Mother-of-Pearl" (Figure 8.2) from the Northern Song Dynasty was discovered. The black lacquer outer wall is inlaid with luminescent mother-of-pearl floral patterns. It is the earliest complete inlaid mother-of-pearl lacquerware in China, now housed in the Suzhou Museum.

Although the technique of inlaying mother-of-pearl was invented by the Tang people, its peak development occurred during the Song and Yuan dynasties. In the Ming Dynasty, *Xiushi Lu* of Huang Cheng noted that "the shell pieces of ancient times were thick, but now they are gradually thin," referring to the evolution of the inlaying of mother-of-pearl technique during the Song and Yuan dynasties. The change lies in the fact that the thick mother-of-pearl pieces, approximately 1 millimeter thick, transformed into pieces less than 0.1 millimeters, generally ranging from 0.03 to 0.04 millimeters. The mother-of-pearl pieces shifted from being applied to a smooth lacquer surface to being applied to a rough lacquer surface. The technique progressed from finely carving floral patterns, veins, and textures on the mother-of-pearl pieces to meticulously selecting conch shell pieces and sawing them into individual patterns. The subsequent steps-covering with lacquer, waiting for it to dry, polishing to reveal the patterns, and finishing with gloss-are the same. Due to the softening of the mother-of-pearl pieces after thinning, thicker pieces are now referred to as "hard-shell inlay" (also known as "houbei" in Japanese and Korean), while thinner pieces are called "thin-shell inlay" (also known as "baobei" in Japanese and Korean). The latter poses double the difficulty in craftsmanship.

Emperor Huizong of the Song Dynasty, Zhao Ji, had a deep passion for calligraphy, painting, and collectibles. The thin-shell inlay craft experienced significant

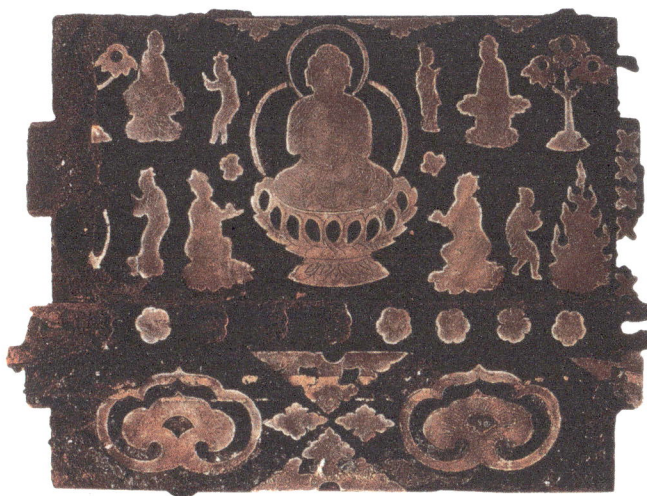

Figure 8.1 [Five Dynasties] Lacquered Sutra Box with Inlaid Mother-of-Pearl, provided by the Huzhou Museum

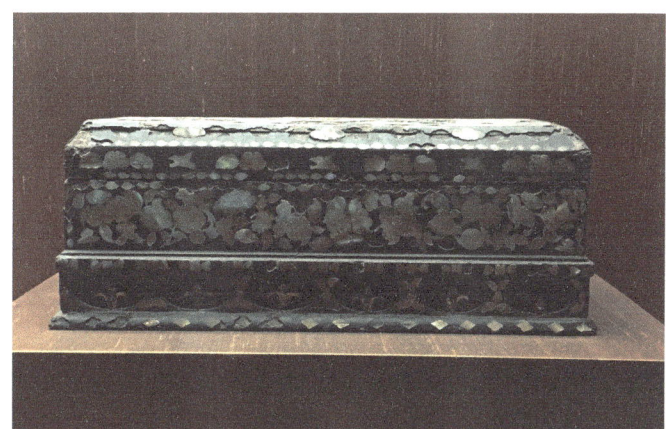

Figure 8.2 [Northern Song] Lacquered Sutra Box with Inlaid Mother-of-Pearl, photographed by the author at the Suzhou Museum

development during his reign, along with other art forms. During the tumultuous events of the Jingkang Incident, Huizong and his successor, Emperor Qinzong, were captured by the Jin forces. The following year, Prince Kang Zhao Gou ascended the throne in Yingtian Fu (present-day Nanjing), becoming Emperor Gaozong, and established the Southern Song Dynasty. In the second year of Jianyan (1128), Emperor Gaozong moved to Yangzhou, where he built the Altar of Heaven and a palace. Jin forces crossed the Huai River the next year, and Emperor Gaozong continued his southward escape. The young emperor, who was just 21 years old, attributed the court's downfall and the nation's humiliation during his exile to Huizong's indulgence in collecting art and calligraphy. Historical records state, "In the year Wushen (1128),

Emperor Gaozong took refuge in Zhenjiang. Previously, this prefecture had collected offerings from Wenzhou and Hangzhou, among which were items adorned with mother-of-pearl. The emperor disliked their fanciness and ordered the prefect Qian Boyan to destroy them."[1] Emperor Gaozong extensively destroyed the delicate and expensive thin-shell inlay lacquerware, incurring massive costs. Various historical records, including *Qingbo Zazhi* (*Qingbbo Magazine*), *Jianyan Yilai Chaoye Zaji* (*Miscellaneous Records of the Court and the Wild Since the Jianyan Era*), *Jianyan Yilai Xinian Yaolu* (*Chronicles of the Jianyan Era*), as well as *Songshi* (*History of the Song Dynasty*) and *Song Huiyao* (*Collected Statutes of the Song Dynasty*), have documented the destruction. *Song Huiyao Jigao* (*Compilation Draft of Collected Statutes of the Song Dynasty*) specifically lists 36 items, including chairs, tables, and footrests, that were destroyed. Thin-shell inlay lacquerware from the Song Dynasty is scarce in domestic collections, perhaps due in part to Emperor Gaozong's extensive destruction of these artworks.

During the Southern Song Dynasty, the Lesser Imperial Court resided in Lin'an (present-day Hangzhou). The four reigns of Emperor Gao, Emperor Xiao, Emperor Guang, and Emperor Ning are collectively referred to as the "Era of Zhongxing." In this period, Wenzhou and Hangzhou continued extensive production of thin-shell inlay lacquerware and lacquer furniture, reaching the pinnacle of the craft. During the reign of Emperor Xiao, there is evidence of the artistry in Su Hanchen's painting *Qiuting Yingxi* (*Autumn Courtyard and Playing Children*), which features a "Thin-Shell Inlay Drum Stool" (Figure 8.3), corroborating with actual artifacts. The craft of thin-shell inlay lacquerware had become so widespread that it even reached the streets and markets of Jiangnan. An anonymous author from the Southern Song recorded in *Xihu Fansheng Lu* (*Records of the Splendors of West Lake*) that in the markets of Lin'an, one could find "thin-shell inlay chairs," "thin-shell inlay throwing drums," "thin-shell inlay drum stands," and various other "thin-shell inlay toys." This further illustrates the prevalence and popularity of thin-shell inlay lacquerware during the Southern Song Dynasty.

From the Jin and Tang dynasties to the Song Dynasty, there was frequent official and civilian interaction between China and Japan. A large number of Song and Yuan Dynasty thin-shell inlay lacquerware items were extensively transmitted to Japan

---

1. [Southern Song] Lu Xian, *Zalu* (*Miscellaneous Records*), vol. 21 of *Jiading Zhenjiang Zhi* (*Gazetteer of Jiading Town in Jiangsu*), bk. 698 of *Xuxiu Siku Quanshu* (*Continuation of the Complete Library in Four Branches*), collection of Wanwei Bookstore (Shanghai Classics Publishing House, 2002), 543.

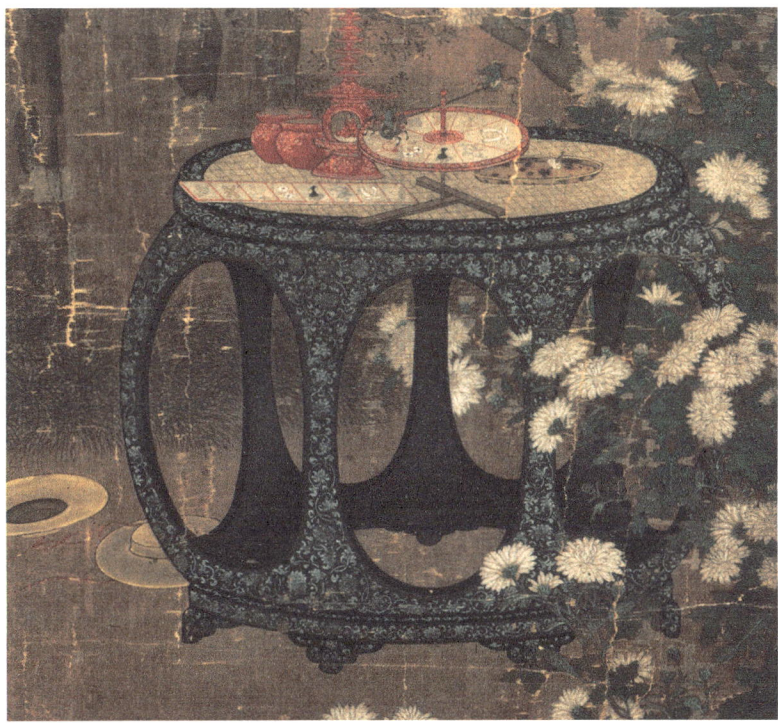

Figure 8.3 [Southern Song] Thin-Shell Inlay Drum Stool, depicted in Su Hanchen's painting *Qiuting Yingxi* (*Autumn Courtyard and Playing Children*), provided by *Hushang Magazine*, painting housed in the National Palace Museum, Taipei

and are now almost entirely housed there. The Eisei Bunko Library in Japan holds a "Thin-Shell Inlay Lacquer Casket with Tower and Figure Patterns" (Figure 8.4) from the Southern Song Dynasty. The casket has lotus petal-shaped multiple layers intricately assembled with meticulous craftsmanship. The multiple layers are tightly stitched together, and the top of the casket is inlaid with thin-shell inlay depicting tower and figure patterns. The octagonal body of the casket features courtyard figures inlaid with thin-shell inlay, and the floral patterns on the clothing are meticulously crafted using thin-shell inlay, creating a rich and orderly design. Another item in the Japanese collection is a "Thin-Shell Inlay Lacquer Plaque with Figure Patterns" (Figure 8.5) from the Song-Yuan transition period. Within a limited height of 56.5 centimeters, this plaque features eleven figures, including the Great Emperor Zhenwu, intricately inlaid with thin-shell inlay. The fine details of the clothing and dynamic cloud patterns are awe-inspiring, making the author wish to kneel before the ancient Chinese craftsmen!

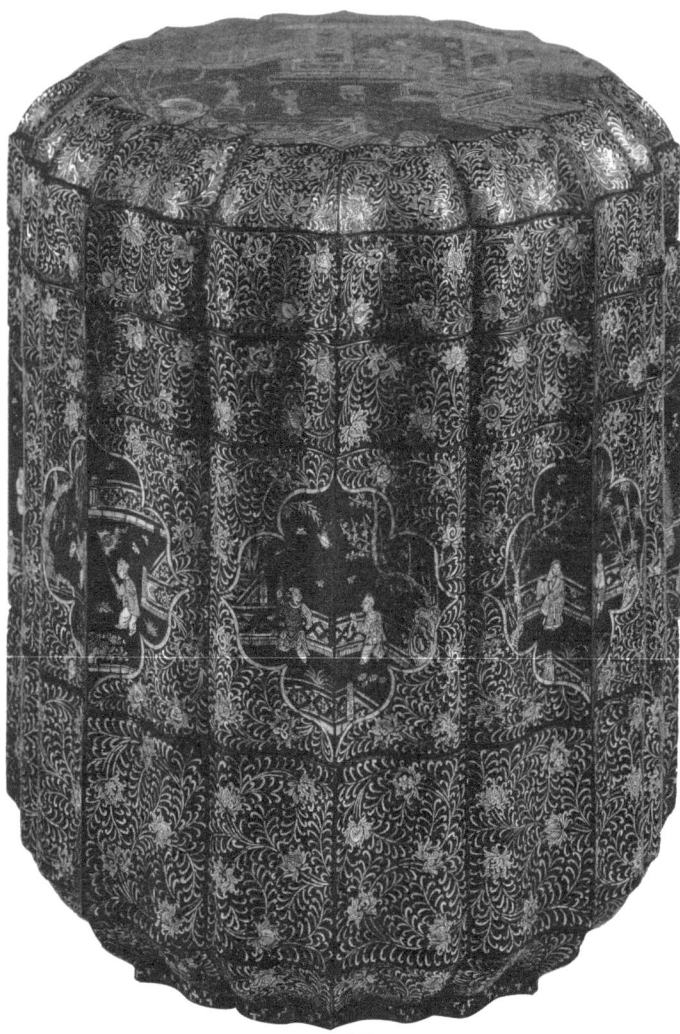

Figure 8.4 [Southern Song] Thin-Shell Inlay Lacquer Casket with Tower and Figure Patterns, held in the Eisei Bunko Museum, Japan, selected from the compilation *Songyuan De Mei* (*Beauty of the Song and Yuan Dynasties*) by the Nezu Museum

Compared to the Song Dynasty, the Yuan Dynasty, especially the later period, maintained the exquisite craftsmanship of thin-shell inlay lacquerware, "rich households undertake construction regardless of the time or month,"[2] and the elegance surpassed that of the Song Dynasty. According to *Zhongguo De Luodian* (*Chinese*

---

2. [Ming] Cao Zhao, *Guqiqi Lun · Luodian* (*Ancient Lacquerware Theor · Thin-Shell Inlay*), vol. 8 of *Xinzeng Gegu Yaolun* (*Newly Expanded Essentials of Ancient and Modern Discourses*), bk. 50 of *Congshu Jicheng Chubian* (*Comprehensive Collection of Series in Initial Compilation*) (The Commercial Press, 1939), 160.

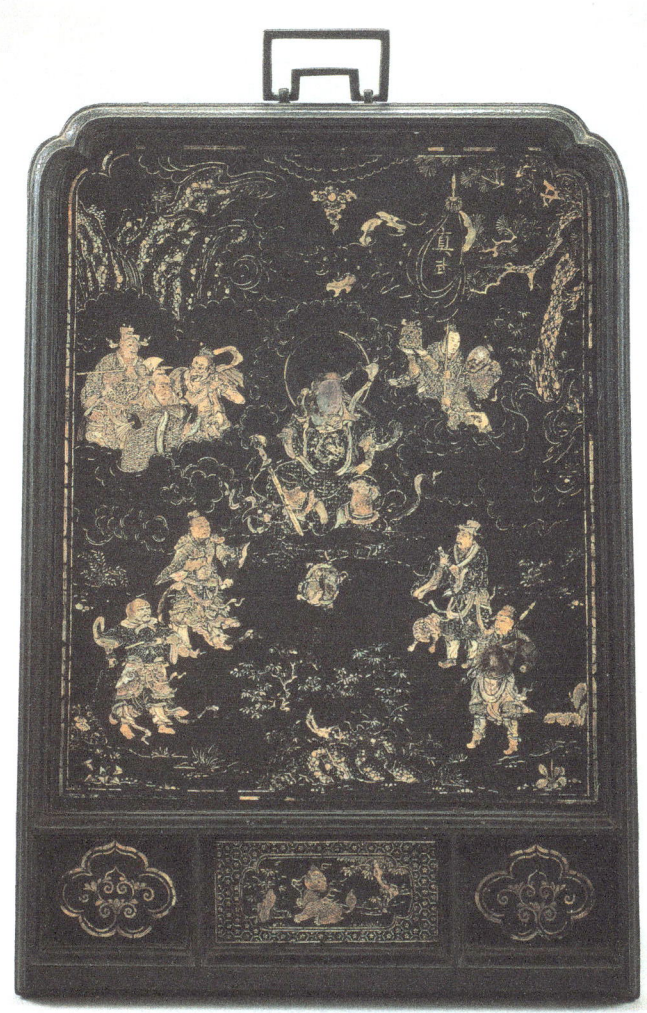

Figure 8.5 [Yuan] Thin-Shell Inlay Lacquer Plaque with Figure Patterns, selected from *Zhongguo De Qigongyi* (*Chinese Lacquer Craft*), edited by Shoto Museum of Art

Thin-Shell Inlay) by Nishioka Yasuhiro, there are 97 Chinese thin-shell inlay lacquerware pieces held in public and private collections in Japan, with 32 of them dating from the Yuan Dynasty's middle and late periods. For instance, the Tokyo National Museum houses a "Thin-Shell Inlay Lacquer Dish with Dragon and Waves Patterns" (Figure 8.6) from the Yuan Dynasty, where cloud patterns, waves, and dragon scales are meticulously inlaid, creating a colorful and radiant appearance. Another example is a privately-owned "Thin-Shell Inlay Lacquer Octagonal Box with Tower and Figure Patterns" with a three-layer heightened lid and legs from the Yuan Dynasty, measuring only 36 centimeters. The inlaid nacre lotus and curling grass on

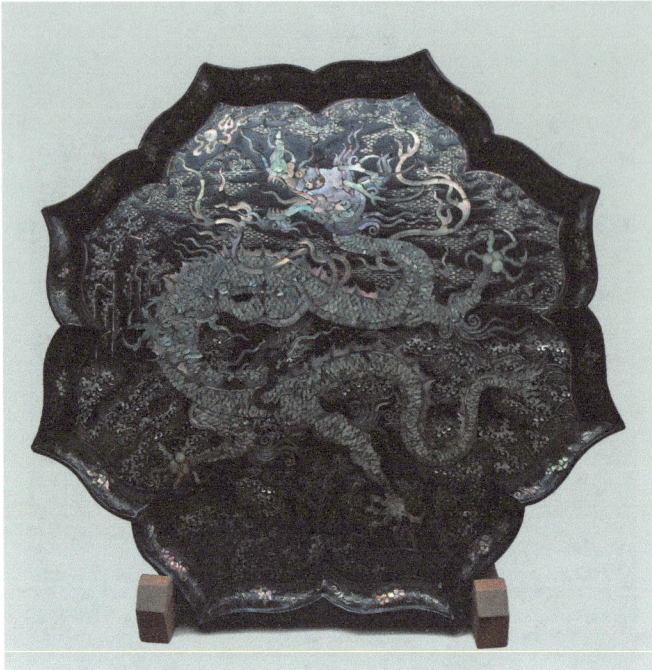

Figure 8.6 [Yuan] Thin-Shell Inlay Lacquer Dish with Dragon and Waves Patterns, photographed by the author at the Tokyo National Museum

the lid rise gracefully, depicting a lush and intricate scene. The intricate craftsmanship leaves one speechless.[3] Some Yuan Dynasty thin-shell inlay lacquerware pieces bear inscriptions like "Craftsmanship by Jishui Tongming," "Luling Hu Zhaogang Iron Pen," and "Yongyang Liu Liangbi Iron Pen," indicating their origin in Ji'an Prefecture, Jiangxi Province. The artistic achievements of Chinese Song and Yuan Dynasty thin-shell inlay lacquerware are rarely paralleled in later periods, and Korean thin-shell inlay lacquerware struggles to compare.

---

3. [Ming] Gao Lian, *Zunsheng Bajian · Yanxian Qingshangjian Shang*, section on "Discussing Carved Red Lacquer, Japanese Lacquer, Carving, and Inlaid Vessels," mentioning the Song Dynasty Thin-Shell Inlay, "For example, carved with snail shells, the bodhisattva is adorned with six kinds of brocade pieces. Regardless of the depth of the snail shell, it is difficult to handle flat objects. Later practitioners rarely achieved its subtleties." It can be seen that the skill of expertly inlaying nacre with uneven surfaces on vessels was already mastered in the Song Dynasty. Quoted from Chang Bei's *Zhongguo Gudai Yishu Lunzhu Jizhu Yu Yanjiu* (*Collection of Annotations and Research on Ancient Chinese Art Treatises*) (Tianjin People's Publishing House, 2008), 322.

CHAPTER IX

Feijin Xiushi

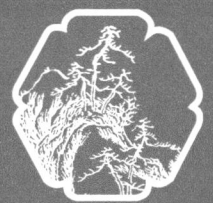

D istinguished from Japanese lacquer artisans who excel in using gold powder and gold leaf flakes, Chinese lacquer artisans excel in using metal leaf powder. The Chinese metal leaf powder *xiushi* technique has developed into a series showcasing the ingenuity and distinctive craftsmanship of Chinese artisans in *xiushi*.

The emergence of the metal leaf powder *xiushi* technique is supported by the material—the introduction of *feijin*. Legend has it that the craft of forging gold leaf was initiated by Ge Hong (AD 283–363) of the Eastern Jin Dynasty. In the Tang Dynasty, gold leaf was used to embellish Buddha statues, and the majestic landscape paintings were pioneered during that era. In the Song Dynasty, renowned artists excelled in creating majestic landscape paintings, and various metal leaf powder *xiushi* techniques, such as gold-leaf application, gold outlining, hidden gold outlining, and raised gold outlining, became popular, forming a diverse series of *feijin xiushi* techniques. In the Song and Yuan dynasties, the *feijin xiushi* technique was documented in literary works. For example, the application of gold leaf is recorded in the official Northern Song Dynasty publication *Yingzao Fashi* (*Architectural Methods*),[1] and the raised gold outlining technique is documented in the late Yuan Dynasty work *Chuogeng Lu* (*A Record of Abandoning Farming*).[2] Written records about the forging of gold leaf, with the earliest being in the Yuan Dynasty by Tao Zongyi in *Chuogeng Lu*, were later elaborated on in the Ming Dynasty by Song Yingxing in *Exploitation of the Works of Nature · Metallurgy Volume Fourteen* and in the Qing Dynasty by Ze Lang in *Huishi Suoyan* (*Idle Talk on Painting*). In contemporary times, the gold leaf forging technique in Nanjing has been recognized as a national-level intangible cultural heritage.

I participated in the Symposium on the Protection and Development of Nanjing Gold Foil Forging Technology, where some scholars traced the history of gold foil forging technology back to the Three Dynasties. I believe it is necessary to clarify some people's vague understanding of gold pieces and gold foil. The processing of metal sheets by humans has undergone a gradual process of thinning from thickness.

---

1. [Northern Song] Li Jie, *Caihuazuo Zhidu* (*System of Color Painting*), vol. 14 of *Yingzao Fashi* (*Architectural Methods*), bk. 3, 2a.

2. [Yuan] Tao Zongyi, *Qiangjin Yinfa* (*Carved Gold and Silver Technique*), vol. 30 of *Chuogeng Lu* (*A Record of Abandoning Farming*), bk. 1040 of *Wenyuange Siku Quanshu* (*Complete Library in Four Branches of Literature from the Wenyuange*) (Commercial Press, Taiwan, 1986), 748–749.

Houhanshu (*Book of Later Han*) records "gold foil,"[3] and the gold thread twisted from Li Chui's tomb in the Tang Dynasty was only 8.956 micrometers thick. The archaeological community refers to it as "gold foil," but in reality, these are gold pieces. *Feijin* is the true meaning of gold foil, with a thickness of only 0.12 micrometers and flying with the wind. Since the advent of *feijin*, historical records have distinguished between gold pieces and gold foil. For example, *Tang Liudian* (*Six Codes of the Tang Dynasty*) separately mentions "attaching gold" (using *feijin*) and "embedding gold" (using gold pieces), indicating that people in the Tang Dynasty were consciously aware of the distinction between *feijin* and gold pieces. In the first year of Xuanhe (1119) during the Northern Song Dynasty, Emperor Huizong mentioned "the use of 567,000 sheets of gold foil for decoration. He said, 'Using gold as a foil to decorate earth and wood, once damaged, it cannot be recovered. It is a great loss.'"[4] The phrase "cannot be recovered" clearly indicates that the decorative material is *feijin*, not gold pieces. It is because people in the Song Dynasty extensively used the emerging material *feijin* that the colorful and rich craft of *feijin xiushi* emerged, forming a series. Nowadays, people should have a conscious awareness to distinguish between *feijin* and gold pieces: anything that can be picked up without backing paper, can be cut into patterns, and can be recycled when embedded in artifacts is a gold piece, formerly known as "thin gold"; anything that flies with the wind, cannot be cut or carved, and cannot be recovered when decorated on artifacts is *feijin*, now called "gold foil." Some scholars trace the origin of lacquerware decorated with impressed gold to gold and silver inlays on Warring States bronze ware. Gold and silver inlays were embedded in gold piece threads, and impressed gold was embedded in *feijin*. The *xiushi* craft of impressed gold into *feijin* can only emerge after the maturity of the *feijin* forging technology.

While there is no physical evidence to prove the existence of foil powder *xiushi* in the Tang Dynasty, in the Northern Song Dynasty, there are many surviving examples of lacquerware adorned with techniques like gold outlining, hidden gold outlining, and impressed gold. Among them, several pieces are classified as national treasures.

---

3. [Jin] Sima Biao, *Houhanshu · Yufu Zhi* (*Book of Later Han · Treatise on Carriages and Clothes*), vol. 12 (Zhonghua Book Company, 1965), 3644. "The carriage ... is adorned with thin gold and dragons, serving as a support for the carriage." This refers to the emperor's carriage in the Han Dynasty, which was inlaid with thin gold pieces rather than *feijin* patterns.

4. [Yuan] Tuitui, *Songshi · Shihuo Zhi* (*The History of the Song Dynasty · Treatise on Food and Commodities*), vol. 13 (Zhonghua Book Company, 2011), 4360.

From 1966 to 1967, a batch of Northern Song Dynasty artifacts was discovered in the heart of the cellar of Huiguang Pagoda in Rui'an City, Zhejiang Province, China. Among them, the "Reliquary Lacquer Box" and the "Sutra Boxes (including Inner Sutra Box and Outer Sutra Box)" are considered national treasures. The Reliquary Lacquer Box has a high cover, a luting top, and a long cover overlapping the body, and the luting top and four walls are built up with lacquer ash in twining lotus patterns and then lacquered with gold. The base is built up with lacquer ash in twining lotus patterns with an openwork, and inside the openwork, lacquer ash is built up with different beasts and then lacquered with gold (Figure 9.1). The four walls of the cover are built up with lacquer ash in Yang patterns, forming a diamond-shaped openwork. Along the openwork lines, pearls are inlaid, and inside the openwork, gold is used to depict a procession of immortals worshipping Buddha (Figure 9.2). The figures are elegant and lifelike, with delicate clothing lines, and the cloud patterns are rendered in varying shades, reminiscent of the famous contemporary painting *Bashiqi Shenxian Juan* (*Eighty-Seven Immortals Scroll*). In contrast to the tall and elongated shape of the Reliquary Lacquer Box, both the Inner Sutra Box and Outer Sutra Box have a horizontal and elongated luting top. The Inner Sutra Box is made of sandalwood and is very elegant. Except for the bottom, all sides are fully gold-plated. The two long walls are surrounded by gold threads, forming a three-dimensional six-petal plum blossom-shaped openwork. Gold-hooked flowers and birds are finely drawn inside the openwork on red-colored ground, forming golden twining lotus patterns and bird patterns. Both inside and outside the openwork, gold and red flowers alternate, creating indescribable exquisite beauty, and the craftsmanship is beyond measure. The later generations' gold plating cannot match it (Figure 9.3). The Outer Sutra Box has a long cover overlapping the body and is mainly decorated with hidden and inscriptive relief gold.[5] The ground pattern is made of relief gold (Figure 9.4). There is an inscription on the bottom of the box, and only a few characters, such as "The Second Year of Qingli Era of Northern Song Dynasty (1042)," can be identified. These three ancient lacquerware masterpieces are exquisitely crafted and serene, serving as treasures in the museum collection of Zhejiang Province.

It is worth noting that in 1978, inside the cellar of Ruiguang Pagoda in Suzhou, a "Pearl Reliquary Stupa" was discovered. The stupa is 122.6 centimeters tall, with an octagonal sandalwood-carved Sumeru base topped by a carved wooden Sumeru

---

5. Hidden relief gold refers to using lacquer mixed with ash to build a relief drawing, decorating it with metal foil powder on the relief drawing; inscriptive relief gold refers to using lacquer mixed with ash to create a sun pattern, decorating it with metal foil powder on the sun pattern.

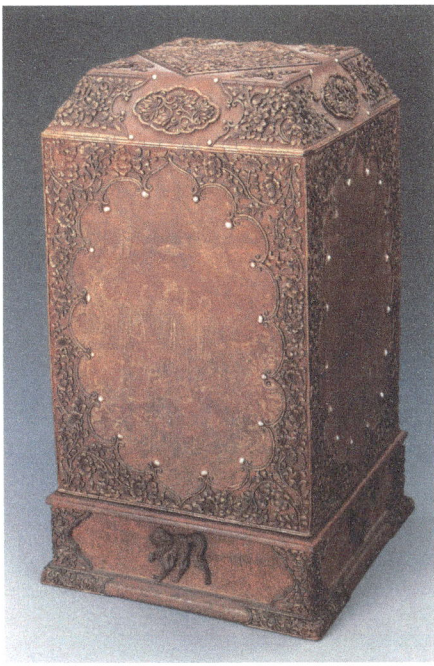

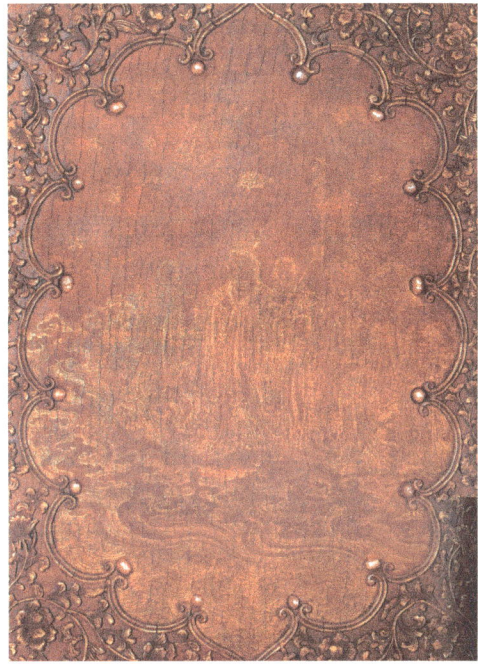

Figure 9.1 [Northern Song] Hidden Gold-Decorated Reliquary Lacquer Box, unearthed from the Huiguang Pagoda in Rui'an, Zhejiang Province, selected from the compilation *Gaomu Qigong* (*Extraordinary Achievements in Weathered Wood*) by the Zhejiang Provincial Museum

Figure 9.2 [Northern Song] Reliquary Lacquer Box with Gold-Decorated Interior Depicting Divine Figures and Buddhist Procession in Diamond Shape, selected from *Zhongguo Meishu Quanji · Gongyi Meishu Pian · Qiqi* (*The Complete Collection of Chinese Art · Applied Arts · Lacquerware*), edited by Wang Shixiang and Zhu Jiajin

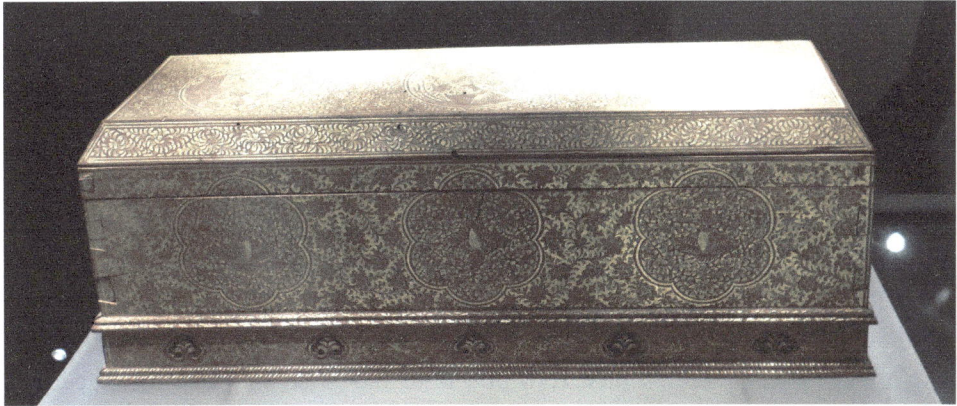

Figure 9.3 [Northern Song] Sandalwood Inner Sutra Box with Gold Decoration, unearthed from the Huiguang Pagoda in Rui'an, Zhejiang Province, photographed by the author at the Zhejiang Provincial Museum

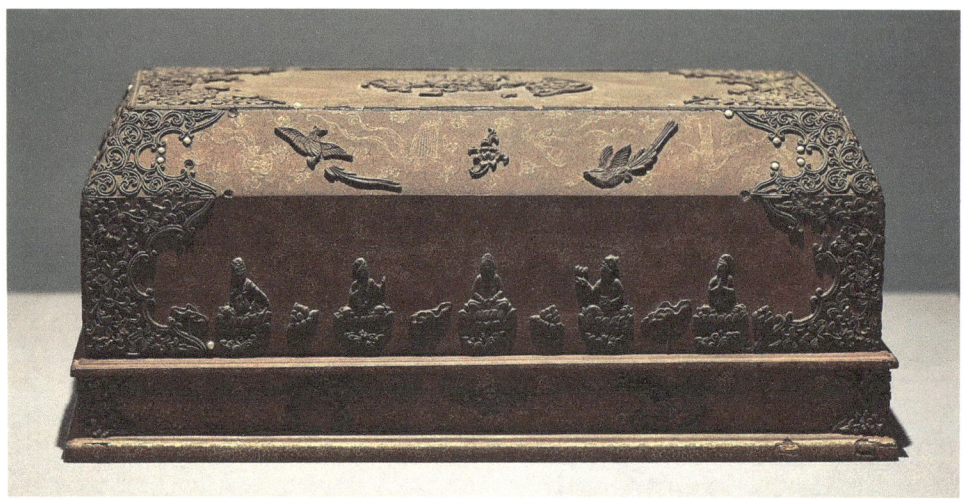

Figure 9.4 [Northern Song] Hidden Gold-Decorated Outer Sutra Box, unearthed from the Huiguang Pagoda in Rui'an, Zhejiang Province, photographed by the author at the Zhejiang Provincial Museum

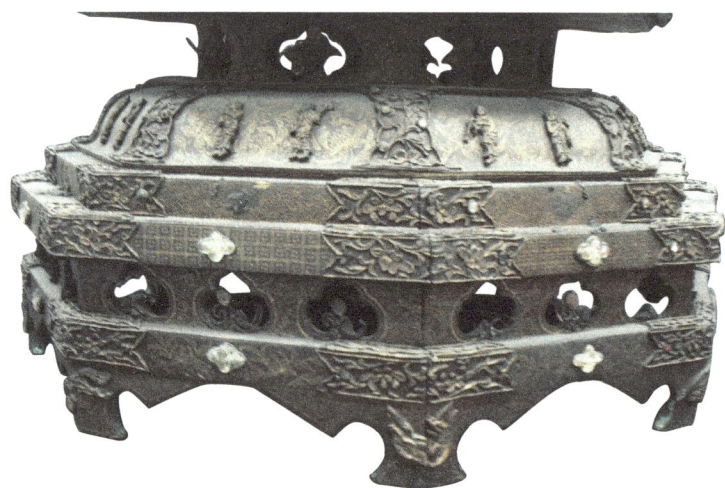

Figure 9.5 [Northern Song] Pearl Reliquary Stupa with Hidden Gold-Decorated Base, photographed by the author in the storage room of the Suzhou Museum

mountain, surrounded by an openwork wooden railing. The Sumeru base is crafted with relief gold techniques, depicting twining lotus and other floral patterns. It features oil paint mixed with ash for sculpting branch flowers, flying deities, and worshippers, followed by mud gold application. Gold lines twist and turn on the wooden-carved and lacquered Sumeru mountain, with rows of pearls and a running dragon. On top of the Sumeru mountain is a wooden lacquered Buddha shrine adorned with a circle of pearls and gemstones. Eight golden dragons soar into the sky, connected to the top of the stupa by eight gold chains. The stupa's top holds a large crystal bead. On the wooden box containing the sacred stupa are painted images of the Four Heavenly Kings and an inscription dated "The Sixth Year of Dazhong Xiangfu (1013)" and more. This discovery, known as the "Pearl Reliquary Stupa," predates the Northern Song Dynasty "Reliquary Lacquer Box" and Inner and Outer Sutra Boxes by 29 years. Its elegant, tall, and slender form, precious materials, and exquisite craftsmanship make it a rare and comprehensive work of art. It is included in the Suzhou Museum as the only artifact prohibited from leaving the country. It is recognized as one of the "Nine Great Treasures of the Nation" by *National Humanities History*. The base of the stupa is the earliest known physical example of wooden carving with hidden relief gold craftsmanship (Figure 9.5). Due to the accumulation of dust in the long-locked storage room, the gold color appears dim. The replica of the "Pearl Reliquary Stupa" displayed in the exhibition hall has a base that has been replaced with wooden carving (Figure 9.6), and viewers are advised to discern this difference themselves.

As a type of foil powder *xiushi*, "qiangjin" refers to the use of a knife to draw patterns on the lacquer surface, and when the gold size in the grooves is dry and adhesive, gold foil powder is applied into the grooves to create gold line drawings. A significant number of *qiangjin* lacquerware items were unearthed from Southern Song Dynasty tombs in Cunqian Township, Wujin District, Changzhou City, Jiangsu Province. These items include lacquer caskets, lacquer boxes, lacquer mirror cases, and lacquer mirror boxes.[6] Due to these discoveries, the Changzhou Museum has become a key institution for the collection of Song Dynasty *qiangjin* lacquerware in China. A brief introduction of these items is provided below.

The "Silver Button Twelve-Faceted Lotus-Petal Shaped *Qiangjin* Courtyard Ladies Painting Vermilion Lacquer Casket" unearthed from Tomb No. 5 of the Southern Song Dynasty in Cunqian Township, Wujin District, Changzhou City, is a national treasure. The casket is only 21.3 centimeters high with a diameter of 19.2 centimeters, and it is made of curled wood in a three-colliding lotus-petal style, coated with vermilion lacquer on the outer surface. The silver buttons along the edges of each collision are thick and sturdy, ensuring the integrity and strength of the

---

6. Chen Jing and Chen Lihua, "Cleaning Summary of Southern Song Tombs in Cunqian Township, Wujin District, Jiangsu," *Archaeology*, no. 3 (1986); Chen Jing, "Remembering the Newly Excavated Precious Lacquerware from Southern Song in Wujin, Jiangsu," *Cultural Relics*, no. 3 (1979).

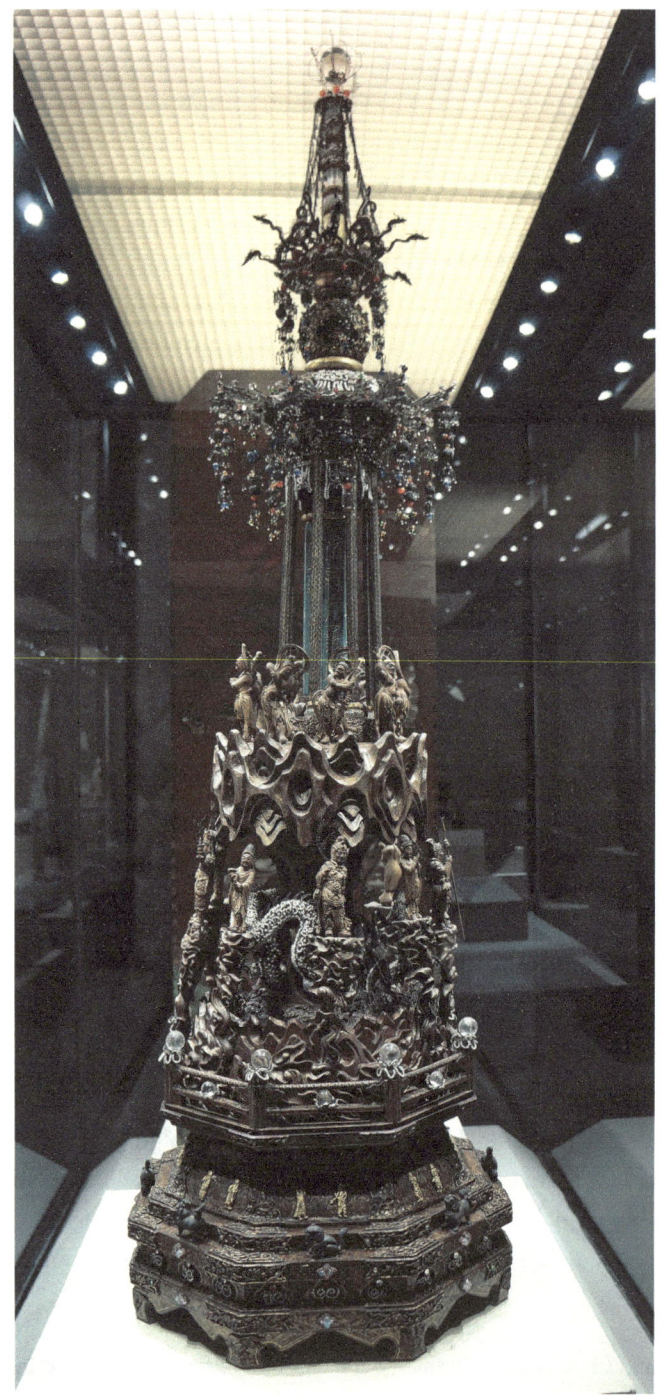

Figure 9.6 [Northern Song] Replica of the Pearl Reliquary Stupa, provided by Leng Jian

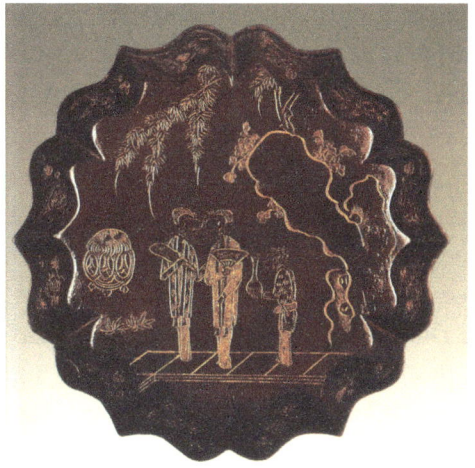

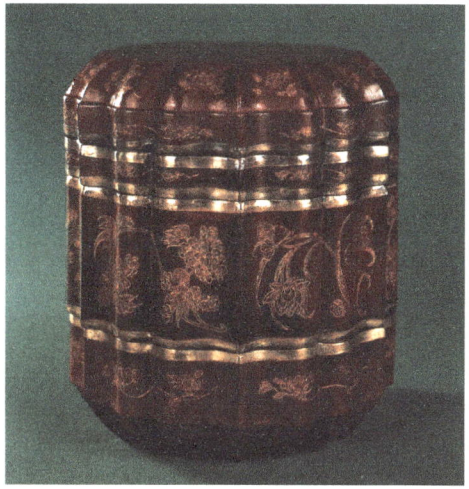

Figure 9.7 [Southern Song] Silver-Buttoned Twelve-Sided Lotus-Shaped Carved Gold Vermilion Lacquer Box Lid, selected from *Zhongguo Meishu Quanji* (*The Complete Collection of Chinese Art*)

Figure 9.8 [Southern Song] Silver-Buttoned Twelve-Sided Lotus-Shaped Carved Gold Vermilion Lacquer Box, selected from *Zhongguo Meishu Quanji* (*The Complete Collection of Chinese Art*)

lacquer casket. The gold foil decoration on the lid depicts the painting *Yuanlin Shinü* (*Court Ladies Painting*) (Figure 9.7): two court ladies wearing Song-style flower-patterned straight-collar robes and floor-length skirts, each holding a circular fan or a folding fan, walking slowly, with a maidservant holding a bottle standing on the side. The gold foil on the clothing of the court ladies forms intricate floral patterns, with delicate details on facial features and thicker application on willow trees and rocks. The gold foil decoration on the outer surface of the casket depicts branching flowers, and fine brushstroke patterns are visible on the flower petals (Figure 9.8). The inside of the lid bears a red lacquer inscription that reads, "Wenzhou Xinhe Jinnian Wulang Shanglao" (Produced in Xinhe, Wenzhou, by Kinnen Goro, Top Quality), consisting of 10 characters.

The "Vermilion Lacquer and *Qiangjin* Figural and Floral Rectangular Box," unearthed from Tomb No. 5 in Cunqian Township, features a lustrous vermilion lacquer exterior with exquisite gold foil decoration. On the lid, a gold foil depiction portrays an elderly person with an exposed belly leisurely walking with a walking stick, displaying a relaxed demeanor. The four walls are adorned with gold foil branching floral patterns, resembling a simple and fresh sketch, with clear brushstroke details on the flowers and leaves. The box exudes an air of elegance, and inside the lid is a red lacquer inscription that reads, "Dingyou Wenzhou Wuma

Zhongnian Erlang Shanglao"(Produced in Wenzhou in the Year of Dingyou by Wuma Zhongnian Erlang, Top Quality), consisting of 12 characters.

The "Black Lacquer with Inlaid Gold Scene of Stacked Xipis and Willow Pond Rectangular Lacquer Box," unearthed from Tomb No. 4 in Cunqian Township, features a black lacquer exterior. On the lid, a gold foil scene depicts a small view of willow branches by a pond. The surrounding walls and the lid walls are adorned with gold foil floral patterns, and pearl-shaped indentations are densely drilled into the gaps of the patterns, filled with bright red lacquer. Inside the lid is a red lacquer inscription that reads, "Gengshen Wenzhou Dingzi Qiaoxiang Xie Qishu Shanglao" (Produced in Dingziqiao Alley, Wenzhou in the Year of Genshen by Xie Qishu, Top Quality), consisting of 13 characters. This type of craftsmanship, known as "stacking *xipi* inlay with gold foil," is recorded in *Xiushi Lu*. This box stands as the earliest known surviving example of stacked *xipi* lacquerware in China. Tomb No. 5 in Cunqian Township also yielded fragments of silver-inlaid *xipi* lacquerware, making it the only known example of Song Dynasty silver-inlaid *xipi* lacquerware, currently housed in the Changzhou Museum.

Japan refers to "qiangjin" as "chinkin" and houses several *qiangjin* lacquerwares from the Yuan Dynasty. The National Museum of Kyushu in Japan possesses a *qiangjin* peacock-patterned sutra box from the Yuan Dynasty. It features black lacquer inscribed with the characters "Second Year of Yanyou (1315), Hangzhou Oil Bureau." This item is designated as an "Important Cultural Property" in their collection. The Tokyo National Museum holds a Yuan Dynasty "Black Lacquer with Inlaid Gold Lotus and Tang Grass Pattern Rectangular Handbox," which exhibits a wide variety of gold line variations, surpassing the intricacy of the lacquerware unearthed from the Cunqain Township tomb. In the 15th and 16th centuries, Ryukyu lacquerware imitating Chinese "qiangjin" reached its peak, featuring distinctive characteristics such as vermilion and green lacquer grounds. Shurijo Castle, the ancient royal palace of Ryukyu, houses *chinkin* lacquerware from the 16th to 19th centuries. Some 16th-century pieces closely imitate Chinese Yuan Dynasty *qiangjin*, with exceptional examples found in the Urasoe Art Museum's collection, such as the "Green Lacquer with Inlaid Gold Phoenix and Cloud Pattern Circular Cabinet" from the 16th century, considered a masterpiece among their collection of *chinkin* lacquerware.

CHAPTER X

Xitang Lacquer Village

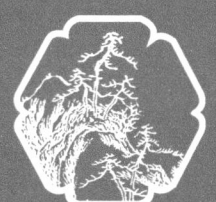

I n ancient China, there was a saying, "Entities that transcend the material world and substantive existence are referred to as the Dao; while those that are materialized, substantiated, and concretized are referred to as artifacts" (*Book of Changes · Appended Judgments*). The overall status of craftsmen was low. During the Qin and Han dynasties, there was a system of "Wule Gongming" (carving the craftsman name), which aimed to "test their sincerity," meaning to examine the sincerity of craftsmen by inspecting the quality of their products. In the Song Dynasty, the literati developed a trend of appreciating and collecting artifacts, leading to the emergence of literary works on the appreciation of artifacts. In the later period of the Yuan Dynasty, Southern Chinese culture experienced a revival. Scholars praised artifacts and craftsmen, and craftsmen's names reappeared on the artifacts. Their deeds were also recorded in local gazetteers. During the Ming and Qing dynasties, the idea of human-centered thinking first sprouted in Jiangnan, and the self-awareness of craftsmen in Jiangnan awakened. They started inscribing their names on artifacts, not to "test their sincerity" but to establish their reputation.

During the Southern Song to Yuan and Ming dynasties, numerous industrial and commercial towns emerged in Jiangnan. In Zhejiang, the waterways of Xitang in Jiaxing were well-connected, fostering prosperous agricultural and trade activities. Craftsmen such as Zhang Cheng, Yang Mao,[1] Zhang Degang, Peng Junbao, and Bao Liang from Xitang in the Yuan Dynasty were recorded in local gazetteers. *Jiaxing Fuzhi* (*Records of Jiaxing Prefecture*) records, "Zhang Degang, a resident of Xitang. His father Cheng, along with Yang Mao from the same village, excelled in lacquerware with carved and red-colored decorations."[2] Since then, Xitang, known as the hometown of lacquerware, gained widespread fame. Names like Zhang Cheng, Yang Mao, and Zhang Degang became renowned. During the Edo period in Japan, there was a lacquer craftsman known as "Yang Cheng. It is said that he inherited his family tradition from Zhang Cheng and Yang Mao of the Yuan Dynasty."[3] Taking one character each from

---

1. Yang Mao (扬茂): In the extant copied version of *Xiushi Lu*, the earliest is the manuscript from Jianjiatang. Later copies and prints have variations in the name, being written or printed as "杨茂." In contemporary interpretations, Mr. Suo Yuming from the National Palace Museum in Taipei and the author have considered the earliest manuscript as "扬茂."

2. *Jiaxing Fuzhi* (*Records of Jiaxing Prefecture*), vol. 17, Nanjing Library collection, Kangxi 21st year (1682), 112b. Originally recorded as Yang (杨) Ming, Mr. Suo Yuming's research revealed that it was actually "Yang" (扬), and the craftsman who made "Carved Red Floral Pattern Waste Bucket" signed his name as "Yang" (扬). See Suo Yuming, "Tihong Kao (Study on Red Carving Lacquer)," *Gugong Jikan* (*Palace Museum Quarterly*) 6, no. 3 (1972).

3. [Qing] Huang Zunxian, *Gongyi Zhi* (*Craftsmanship Records*), vol. 10 of *Riben Guozhi* (*Japan's Annals*) (Shanghai Ancient Books Publishing House, 2001), 430–431.

the names of Zhang Cheng and Yang Mao, he adopted the name "Duizhu Yangcheng." The Tokyo National Museum houses his work called "Piled Vermilion Tray with Pine, Bamboo, and Plum Motifs." Another Chinese artisan, Ouyang Yuntai, resided in Nagasaki for an extended period, creating lacquerware with carved designs. He became known as "Yuntai Diao" among the people of Nagasaki.

Zhang Cheng and Yang Mao were not the creators of the red-carving craft. In terms of its origins, this craft can be traced back to the Jin and Tang dynasties. The technique involves layering accumulated transparent lacquer, which becomes extremely hard after drying. Lacquer craftsmen discovered that by incorporating layers of well-cooked tung oil into natural lacquer to a certain thickness, the lacquer layer becomes soft and convenient for carving. The exploration of the potential of lacquer and tung oil led to the birth of the intricate carved lacquer craft known as "tixi" in the Six Dynasties of southern China. A 5th-century Chinese carved lacquer box featuring the technique of *tixi* is housed in the Shanghai Museum, as documented in publications such as *Zhongguo De Qigongyi* (*Chinese Lacquer Craft*) by the Shoto Museum of Art and *Zhongguo Qiyi Erqiannian* (*Two Thousand Years of Chinese Lacquer Art*) by the Chinese University of Hong Kong Art Museum. The red-carving technique was invented by lacquer craftsmen during the Tang Dynasty. Historical records state, "The Tang production is mostly like printing boards, engraved with flat brocade, vermilion color, and the carving method is ancient and simple, worthy of appreciation ... The Song and Yuan productions have clear hidden edges, smooth rising, and delicate details." (Huang Cheng, *Xiushi Lu*). In other words, the Tang Dynasty red-carving exhibited an ancient and simple appearance that resembled printing boards, while the Song and Yuan dynasties mastered the red-carving technique, showcasing exquisite craftsmanship. During the Song Dynasty, lacquer craftsmen also developed various types of carved lacquer, such as black carving and colored carving.

The Tang-era red-carving technique is no longer extant. Physical examples of Song Dynasty carved lacquer are scarce within China but are predominantly found in collections in Japan. The Tokyo National Museum, Nezu Museum, and Kyushu National Museum in Japan house a considerable number of Chinese Song and Yuan Dynasty carved lacquer artifacts. Examples include the Song Dynasty "Red-Carved Zuiweng Pavilion Round Plate" from the Enkaku-ji Temple collection in Kanagawa and the Song Dynasty "Red-Carved Landscape with after Red Cliffs Poetry Round Plate" from the Kyushu National Museum, both displaying a flat visual effect, disregarding spatial depth, reminiscent of early carved lacquer with a plate-like appearance. Private collections in Japan also feature a Northern Song "Red-Carved

Peony and Tang Grass Pattern Dish Stand" (Figure 10.1) showcasing voluptuous and twisting peony and tang grass patterns with shallow carving, delicately engraved with six-petaled flowers in the gaps of the patterns against a beige lacquer background, exuding a harmonious and luscious beauty. The Tokyo National Museum holds a Southern Song "Black-Carved Floral Pattern Lacquer Plate" (Figure 10.2), with shallow carving, gracefully displayed flowers and leaves, and a worn edge revealing a hidden red lacquer layer within the black lacquer, forming a red lacquer line contours, finely polished without sharp angles, imparting a subtle and warm aesthetic. The Hayashibara Museum of Art in Japan houses a Southern Song "Black-Carved Dragon Pattern Lacquer Box" (Figure 10.3), depicting twin dragons moving in a Tai Chi pattern, surrounded by cloud patterns, with a thicker lacquer layer. The carving reveals red lacquer beneath the black layer, creating a looped and repetitive red line, presenting

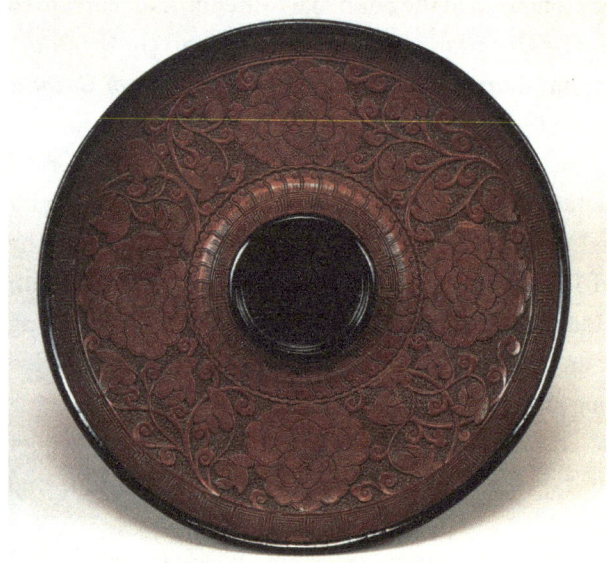

Figure 10.1 [Northern Song] Red-Carved Peony and Tang Grass Pattern Dish Stand, selected from *Zhongguo De Qigongyi* (*Chinese Lacquer Craft*), edited by Shoto Museum of Art

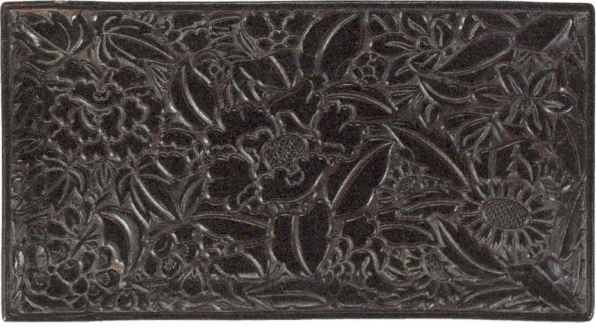

Figure 10.2 [Southern Song] Black-Carved Floral Pattern Lacquer Plate, photographed in the storage of the Tokyo National Museum by the author

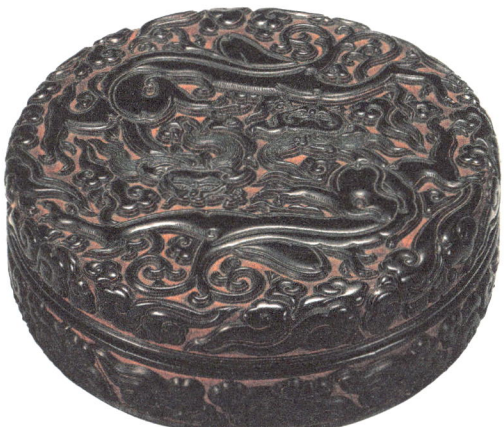

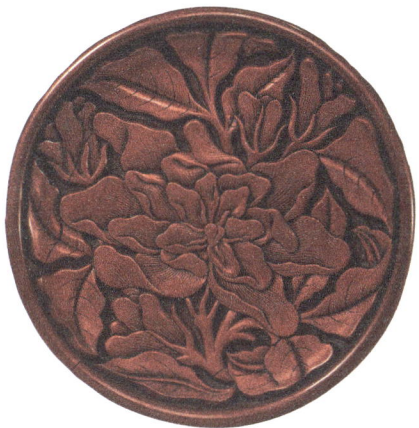

Figure 10.3 [Southern Song] Black-Carved Dragon Pattern Lacquer Box, in the collection of the Hayashibara Museum in Japan, selected from *Songyuan De Mei* (*Beauty of the Song and Yuan Dynasties*), edited by the Nezu Museum

Figure 10.4 [Yuan] Red-Carved Gardenia Round Plate, selected from *Gugong Bowuyuan Cang Diaoqi* (*Carved Lacquerware in the Palace Museum*)

an exquisite and beautiful appearance. The red-carving tradition continued into the Yuan Dynasty, with artifacts like the "Red-Carved Gardenia Round Plate" (Figure 10.4) crafted by Zhang Cheng and held in the Palace Museum in Beijing. The plate features a single flower intricately carved across the entire surface, with plump and gracefully unfurled petals, a rounded finish, and a glossy sheen. Another artifact from the Forbidden City Museum in Beijing is the "Red-Carved Landscape and Figures Eight-Sided Plate" (Figure 10.5) signed by Yang Mao. The center of the plate depicts a scene of literati life in southern China, with precise and well-polished carving devoid of sharp edges. However, in terms of nat-

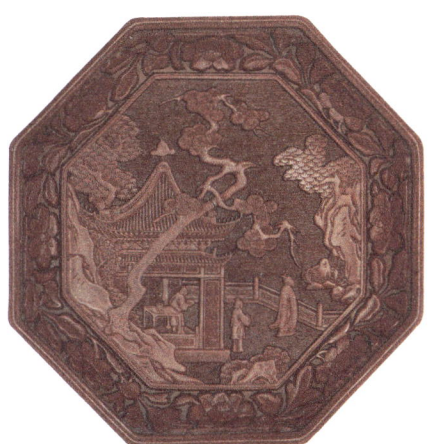

Figure 10.5 [Yuan] Red-Carved Landscape and Figures Eight-Sided Plate, selected from *Zhongguo Lidai Yishu · Gongyi Meishu Bian* (*Chinese Art and Craftsmanship through the Ages*), edited by Li Zhongyue, Zhang Dunsheng, and Li Hong

ural appeal, the Yuan Dynasty carved lacquer surpasses that of the Song Dynasty. Nowadays, on the market, one can occasionally encounter red-carved lacquerware with inscriptions attributed to Zhang Cheng and Yang Mao, though the majority of these are considered modern forgeries.

In the early Ming Dynasty, the red-carving technique inherited the style of red carving from the Yuan Dynasty in Jiaxing, characterized by "clearly hidden knives, smooth pressing techniques, and delicate engraving methods for brocade patterns. This method was used from the Song and Yuan dynasties to the Ming Dynasty." (Huang Cheng, *Xiushi Lu*). In the first, fourth, and fifth years of the Yongle era, the emperor gifted more than 200 red-carved lacquer items to Japan.[4] Initially, Emperor Yongle did not prioritize the creation of objects for enjoyment, and the lacquerware he gifted to Japan originated from the Hongwu period in Nanjing and its surrounding areas.[5] In the late Ming Dynasty, records by Liu Dong and Yu Yizheng mention, "For red carving, in the Song Dynasty, gold and silver were often used as a base, in the Ming Dynasty, tin-wood became the base, and during the Yongle period, it was produced in the Guoyuan Factory. Trays, plates, and boxes varied ... The technique involved thirty-six layers of red lacquer, intricately carved with fine brocade and a glossy black lacquer base. The phrase 'Made in the Yongle Reign of the Great Ming' was needle-engraved ... Afterward, the factory's products never matched those of the past. The craftsmen were often punished, so they privately purchased concealed trays, plates, and boxes and presented them, grinding away the Yongle inscriptions with needle writing and engraving large characters of the Xuande reign, with thick gold applied over them. Therefore, inscriptions of the Xuande period are all products of the Yongle era. Genuine original inscriptions from the Yongle period are rare."[6] Emperor Yongle reigned for 22 years, and it was only 19 years (1421) after his reign began that the capital was moved. Given the initial challenges associated with relocating the capital, it can be inferred that the "Guoyuan Factory" was in Nanjing. *Jiaxing Fuzhi* records: "Zhang Degang, a native of Xitang. His father, Cheng, along with his fellow villager Yang Mao, were skilled in lacquerwork and red carving. During the Yongle era, their works were purchased by Japan and Ryukyu, and upon hearing of this, Emperor Chengzu summoned them to the capital. By then, both had passed away. Degang continued his father's legacy, and after being summoned to the capital for an interview and proving his skills, he was appointed as a deputy in the construction

---

4. The detailed list of Japanese gifts received during the Yongle period includes 203 pieces of *tihong* lacquerware; see *Diaoqi* (*Carved Lacquer*) compiled by Tokugawa Art Museum and Nezu Museum (1984), 237–238.

5. Lee King-tsi and Hu Shih-chang, "Carved Lacquer of the Hongwu Period," *Oriental Art* 4, no. 1 (2001).

6. [Ming] Liu Dong and Yu Yizheng, *Dijing Jingwu Lue* (*Brief Record of the Scenery of the Imperial Capital*), vol. 4 (Classical Literature Publishing House, 1957), 68.

and repair office."[7] Here, "the capital" clearly refers to Nanjing, and the "construction and repair office" was located in Nanjing, with the "Guoyuan Factory" subordinate to the "construction and repair office." During the Xuande period, the Guoyuan Factory moved to Beijing. The emperor summoned the renowned Jiaxing craftsman, Bao Liang, as the deputy of the "construction and repair office." However, the craftsmen from the north did not match those from the south. Considering that the northern climate lacked the advantages of lacquerwork that the southern climate possessed, red carving began to decline towards the end of the Xuande era. This is evidenced by records stating that during the Xuande period, lacquer workers "ground away the Yongle inscriptions with needle writing and engraved large characters of the Xuande reign, with thick gold applied over them."[8] Mr. Xia Gengqi from the Palace Museum gradually explored the Xuande-era red-carved items stored in the warehouse and discovered that many were altered. Xuande red-carved items were rare, to the extent that Emperor Qianlong, upon finding a needle-engraved "Made in the Yongle Reign of the Great Ming" inscription on the base of a "Peony Red-Carved Lacquer Round Box," joyously composed a poem within the lid, expressing gratitude for obtaining this treasure from a previous era and wondering which god was protecting him.[9]

During the Song Dynasty, lacquer craftsmen also invented the technique of "ticai," as noted by Gao Lian in *Zunsheng Bajian · Yanxian Qingshangjian Shang*. Gao Lian mentioned, "Using five-colored lacquer as the base, with varying depths of carving, revealing colors in accordance with the design, such as red flowers with green leaves, yellow centers with black stones, etc., it is striking and visually appealing, but very few have been handed down."[10] The lacquerware with *ticai* from the Song Dynasty has been collected in places like the Tokugawa Art Museum in Japan. However, domestically, collections of *ticai* lacquerware do not date back earlier than the Ming Dynasty. An example is the design of the Xuande "Carved Polychrome Large Offering

---

7. *Jiaxing Fuzhi* (*Records of Jiaxing Prefecture*), vol. 17, Nanjing Library collection, Kangxi 21st year (1682), 112b.

8. [Qing] Gao Shiqi, *Jin'ao Tuishi Biji* (*Golden Arowana Retreat Notes*), bk. 588 of *Wenyuange Siku Quanshu* (*Complete Library in Four Branches of Literature from the Wenyuange*) (Commercial Press, Taiwan, 1986), 425.

9. The "Peony Red-Carved Lacquer Round Box" with the Yongle mark, about which Emperor Qianlong composed a poem, is preserved in the National Palace Museum in Taipei.

10. [Ming] Gao Lian, *Zunsheng Bajian*, selected edition in *Zhongguo Gudai Yishu Lunzhu Jizhu Yu Yanjiu* (*Collection and Research on Ancient Chinese Art Theories*) (Tianjin People's Publishing House, 2008), 321.

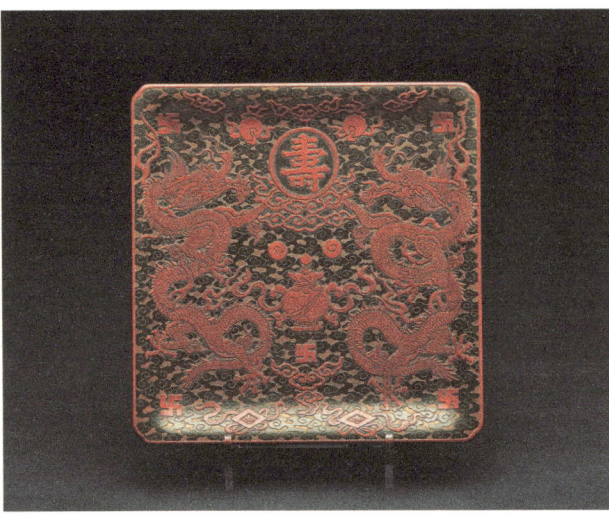

Figure 10.6 [Qing] Carved Lacquer Plate with Dragon Pattern in Horizontal Colors, selected from Special Exhibition of Nanjing Weaving Museum (Lacquerware of the Yuan, Ming, and Qing Dynasties)

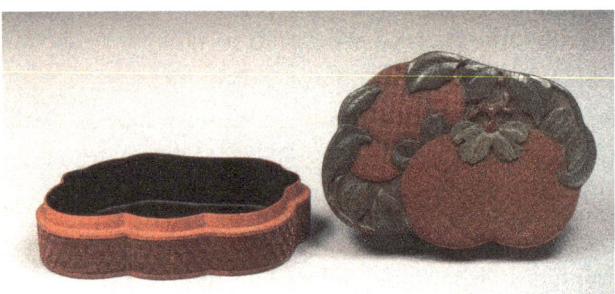

Figure 10.7 [Qing] Carved Lacquer Box with Persimmon Pattern in Layered Colors, selected from *Heguang Ticai—Gugong Cangqi* (*Radiance and Refinement—Lacquerware in the Collection of the National Palace Museum, Taipei*)

Box with Apple and Double Magpie Pattern" preserved in the Beijing Palace Museum, which is a first-class cultural relic. In the Qing Dynasty, the number of domestically preserved *ticai* lacquerware items increased, featuring both "zhongse" (horizontal colors), as seen in Figure 10.6, and "duise" (vertical colors), as seen in Figure 10.7.[11]

---

11. Carved Lacquerware in horizontal Colors and layered carved lacquerware, refer to techniques mentioned in *Xiushi Lu* of Huang Cheng during the Ming Dynasty.

CHAPTER XI

Treasury of Craftsmanship

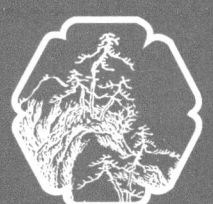

During the Longqing period (1567–1572), Huang Cheng, a renowned lacquer craftsman from Xin'an, Anhui, summarized the experiences of his predecessors and wrote the only ancient treatise on *xiushi*—*Xiushi Lu*. *Xiushi* has been explained before; *Xiushi Lu*, as the name suggests, is a systematic record of *xiushi* techniques. Half a century later, during the Tianqi period (1621–1627), Yang Ming from Xitang, Jiaxing, meticulously annotated and wrote a preface for it. Since then, *Xiushi Lu* has become a classic work in the history of *xiushi* craftsmanship in China, East Asia, and even the world.

After the publication of *Xiushi Lu*, it circulated among craftsmen in the form of handwritten copies, but it soon disappeared from the domestic scene. The Qing Dynasty's compilation of *Siku Quanshu* (*Complete Library in Four Branches of Literature*) did not include it, and literary notes did not pay attention to it. This indicates that *Xiushi Lu* was not highly valued by the imperial court and literati. In the mid-Edo period in Japan (roughly the early Jiaqing period of the Qing Dynasty in China), the owner of Jianjiatang possessed a handwritten copy of *Xiushi Lu* known as the "Jianjiatang manuscript" (Figure 11.1), which eventually made its way to the Imperial Museum (now the Tokyo National Museum). In 1972, Mr. Suo Yuming, a researcher

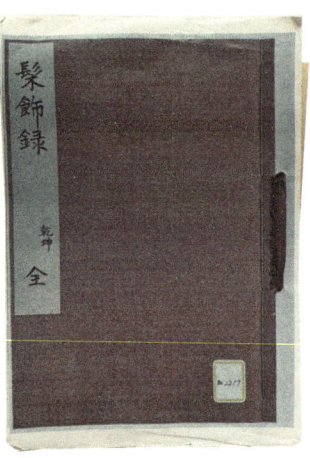

Figure 11.1 Color reproduction of Jianjiatang manuscript of *Xiushi Lu*, gifted by a Japanese friend

at the National Palace Museum in Taipei, obtained a photocopy of the Jianjiatang manuscript from his Japanese friend Inoue Kei, and it was reproduced in the October issue of the Taipei *Palace Museum Monthly* the same year. Since then, the Jianjiatang Manuscript of *Xiushi Lu* has spread in the Chinese-speaking world. What did *Xiushi Lu* write, and what are its characteristics?

This book is divided into two volumes, with a total of 18 chapters. The first volume is titled *Qian Ji*. The first chapter, "Utilization First," describes celestial phenomena such as heaven, earth, sun, moon, stars, wind, thunder, lightning, clouds, rainbow, dawn, rain, dew, frost, snow, hail, and other astronomical phenomena. It metaphorically compares the manufacturing of lacquerware to the materials and tools of nature, including mountains, water, seas, tides, rivers, Luo River, and springs. To the unfamiliar reader, this chapter may seem like reading a celestial book, but careful contemplation by craftsmen is required to comprehend its philosophical depth. The metaphors used in the writing make it concise and imbued with philosophical insight.

The second chapter, "Kai Fa," emphasizes the principles of *xiushi* and lists various potential flaws that may arise in various crafts. It highly emphasizes the dedication and pursuit of excellence as ethical principles for craftsmen. It introduces the "Three Principles": "craftsmanship of nature" suggests emulating nature; "quality mimics the human form" implies that the materials of lacquerware (body, ashes, cloth, lacquer) correspond to the bones, flesh, tendons, and skin of the human body; "design reflects *yin* and *yang*" indicates that the patterns on lacquerware are based on the principles of *yin* and *yang*. It then presents the "Two Cautions": caution against excessive cleverness and distraction of the heart and caution against excessive elaboration that dazzles the eyes but lacks substance. This implies opposition to the prevailing trend of excessive sophistication, advocating practicality over superficial aesthetics. Additionally, it introduces the "Four Failures": borrowing admonitions from ancient classics like the *Book of Rites* and *Analects of Confucius*, emphasizing meticulousness in craftsmanship and the need for careful inspection after completion. Lacquerware that deviates from established rules should not be sold in the market. The annotation by Yang Ming includes the phrase "not to be carved," a reference to the saying in *Analects of Confucius* that "decayed wood cannot be carved," explicitly pointing to the craftsman's conduct. Finally, it presents the "Three Illnesses": opposition to keeping one's unique skills secret, opposition to the lack of unity between local interests and overall design, and opposition to disharmony between patterns and colors. The "Three Principles," "Two Cautions," "Four Failures," and "Three Illnesses" not only discuss the principles of lacquerware craftsmanship but also serve as ethical guidelines for craftsmen to follow in their behavior.

The second volume is titled *Kun Ji*. Chapters three to sixteen, from "Quality and Color" to "Single Color," comprise a total of 14 chapters, each documenting a specific type of lacquerware decoration technique. Chapter Seventeen, "Quality Method," details the craftsmanship of lacquerware fabrication, while Chapter Eighteen, "Admiring Antiquity," focuses on the imitation of antique, contemporary, and restoration techniques in lacquerware. These sixteen chapters systematically outline the extensive system of Chinese *xiushi* techniques. They vividly depict the flourishing era of *xiushi* in the mid-to-late Ming Dynasty, showcasing a multitude of patterns and decorations that are beyond comprehension. Using the changes of *yin* and *yang* as the standard for classifying lacquerware decoration techniques, the work exhibits a rich creation with distinct Chinese characteristics. The final chapter, "Admiring Antiquity," serves as a dedicated section advocating the value of "respecting the old while knowing the new." It encourages future craftsmen to honor traditions while exploring new possibilities. The last section of the "Admiring Antiquity" chapter is titled Imitation, where the author classifies imitative works into two categories: imitating the ancient and imitating the contemporary. Those who imitate the ancient should capture the subtleties of ancient craftsmanship, while those imitating the contemporary should understand the local styles. Yang Ming adds a note stating that all imitative works should be marked with the name of the imitator. *Xiushi Lu* emphasizes the ethical conduct of craftsmen, reflecting the principle that, in establishing a career, one must first establish one's character.

In the mid to late Ming Dynasty, the handicraft and commercial sectors in Jiangnan thrived, leading to a flourishing cultural environment among the urban population. The trend of collecting and appreciating art became prevalent, prompting lacquerware to move from uniformity to seeking uniqueness. During this period, the forms and patterns of lacquerware underwent innovation, showcasing a myriad of creative and intricate decorations. In the late Ming era, western missionaries introduced practical utensils from the West. Chinese literati began to reconsider the longstanding practice of treating craftsmanship as trivial and started shifting their focus from "Dao" to "Technique." Works such as Xu Guangqi's *Nongzheng Quanshu* (*Complete Book on Agriculture and Administration*), Song Yingxing's *Tiangong Kaiwu* (*Exploitation of the Works of Nature*), Ji Cheng's *Yuan Ye* (*Gardens and Furnaces*), Huang Cheng's *Xiushi Lu*, Wang Zheng's *Yuanxi Qiqi Tushuo* (*Illustrated Explanation of Exotic Artifacts from the Far West*), among others, were the products of the practical learning trend of late Ming. These works distanced themselves from the conventional notes of most literati, delving into the field and workshops to document practical production and design practices. After the publication of *Xiushi Lu*, lacquerware craftsmanship in East Asia continued to grow, evolve, and advance. It is largely built upon the craft system documented in *Xiushi Lu*, demonstrating adaptability, innovation, and transcendence. *Xiushi Lu* became a significant work in ancient China, establishing its own systematic and philosophically profound approach to craftsmanship after *Kaogong Ji*. Simultaneously, it gained recognition worldwide as a classic in the field of lacquerware craftsmanship.

In modern times, Chinese scholars have written several commentaries on *Xiushi Lu*. Broadly speaking, Mr. Wang Shixiang's *Commentary on Xiushi Lu* is based on the "Zhu's Carved Edition," specifically the version that was copied and annotated by Zhu Qiqian under the supervision of Kan Duo, after being copied from the Jianjiatang manuscript by the Japanese Omura Seigai. This version has undergone multiple reproductions and reprints. Mr. Suo Yuming's *Commentary on Xiushi Lu*, and Chang Bei's *Illustrations and Discussions on Xiushi Lu*, *Xiushi Lu and East Asian Lacquer Art*, and *Analysis of Xiushi Lu* all use the original manuscript, the Jianjiatang manuscript as their base text, encompassing all versions that have been passed down worldwide. The 2021 edition of Chang Bei's *Illustrations and Discussions on Xiushi Lu* and the 2014 edition of *Xiushi Lu and East Asian Lacquer Art* provide a comparative commentary using both the Jianjiatang manuscript and a later manuscript, the Tokugawa manuscript. Mr. Suo Yuming's *Commentary on Xiushi Lu* is concise and accessible, suitable for all readers (Figure 11.2). Mr. Wang Shixiang's *Commentary Xiushi Lu* is scholarly and well-referenced, suitable for scholars in a study environment (Figure 11.3). Chang Bei's *Xiushi Lu and East Asian Lacquer Art* comprehensively reviews the East Asian 8,000-year *xiushi* craft system, with a wealth of information, emphasis on field investigation and original documents and strong visual appreciation through images, and the recorded craftsmanship is practical and reproducible (Figure 11.4). Chang Bei's *Analysis of Xiushi Lu* interprets *Xiushi Lu* according to the actual process of lacquer decoration craft, suitable for workers and the general public (Figure 11.5). The 2021 edition of Chang Bei's *Illustrations and Discussions on Xiushi Lu* (Figure 11.6) presents a three-dimensional perspective compared to the 2007 edition. The textual criticism is more rigorous and comprehensive, with tighter explanations and more typical, comprehensive, and rigorous data selection. It respects the original context and is suitable for multidisciplinary scholars to read. *Xiushi Lu* remains intertwined with Chinese and East Asian history, flowing through the great rivers of East Asian culture and human culture.

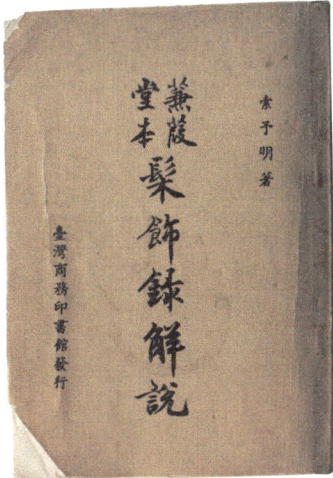

Figure 11.2 *Commentary on Xiushi Lu* by Suo Yuming, published by Commercial Press, Taiwan, in 1974

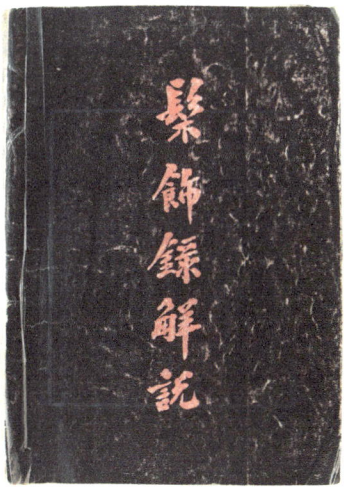

Figure 11.3 *Commentary Xiushi Lu* by Wang Shixiang, published by Cultural Relics Press in 1983

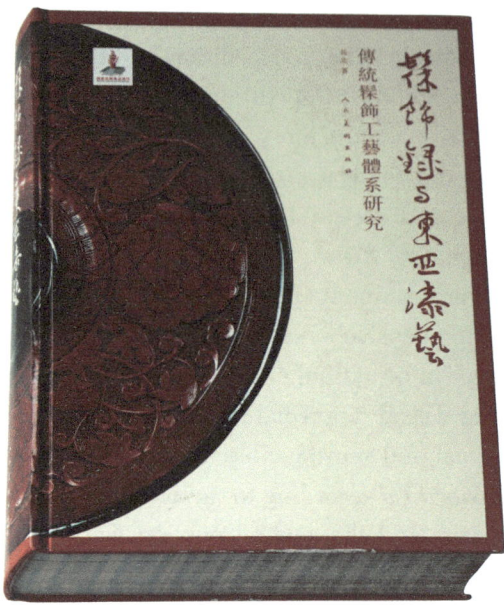

Figure 11.4 *Xiushi Lu and East Asian Lacquer Art* by Chang Bei, published by People's Fine Arts Publishing House in 2014

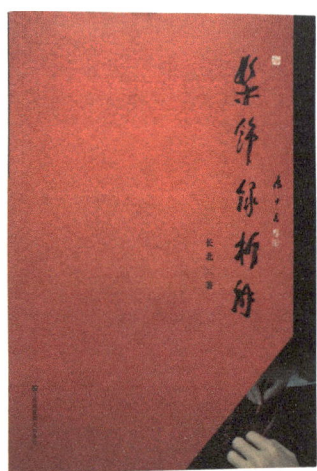

Figure 11.5 *Analysis of Xiushi Lu* by Chang Bei, published by Jiangsu Phoenix Fine Arts Publishing House in 2017

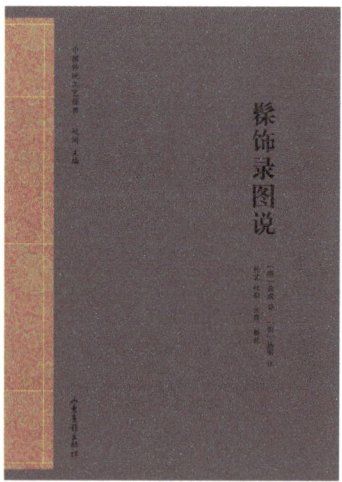

Figure 11.6 Revised Edition of *Illustrations and Discussions on Xiushi Lu* by Chang Bei, published by Shandong Pictorial Publishing House in 2021

CHAPTER XII

The Rise of Foreign Lacquer

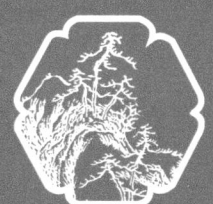

T he term "yangqi" (foreign lacquer) refers not to industrial paint but specifically to Japanese lacquerware that entered China during the Ming and Qing
dynasties. Emperor Kangxi first introduced this term, and subsequently, the
Qing palace archives used "yangqi" to refer to lacquerware imitating Japanese styles
and gold-painted lacquerware from various regions.

As is well known, before the Ming Dynasty, Japan extensively studied Chinese
culture. During the Ming Dynasty, Japanese lacquerware and decorative techniques
were transmitted back to China, marking a new stage of frequent cultural exchanges
between China and Japan. "During the Xuande period, a lacquer craftsman named
Yang was sent to Japan to impart his skills. Yang's son, Xun, mastered the techniques
and, with his own innovative ideas, applied multicolored gold and gems, going beyond
the traditional methods. The artworks were so exquisite that when the Japanese saw
them in China, they pointed and admired them, thinking that although their country
had originated the method, they could not achieve this level of excellence."[1] *Xiushi Lu*
documented many *xiushi* techniques unprecedented before the Xuande period, such
as gold painting with inserts, gold painting with inserts and contrasting colors, gold
painting with scattered gold, gold painting with scattered gold and inserts, colored
oil with contrasting mud and gold with inserts of gold and silver pieces. These were
precise techniques either from foreign lacquer or imitated by Chinese lacquer artisans
influenced by foreign lacquer techniques. *Zunsheng Bajian · Yanxian Qingshang
Jian* (*Treatise on the Eight Essentials of Nurturing Life: Record of Appreciation · On
Carved Red Lacquer, Japanese Lacquer, Carving, and Inlaid Vessels*) by Gao Lian
from the Ming Dynasty provides insights into this trend during late Ming, stating that
there were imitations of Japanese lacquerware, especially by craftsmen Jiang Huihui
in Wu, who excelled in mimicking the techniques. They used lead-sealed mouths, gold
and silver floral pieces, inlaying with gems, gold painting, and various techniques that
closely resembled the Japanese style. However, many of the imitations in the present
day are considered fake. It can be seen that imitating the foreign lacquer became
fashionable among Chinese lacquer workers during the late Ming Dynasty.

The prerequisite for Chinese lacquer artisans to imitate foreign lacquer was
having objects to reference. Gao Lian from the late Ming mentioned, "Japanese
lacquerware is considered the best, and their techniques for making the base are

---

1. [Qing] Chen Ting, vol. 18 of *Liangshan Motan* (*Dialogue on Two Mountains*), bk. 1143 of *Xuxiu
Siku Quanshu* (*Continuation of the Complete Library in Four Branches*) (Shanghai Classics
Publishing House, 2002), 354.

also excellent. For instance, they make round boxes with three small boxes nested inside, extending to five, seven, or nine nested boxes, with an outer diameter of about an inch and a half. The inner boxes resemble lotus seed shells, meticulously adorned with gold details. The smaller boxes each weigh three parts. How are they made? There are square boxes with four, six, and nine nested boxes, as well as chests, writing instrument replacement boxes, hairpin boxes, gold-bordered red lacquer trinket boxes, gold-sprinkled writing desks, handboxes with gold decorations, gold-sprinkled powder boxes, pen holders, gold-pasted fan boxes, gold-sprinkled wooden lid corner washbasin covers, and many others with covers, ranging from large to small square boxes. There are even cabinets for books that are exquisitely crafted. There are gold and silver pieces embedded in various round boxes, bamboo-segment boxes, knot boxes, waist boxes, and inkstone boxes. There are secret cabinets, single-flower vases, wine decanters with gold-copper-inlaid spouts, folding wine cups with a large cup-like top, and an embedded tube used to cover a large bowl. The outer part of the bowl is adorned with mud, gold, and colored flowers, suitable for pouring wine to prevent spills. There are bowls and dishes, red as cinnabar. There are gold-sprinkled and inlaid silver wine trays. There are magistrate plates containing Japanese stone inkstones, water containers, knives, and dusters. There are lead (tin) inlaid and capped small rectangular boxes, pen holders, tea caskets, lacquer niches with Guanyin, and Zhunti Mahala Buddhas. There are small round incense burners with three or four layers and hanging waist incense burners with five and three compartments. There are octagonal tea trays, tea cups, pointed-bottom persuasion cups, copper-covered smoking blankets, mirror cases, and gold and silver inlaid mountain and water bird Japanese desks, measuring over two feet in length and slightly over one foot in width, with a height of two inches. There are incense desks measuring two feet in height, with gold and silver inlaid *Zhaoyun Tu (Portrait of Zhaojun)*, exquisitely detailed. There are various utensils, and it is impossible to enumerate them all. The lacquerware crafted by the Japanese is incredibly skillful and refined!" It is evident that in the late Ming, Japanese lacquerware made a significant entry into China. The National Palace Museum in Taipei once held an exhibition and published *Splendid Lacquerware from the Qing Palace—Special Exhibition of Japanese Lacquerware from the Imperial Court Collection* (Figure 12.1) based on the Qing Dynasty's secret collection of Japanese lacquerware.

Collecting Japanese lacquerware still couldn't satisfy the emperor's insatiable desire for possession. The Qing Palace archives reveal that the emperor ordered craftsmen to replicate foreign lacquerware in the palace. In the eighth year of

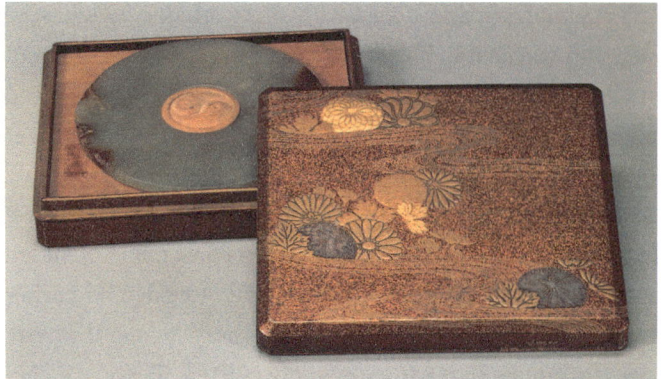

Figure 12.1 [Edo] Handbox with Fan Pattern and Scattered Flowers, selected from Chen Huixia's compilation *Splendid Lacquerware from the Qing Palace—Special Exhibition of Japanese Lacquerware from the Imperial Court Collection*

Yongzheng (1730), the emperor commanded to build "a cellar specializing in imitating foreign lacquer" in the palace.[2] Various places, including Nanjing, Suzhou, Yangzhou, and Fuzhou, contributed imitated Western lacquerware to the palace, uninterrupted for over a century from the Kangxi to Jiaqing reigns. For instance, in the thirty-second year of Kangxi (1693), Li Xu from Suzhou presented 26 pieces of imitated Western lacquerware, such as "lacquer boxes with gold and silver pieces and drum-shaped lacquer boxes."[3] In the seventh year of Yongzheng (1729), "Eunuchs Zhang Yuzhu and Wang Changgui brought offerings, including a golden lacquer Wanshou tripod, an imitated Foreign lacquer Wanshou screen for foreign envoys, a carved lacquer five-dragon throne (split with brocade cushions), an imitated foreign lacquer sweet-scented kangs armrest, two imitated foreign lacquer cloud-shaped side tables, four imitated foreign lacquer hundred-step lanterns, three palace-design furnace vases, a Wuanfu Youtong sweet-scented kang table, a small sweet-scented kangs table, a sweet-scented flower vase, and a palace-design incense plate, all presented by Sui Hede."[4] In the eighth year of Yongzheng (1730), Gao Bin, the Suzhou Provincial Governor, contributed "a dozen pairs of Suzhou-made imitated foreign

2. Zhu Jiajin, *Yangxindian Zaobanchu Shiliao Jilan* (*Compilation of Historical Materials from the Department of Construction and Management of Yangxin Hall*), vol. 1 (Forbidden City Publishing House, 2003), 202.

3. In December of the thirty-second year of Kangxi, Suzhou weaver Li Xu submitted a report on the New Year's dragon robe and lacquerware folds (with a list), included in *Kangxichao Hanwen Zhupi Zouzhe Huibian* (*Compiled Memorial to Emperor Kangxi in Han Characters*), vol. 1 (Archives Publishing House, 1984), 8.

4. Chinese First Historical Archives and Hong Kong Chinese University Museum, eds., *Qinggong Neiwufu Zaobanchu Dangan Zonghui* (*Archives Compilation of the Imperial Household Department of the Forbidden City*), vol. 4 (People's Publishing House, 2005), 199–200, "Record of Events."

lacquer side tables."[5] "In the twelfth year of Yongzheng (1735), the treasury regularly received four imitated foreign lacquer kangs tables and two imitated Foreign lacquer bookshelves from Gao Qizhuo."[6] In the tenth year of Qianlong (1745), the Suzhou Provincial Governor, An Ning, presented "two pairs of imitated foreign lacquer bookshelves, a pair of imitated foreign lacquer bookcases, a pair of imitated foreign lacquer zither tables, a pair of imitated foreign lacquer screen stands, and a pair of imitated foreign lacquer chrysanthemum and *ruyi*-pattern natural kangs tables,"[7] and so on. The Palace Museum in Beijing houses more than 2,400 pieces of Western lacquerware and over 1,600 pieces of imitated Western lacquerware, second only to carved lacquerware.[8] Some items, such as the "Imitated Foreign Lacquer Filled Kangs Armrest" (Figure 12.2) presented by Sui Hede from Jiangning Weaving, are still preserved in the Forbidden City in Beijing.

In late Ming, it was noted that "the Japanese use crushed gold in lacquer, grinding the lacquer until the gold is visible, and the particles are round and sharp, hence distinct. The Jiang (Huihui) uses scattered gold leaves, which are thin and

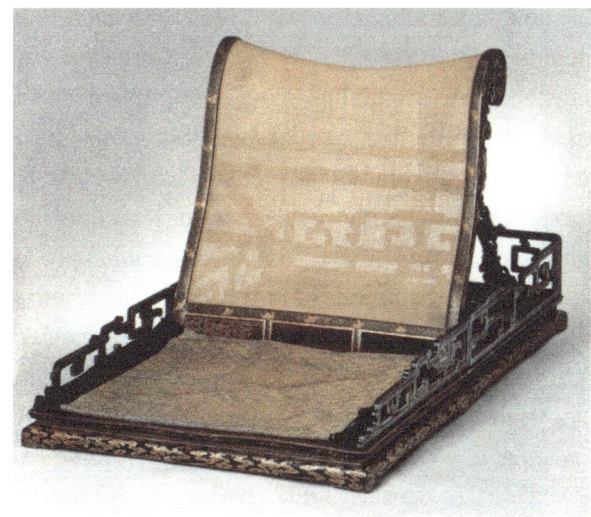

Figure 12.2 [Qing] Imitated Foreign Lacquer Filled Kangs Armrest, collected in the Palace Museum in Beijing, selected from *Yangxindian Zaobanchu Shiliao Jilan* (*Compilation of Historical Materials from the Department of Construction and Management of Yangxin Hall*), complied by Zhu Jiajin

---

5. Xia Gengqi, "Exploring the Origins of Foreign Lacquer and Imitation Foreign Lacquer in the Collection of the Palace Museum," *Palace Museum Journal*, no. 6 (2015).

6. Li Jiufang, ed., *Gugong Bowuyuancang Wenwu Zhenpin Daxi Qingdai Qiqi* (*Cultural Relics and Treasures in the Palace Museum Collection Series: Qing Dynasty Lacquerware*) (Shanghai Science and Technology Press, 2006), 29.

7. Xia Gengqi, "Exploring the Origins of Foreign Lacquer and Imitation Foreign Lacquer in the Collection of the Palace Museum," *Palace Museum Journal*, no. 6 (2015).

8. Ibid.

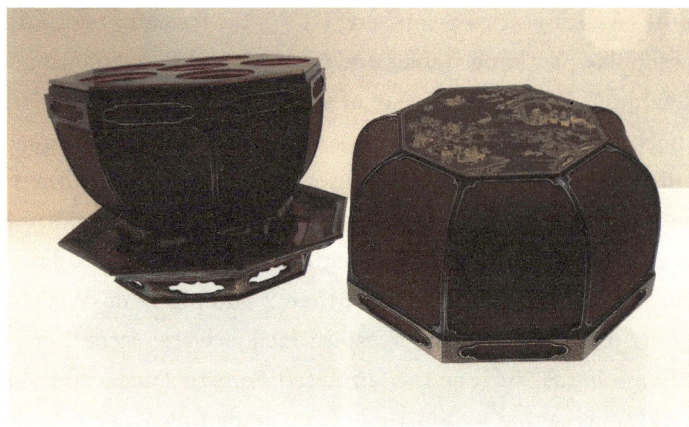

Figure 12.3 [Qing] Octagonal Box with Eight Immortals Birthday Celebration Using Black Lacquer, Gold Paint, and Imitation Foreign Lacquer, photographed by the author at the Shanghai Museum

indistinct.["9] Emperor Yongzheng criticized the production of foreign lacquer boxes, stating, "Although the lacquer is good, the patterns cannot penetrate the substance" (Figure 12.3).[10] Here, "lacquer" refers to the deep and transparent coating of imitated lacquer, resembling clear water when exposed to light. The phrase "patterns cannot penetrate the substance" is because Chinese lacquer workers at that time had not mastered the "original painting" technique of sprinkling gold powder on the lacquer base, solidifying the powder, and then polishing it. Instead, they used gold leaf to imitate painting on the lacquer surface. As a result, the gold on Chinese lacquerware appeared "either diffuse when light or heavy, swollen, and lacking luster." In contrast, on Japanese *maki-e* lacquerware, the gold appeared "with varying intensity, density, resembling a painting, and the lacquer color and gold color never mixed, and dust did not adhere."[11] This indicates that, until the early Qing Dynasty, Chinese lacquer workers had not fully grasped the essence of imitating Western lacquer.

In the mid-Ming period, the cross-cultural *xiushi* technique "piaoxia" was first recorded in works such as the *Hongzhi Wenzhou Fuzhi* (*Prefecture Records of Hongzhi Wenzhou*). In the early Qing Dynasty, Anhui native Fang Yizhi (1611–1671) explained

---

9. [Ming] Liu Dong and Yu Yizheng, *Dijing Jingwu Lue* (*Brief Record of the Scenery of the Imperial Capital*), vol. 4 (Classical Literature Publishing House, 1957), 68.

10. Zhu Jiajin, *Yangxindian Zaobanchu Shiliao Jilan* (*Compilation of Historical Materials from the Department of Construction and Management of Yangxin Hall*), vol. 1 (Forbidden City Publishing House, 2003), 235.

11. [Qing] Xie Kun, *Jinyu Suosui* (*Golden Jade Trifles*), in *Meishu Congshu* (*Art Series*), ed. Huang Binhong and Deng Shi, vol. 2 (Jiangsu Ancient Books Publishing House, 1986), 1820, section "East Asian Lacquer, Deer Antler Ash, and Eight Treasures Ash."

"piaoxia" in his work *Wuli Xiaoshi* (*A Brief Introduction to Physics*), stating, "*Piaoxia* is hiding lacquer. First, paint the flowers and then lacquer them. The result is polished,"[12] indicating that the key to the technique of "piaoxia" is "hiding lacquer." "Hiding lacquer" refers to covering transparent lacquer over the raised flower patterns on the lacquer base. Chinese lacquer workers call them "hidden flowers," "shadow flowers," "sunk flowers," or "dark flowers" (Figures 12.4, 12.5). If *piaoxia* is combined with gold, the gilded patterns are concealed beneath the transparent lacquer, ensuring durability and avoiding the problem of being "thin and indistinct." In modern China, lacquer workers often use aluminum foil powder instead of gold foil powder. The transparent lacquer's reddish-brown color is layered over the silver-colored foil powder. Depending on the height of the raised flowers and the thickness of the transparent lacquer, it presents an extremely rich and layered gold color, such as light gold, yellow gold, and red gold. The gold light is deeply hidden beneath the transparent lacquer, and the polishing can reveal the transparent lacquer surface. The depth, intensity, and variation create a profound and mysterious aesthetic (Figure 12.6).

 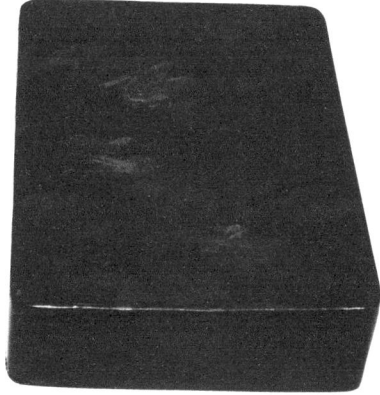

Figure 12.4 [Late Ming to early Qing] *Piaoxia* Lacquer Inkstone Box Inscript by Dai Zhen from Dongyuan, photographed by the author at the Huizhou Cultural Museum in China

---

12. [Qing] Fang Yizhi, *Lacquerware Method*, vol. 8 of *Wuli Xiaoshi* (*A Brief Introduction to Physics*), bk. 867 of *Wenyuange Siku Quanshu* (*Complete Library in Four Branches of Literature from the Wenyuange*) (Commercial Press, Taiwan, 1986), 912.

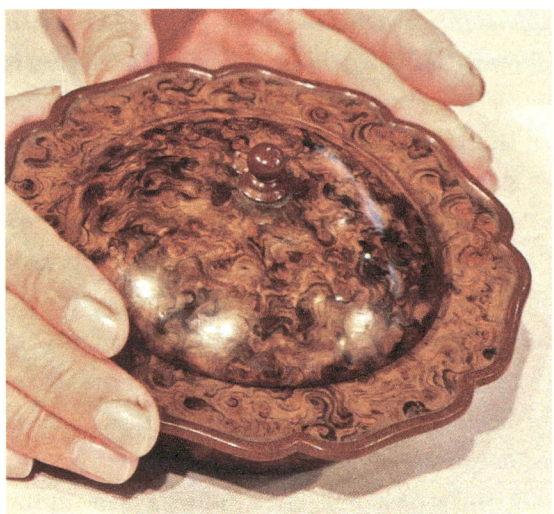

Figure 12.5 [Qing Dynasty] *Piaoxia* Lacquer Covered Cup with Drifting Clouds, held in the collection of the Palace Museum in Beijing, offered by Gan Erke

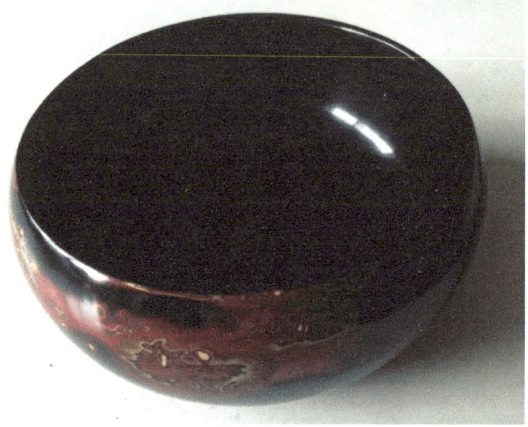

Figure 12.6 [Modern] *Piaoxia* Lacquerware, purchased by the author at the "Boutique Exhibition of Chinese Lacquerware" in Yangzhou

CHAPTER XIII

Avalanche of the Iceberg

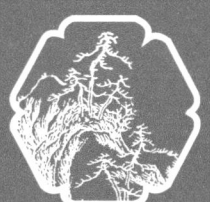

During the Jiajing period of the Ming Dynasty, the craftsman Zhou Zhu from Yangzhou used precious decorative materials such as pearls, gemstones, coral, jadeite, jade, crystal, agate, tortoiseshell, conch shell, malachite, gold, turquoise, ivory, and others. He intricately carved landscapes, figures, trees, pavilions, flowers, and birds and then embedded them into sandalwood, pearwood furniture, or lacquerware. These exquisite pieces ranged from large items like tables, chairs, bookshelves, and screens to smaller objects like pen holders, tea sets, inkstone cases, and book boxes. This style of craftsmanship was known as "zhouzhi" (Made by Zhou) or "zhouqian" (Inlaid by Zhou) during that time.

The inlaying of jade in lacquerware has a long history, but the "zhouzhi" style emerged as an extreme manifestation of decoration during the Ming Dynasty, and "baibao qian" (inlaid with all kinds of treasures) is the term used in *Xiushi Lu* to describe such craftsmanship. The driving force behind this trend was the continuous influx of redwood from Southeast Asia into China, leading to the popularity of hardwood furniture in Jiangnan. Additionally, the flourishing jade carving industry in Jiangnan during the Ming and Qing dynasties made the inlaying of various treasures a byproduct of jade processing. *Yangzhou Huafang Lu* (*Record of the Yangzhou Art Boat*) states, "Excessively carved jade remnants are taken for use in cloisonné. Those that are too small and fragile are ground, sifted, mixed with ash, and applied to screens, hanging screens, and plaques, called 'jeweled craftsmanship.'"[1] The *baibao qian* created by Zhou Zhu was hailed as the "unique skill of Wu region." In the Qing Dynasty, Ruan Kuisheng noted in *Chayu Kehua* (*Tea Leisure Conversations*), "Zhou Zhu's inlaying skills ... are renowned far and wide, and there is no doubt that they have been passed down through the generations."[2]

In the era when Zhou Zhu gained fame, the notorious official Yan Song (1480–1567) controlled the state affairs. Yan Song, known for his corruption and abuse of power, unlawfully seized rare treasures and even kept craftsmen in his home to produce exquisite items for him. Zhou Zhu was among those who were taken into Yan Song's household. Yan Song was eventually accused, had his property confiscated, and an extensive collection of gold, silver, jewels, and antiques was uncovered. The confiscated antiques and items were meticulously recorded, with a list of paintings

---

1. [Qing] Li Dou, *Gongduan Yingzao Lu* (*Craftsmanship Construction Record*), vol. 17 of *Yangzhou Huafang Lu* (*Record of the Yangzhou Art Boat*) (Jiangsu Guangling Ancient Book Printing Society, 1984), 401.
2. Ruan Kuisheng, "A Craft Gains Fame," in vol. 10 of *Chayu Kehua* (*Tea Leisure Conversations*), bk. 19 of *Biji Xiaoshuo Daguan* (*A Comprehensive Collection of Notes Novels*) (Jiangsu Guangling Ancient Book Printing Society, 1983), 376.

and calligraphy titled *Qianshantang Shuhua Ji* (*Record of Calligraphy and Painting in Qianshan Hall*) and a list of artifacts named *Tianshui Bingshan Lu* (*Record of Tianshui Iceberg*). "Tianshui" refers to Yan Song's hometown, and "Bingshan" signifies Yan Song's downfall, symbolizing a complete and utter defeat. The records include 108 framed screens, 17 beds, 54 *qins* (musical instruments), 230 carved lacquer trays and boxes, 531 gilt trays and boxes, and much more. There were also 96 lacquered wooden screens, 185 screens of various ages, and 41 colored and gilt lacquer shrines ...[3] This collection is sufficient to establish a large-scale exhibition of lacquer art. Among the lacquerware and furniture confiscated from Yan Song, there must have been many pieces crafted by Zhou Zhu or under his leadership.

There are hardwood *baibao qian* with Zhou Zhu's signature, such as the "Purple Sandalwood Hundred-Treasure Inlaid Round Inkstone Box" held in the National Palace Museum in Taipei (Figure 13.1). The lid of the box is inlaid with plum blossoms, camellias, and a wax-billed bird. The wooden trunk is carved with wrinkles, and the

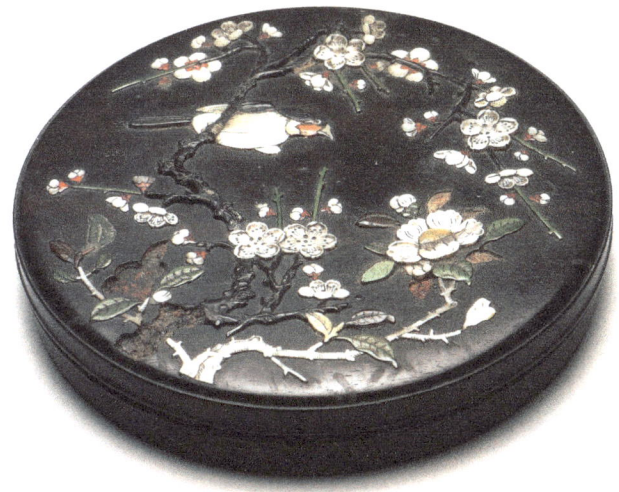

Figure 13.1 [Ming] Purple Sandalwood Hundred-Treasure Inlaid Round Inkstone Box, selected from the compilation *Heguang Ticai—Gugong Cangqi* (*Radiance and Refinement—Lacquerware in the Collection of the National Palace Museum, Taipei*)

---

3. [Ming] Anonymous, *Tianshui Bingshan Lu* (*Record of Tianshui Iceberg*), vol. 48 of *Congshu Jicheng Xinbian* (*A New Compilation of Collected Works*) (New Wenfeng Publishing Company, 1985), 473, 477, 503–504.

finely carved stamen silk on the mother-of-pearl plum blossoms is dyed ivory to represent the leaves. Inside the lid is an engraved poem in clerical script from the Qianlong period, along with an inscription, "Palaces and immortal mountains emerge from the sea waves, crafted following the style of Xuande to imitate Xuanhe. Despite being in the same craft, painting and calligraphy differ in political significance, with Emperor Ming having more than Emperor Song. Qianlong, the year of Jia Chen, composed this imperial poem." The bottom of the box features an inlaid silver-thread seal script inscription reading "Zhou Zhu of Wu." Strictly speaking, this Zhou Zhu-marked inkstone box made of hardwood is not lacquered, so it cannot be classified as lacquerware. However, as a *baibao qian* on hardwood furniture or lacquerware, both the Palace Museum in Beijing and the National Palace Museum in Taipei have their respective collections (Figure 13.2). From this point on, regardless of whether it was crafted by Zhou Zhu, whenever there is a *baibao qian* on hardwood furniture or lacquerware, it is often noted in literary records as "zhouzhi."

The craftsmanship of Zhou Zhu's *baibao qian* received mixed reviews from contemporaries. Zhang Dai, a resident of Zhejiang during the late Ming period,

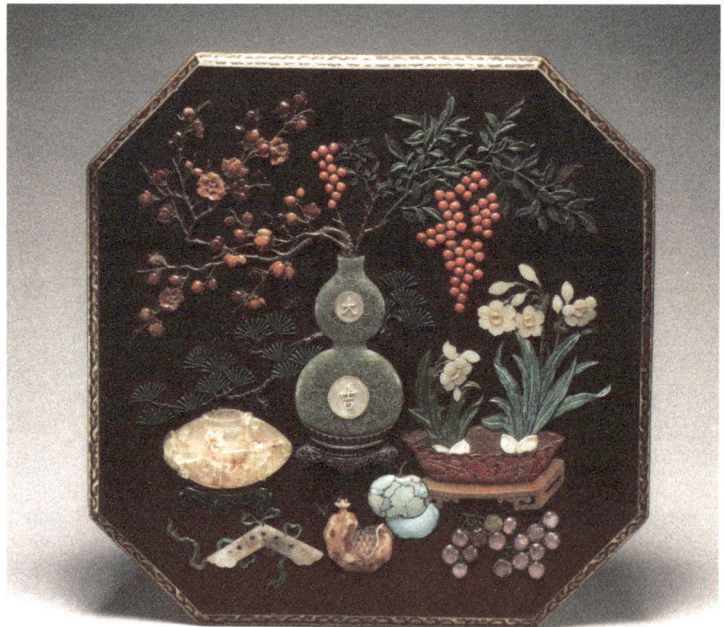

Figure 13.2 [Qing] Octagonal Lacquer Box with Gold-Painted Ancient Motifs, selected from the compilation *Heguang Ticai—Gugong Cangqi* (*Radiance and Refinement—Lacquerware in the Collection of the National Palace Museum, Taipei*)

praised Zhou Zhu's skill, mentioning it alongside other accomplished artisans of the time, "The unique skills of Wuzhong ... Zhou Zhu's treatment of inlays, Zhao Liangbi's treatment of combs, Zhu Bishan's treatment of gold and silver, Ma Xun and He Yeli's treatment of fans, Zhang Jixiu's treatment of *qins* ... all could dominate for a hundred years. However, the skill and effort of these craftsmen are truly remarkable. As for the thickness, depth, intensity, and density, matching the tastes and discernment of connoisseurs in later generations, it is subjective, and can craftsmen truly achieve it?"[4] He expressed doubts about whether Zhou's intricate carvings would truly please future generations. Another critic from Zhejiang in the late Ming period, Gao Lian, remarked, "As for carvings, precious inlays, and purple sandalwood objects, they demand meticulous effort and craftsmanship, representing a peak of their time. However, they may only provide momentary enjoyment, as the adhesives may decay over time, or the boxes may experience shrinkage and expansion due to drying. It seems impractical for long-term preservation ... Moreover, inlaying is commonplace now and differs significantly from Zhou's initial creations; the value has also decreased" (*Zunsheng Bajian · Yanxian Qingshang Jian*). Gao Lian pointed out that the items crafted in the Zhou style were already being imitated in the late Ming period. By the early Qing period, merchants seeking profit from coral and gemstones were damaging Zhou-style items by creating fakes.[5] How do you view the historical events and controversies surrounding Zhou Zhu and the craftsmanship of *baibao qian*?

---

4. [Ming] Zhang Dai, "Wuzhong's Unique Skills," in *Tao'an Mengyi* (*Dreams of Tao'an*), vol. 1 (Shanghai Ancient Books Publishing House, 1982), 9.

5. Regarding this, see Xie Kun's *Jinyu Suosui* (*Golden Jade Trifles*), vol. 3, section "Zhou Zhu and Lacquerware": "Zhou Zhu used lacquer to make screens, cabinets, tables, and desks, purely using the eight treasures for inlaying. Figures, flowers, and birds were also quite exquisite. Foolish merchants took advantage of its coral and gemstones, all digging for genuine and patching with fakes, making it a discarded item, sighing alongside carved lacquer. In my childhood, I still saw its complete beauty. The term 'Zhou Zhi' refers to the name of the person who made the item." Included in *Meishu Congshu* (*Art Series*), eds. Huang Binhong and Deng Shi, vol. 2 (Jiangsu Ancient Book Publishing House, 1986), 1820.

CHAPTER XIV

Dreaming of Returning
Thousands of Miles

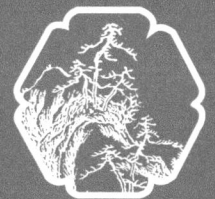

The true fame of Chinese craftsmen arose from their interaction with scholars and officials. From the mid-Ming Dynasty onwards, the court became obscure, and the national fortune declined day by day, but it ironically gave rise to a romantic wave of thought, liberating societal thinking unprecedentedly. During this period, the economy of Jiangnan was extremely prosperous, its culture was highly mature, and the handicraft industry was extremely thriving. Observing the chaotic state of affairs and the diminishing hope for official success, the literati of Jiangnan immersed themselves in music, books, and the appreciation of paintings and calligraphy. They attached great importance to enjoying life. They diligently constructed gardens and residences and sought artisans who could understand their design ideas to customize handicrafts. Suzhou, Yangzhou, Nanjing, Hangzhou, and other places became the most concentrated and developed regions for private gardens in China. Jiangnan workshops aim to meet literati's demands and create handicrafts that cater to their psychological needs. The craftsmen, deeply influenced by the cultural atmosphere of Jiangnan, boasted individuality and proficiency in poetry and painting as fashion trends. Liberated from the authoritarian control of the early Ming, the creative thinking of Jiangnan craftsmen leaped ahead of the workshops in the north, whether state-owned or private. The appreciation, collection, praise, and documentation by literati elevated the reputation of Jiangnan craftsmanship, with craftsmen even becoming "known throughout the country" and "renowned nationwide" for their skills. In the early Jiajing period, Wang Shizhen recorded, "Now in my Wu region, Lu Zigan excels in jade crafting, Bao Tiancheng excels in rhinoceros horn crafting, Zhu Bishan excels in silver crafting, Zhao Liangbi excels in tin crafting, Ma Xun specializes in fans, Zhou Zhizhi specializes in commercial inlay crafting, along with Lü Aishan in Shexian excelling in gold crafting, Wang Xiaoxi excelling in agate crafting, Jiang Baoyun excelling in copper crafting. All of them charge twice the regular price, and there are even those who sit on par with the gentry."[1] In the late Ming Dynasty, Jiangnan became the leader in national handicrafts, and Jiang Qianli was a renowned craftsman in the highland of late Ming Jiangnan craftsmanship.

Jiang (江) Qianli, also known by the courtesy name Qiushui, was a Wu native from the late Ming to early Qing Dynasty who spent considerable time residing in Yangzhou. Wang Shizhen in *Chibei Outan (Conversations in the North of the Pool)*, Zhu Yan in *Tao Shuo (Discourses on Pottery)*, and Zheng Shixu in *Qiqi Kao (Study*

---

1. [Ming] Wang Shizhen, *Gubugu Lu (Record of Gubugu)*, bk. 1041 of *Wenyuange Siku Quanshu (Complete Library in Four Branches of Literature from the Wenyuange)* (Commercial Press, Taiwan, 1986), 440.

on Lacquerware) all referred to him as Jiang (姜) Qianli. Throughout his life, he had a penchant for crafting lacquerware with inserted mother-of-pearl decorations, using conch shells, and adding gold and silver pieces to depict literary stories and intricate patterns. Silver powder, conch shell fragments, lacquer crumbs, and other materials were employed to enhance the luster, with some pieces featuring additional gold and silver detailing. His depictions of characters and patterns were exceptionally exquisite. The *Jiaqing Yangzhou Fuzhi* (*The Annals of Yangzhou Prefecture during the Jiaqing Reign*) recorded, "In the early Kangxi period, there were literati in Yangzhou such as Zha Erzhan who excelled in painting distant landscapes and the rice paper family paintings. There was also Jiang Qiushui, whose conch shell utensils were the most refined and exquisite; they were used in every banquet. At that time, there was a couplet: 'Everywhere there are Jiang Qianli's cups and plates; in every household, there are Zha Erzhan's scrolls.'"[2] This coupled Jiang Qianli with the Xin'an School painter Zha Shibiao, who resided in Yangzhou. In the Qing Dynasty, Ruan Kuisheng noted, "Jiang Qianli's inlay lacquerware ... all were renowned throughout the country, and there is no doubt that their fame continues today."[3] During this period, the poet Liu Yingbin lived in Yangzhou and yearned to acquire lacquerware crafted by Jiang Qianli, adorned with conch shells and gold and silver pieces. Liu Yingbin's deep desire for these lacquerware pieces led him to dream about them. Upon awakening, he ecstatically wrote, "The conch shell decorations have turned into jade-like radiance, the purple clouds of autumn are clear like the fragrance of Wuzhou. ... Both in form and spirit, it is truly extraordinary. In my dreams, I still hope to visit this dreamland."[4] (In essence, Jiang Qianli's lacquerware, adorned with conch shells and gold and silver decorations, shines with a jade-like brilliance reminiscent of the clear autumn skies

2. The preface of *Zhongguo Meishu Quanji · Gongyi Meishu Pian · Qiqi* (*The Complete Collection of Chinese Art · Applied Arts · Lacquerware* edited by Wang Shixiang and Zhu Jiajin quotes a couplet from the *Jiaqing Yangzhou Fuzhi* (*The Annals of Yangzhou Prefecture during the Jiaqing Reign*) stating, "Every family has trays inlaid by Jiang Qianli, and every household has scrolls painted by Zha Erzhan." The author cross-referenced the *Jiaqing Yangzhou Fuzhi* and found that the actual couplet is "at every cup and dish, there is the artistry of Jiang Qiushi; in every household's scroll, there is the inspection of Erzhan." To address this, the author corresponded with Mr. Wang to clarify the discrepancy. Mr. Wang responded that he had made adjustments to the ancient text for the sake of rhyme. The original couplet from the *Jiaqing Yangzhou Fuzhi* is cited in this book.

3. [Qing] Ruan Kuisheng, "One Art Achieves Fame," in vol. 10 of *Chayu Kehua* (*Tea Leisure Conversations*), bk. 19 of *Biji Xiaoshuo Daguan* (*A Comprehensive Collection of Notes Novels*) (Jiangsu Guangling Ancient Book Printing Society, 1983), 376.

4. [Qing] Liu Yingbin, *Qiyan Lü* (*Seven-Character Regulated Verse*), vol. 2 of *Pingtangshan Shiji* (*Poetry Collection of Pingshantang*), Kangxi edition preserved in Nanjing Library, 45.

and the fragrance of fine liquor from Wuzhou. The exquisite craftsmanship captivates both form and spirit, leaving a lasting impression. The poet expresses his fervent desire to dream again of Jiang Qianli's lacquerware rather than dreaming about fanciful illusions.)

As mentioned earlier, the craft of gold and silver *pingtuo* in China became dormant after the Tang and Five Dynasties period. In the Yuan Dynasty, clever Chinese craftsmen began to intricately inlay gold and silver threads and pieces with conch shells into lacquerware. "Conch" and "dian" were originally two different materials, where "conch" referred to the shells of mollusks found in rivers, lakes, and seas, and "dian" referred to gold, silver, and gemstones. In the mid-Yuan Dynasty, the inlaying of "dian" on lacquerware with conch shells can be considered a revival of this technique. The poet Jie Xisi wrote a poem titled "To the Lacquerer Huang Sheng," which includes the line, "amidst golden strands and fine hairs, intricate patterns of conch shells intertwine,"[5] describing lacquerware adorned with conch shells and gold and silver pieces. By the late Ming Dynasty, the inlaying of conch shells with gold and silver pieces had become a popular craft in lacquerware, and beyond Jiang Qianli, Wu Yuezhen of Huizhou was also a renowned craftsman in this field.

Jiang Qianli crafted lacquerware with inlaid conch shells and added gold and silver pieces. These lacquerware pieces are held in collections at institutions such as the Palace Museum in Beijing and the National Museum of China, as well as museums in Yangzhou, Suzhou, Nanjing, Shanghai, and various overseas locations. Many of these items are later imitations from the Qing Dynasty. The Palace Museum in Beijing has over 20 pieces in its collection, including square and round boxes, trays, and wine cups, showcasing a wide variety of shapes and sizes. Various museums in Jiangnan also hold pieces with Jiang Qianli's signature, featuring inlaid conch shells and added gold and silver pieces. The Yangzhou Museum, for example, possesses four pieces of "Round Lacquer Tray with Inlaid Conch Shells and Added Gold and Silver Pieces" with Jiang Qianli's signature, along with 17 unsigned pieces featuring the same technique. These pieces come in round or square shapes with curved edges, measuring between 10 to 12 centimeters in diameter or side length. The center of the tray often features landscapes and figures, while the edges showcase continuous patterns. Ten square trays are identified as imitations from the Qing Dynasty. The Shanghai Museum holds one piece of "Square Tray with Inlaid Conch Shells and Added Gold and Silver Pieces" with Jiang Qianli's signature, as well as three unsigned pieces of "Round Lacquer Tray

---

5. [Yuan] Jie Xisi, *Zeng Xiuzhe Huang Sheng* (*To the Lacquerer Huang Sheng*), vol. 27 of *Quan Yuan Shi* (*Complete Yuan Poetry*), ed. Yang Lian (Zhonghua Book Company, 2013), 237.

with Inlaid Conch Shells and Added Gold and Silver Pieces" (see Figure 14.1). Similar styles of small lacquerware dishes with inlaid conch shells and added gold and silver pieces from the late Ming to early Qing Dynasty are found in collections at institutions such as the Anhui Museum, the Lu Xun Academy of Fine Arts Museum in Shenyang, the Chinese University of Hong Kong Art Museum, the Tokyo National Museum in Japan, the Bukchon Art Museum in South Korea, and the Asian Art Museum in San Francisco, USA. The Chinese University of Hong Kong Art Museum holds a "Black Lacquer Vase with Inlaid Conch Shells and Added Gold and Silver Pieces" from the early Qing Dynasty (see Figure 14.2). Standing at

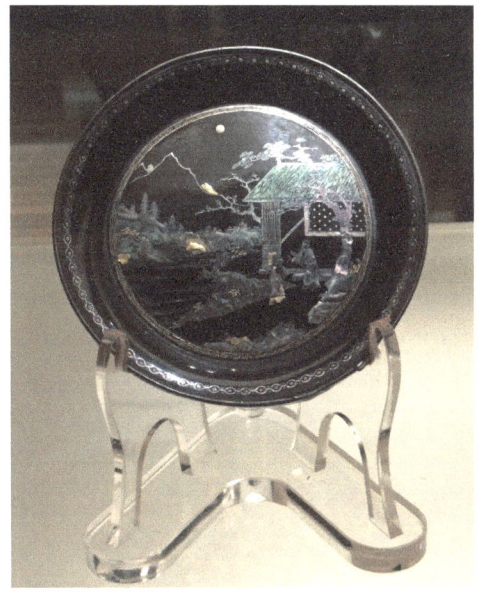

Figure 14.1 [Qing] Round Lacquer Tray with Inlaid Conch Shells and Added Gold and Silver Pieces, photographed by the author at the Shanghai Museum

10.7 centimeters in height, the vase features continuous circular gold pieces forming a vortex pattern, dividing the vase's body into several decorative zones. Conch shells and gold pieces are inlaid within each zone to create intricate patterns. The neck of the vase is adorned with interwoven gold and spiral shell leaf patterns, creating a splendid and beautiful composition. Although the museum dates this piece to the early Qing Dynasty, the author believes that its exquisite and dynamic composition suggests a work from the height of the Qing period.

Inlaid lacquerware with conch shells and added gold and silver pieces provides a first impression of visual beauty and a second impression of the difficulty of the craftsmanship. The challenges are manifested in the following aspects: selecting materials, cutting, and inlaying. The first difficulty lies in selecting materials. Colored shells are boiled, ground, or oil-fried to become thin shell pieces, often displaying a variegated palette of five colors. Selecting red flowers, green leaves, and yellow fruits from these shells requires creating a pure, rich, harmonious, and orderly composition without clutter. The second lies in cutting. Crafting a thin lacquerware piece with inlaid conch shells and added gold and silver pieces involves planting tens of thousands of small conch shell inlays, each as small as a grain of millet. Craftsmen often need to create dozens of similar chisel-like cutting tools to improve cutting speed and maintain uniformity across identical components. The third lies in inlaying. Inlaying tens of thousands of silk pieces requires precision without any height deviation. The slightest error could result in some conch pieces wearing through or being buried beneath the lacquer without being revealed. Describing the labor of thin conch shell workers as "meticulous as hair" is an apt characterization. Contemporary understanding of the complexity of this craft does not necessarily promote the widespread adoption of such intricate techniques. Instead, it emphasizes the inheritance of the artisan spirit akin to "grinding an iron rod into a needle." This spirit aims to preserve the creative essence of Jiangnan craftsmen based on the ideals of life and freedom.

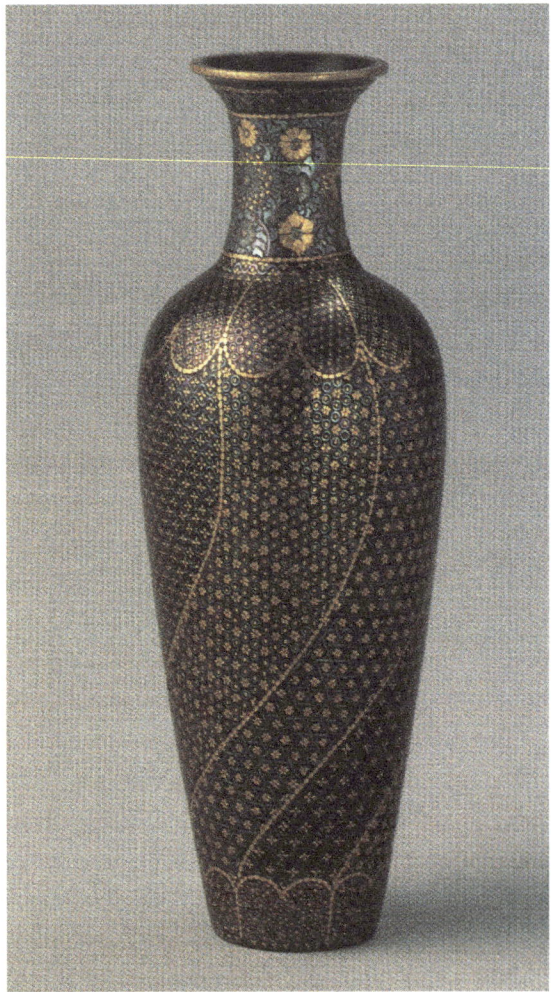

Figure 14.2 [Qing Dynasty] Black Lacquer Vase with Inlaid Conch Shells and Added Gold and Silver Pieces, selected from *Zhongguo Qiyi Liangqiannian* (*Two Thousand Years of Chinese Lacquer Art*) by the Chinese University of Hong Kong Art Museum

CHAPTER XV

Exclusive Use by the Qing
Imperial Palace

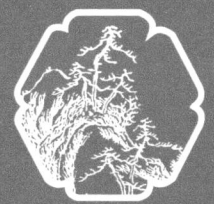

During the reigns of Kangxi, Yongzheng, and Qianlong, as economic accumulation gradually became abundant, the emperors didn't use the national treasury for the well-being of the common people. Instead, they extravagantly spent it by sending craftsmen to the Department of Construction to produce exclusive items for imperial use. Simultaneously, various provinces were allowed to contribute a plethora of rare and exotic treasures. A large number of lacquerware and lacquer-crafted furniture created by skilled artisans engaged in fierce competition became a secret collection within the Qing Imperial Palace, with the products from the Qianlong period particularly renowned for their exquisite quality and craftsmanship.

The Palace Museum in Beijing houses numerous handmade crafts produced by artisans recruited by the Qing Imperial Workshops during that era. The overall characteristics of these crafts are a willingness to invest time and money in pursuit of exquisite materials and craftsmanship. As an example, the series of "moxian tianqi" (polish and fill with lacquer), most of which was invented during the Tang Dynasty, while "louqian tianqi" (inlay and fill with lacquer) was a creation of the Ming Dynasty. The difference lies in the fact that "moxian tianqi" sets patterns on the lacquer base, while "louqian tianqi" carves patterns on the completed lacquer surface. The former involves carving after the lacquer has dried, while the latter fills the pattern with lacquer and only carves it after it has dried. The common feature is that the finished products are uniform, with a smooth and attractive appearance. In late Ming, Liu Dong and Yu Yizheng recorded in *Dijing Jingwu Lue* (*Brief Record of the Scenery of the Imperial Capital*), "*Tianqi* with carved flowers and birds, densely filled with colored lacquer, polished flat like a painting, looks newer after a long time. The high-quality ones have a thick edge with colorful Ganoderma; the shallow ones have a repeating pattern with gold edges. Its antique colors are clear and bright, and the number of such items is extremely limited, making them several times more valuable than carved red lacquer."[1] This description precisely refers to *louqian tianqi*. In the Qing Dynasty, *Louqian tianqi* lacquerware entered the imperial palace, such as the Qing Dynasty "*Louqian Tianqi* Large Vase" from the collection of the Palace Museum in Beijing (Figure 15.1), exuding a dignified atmosphere that clearly indicates its origin from the imperial workshops. After the Qing Dynasty closed itself off from the outside world, the supply of seashells decreased, leading to a resurgence of the craft of thick inlay of seashells. The thick seashell pattern inlaid on circular utensils is difficult to conform perfectly to the utensil's surface. However,

---

1. [Ming] Liu Dong and Yu Yizheng, *Dijing Jingwu Lue* (*Brief Record of the Scenery of the Imperial Capital*), vol. 4 (Classical Literature Publishing House, 1957), 68.

the Palace Museum in Beijing has a mid-Qing period "Red Lacquer Inlaid with Hard Seashell Pattern Gathered Box" (Figure 15.2), with deep and beautiful red lacquer and luminescent seashell treasures shining brilliantly. The inlaid hard seashell pattern is neither hidden beneath the lacquer nor worn or damaged by grinding, indicating the exquisite skill of the court artisans in the mid-Qing period.

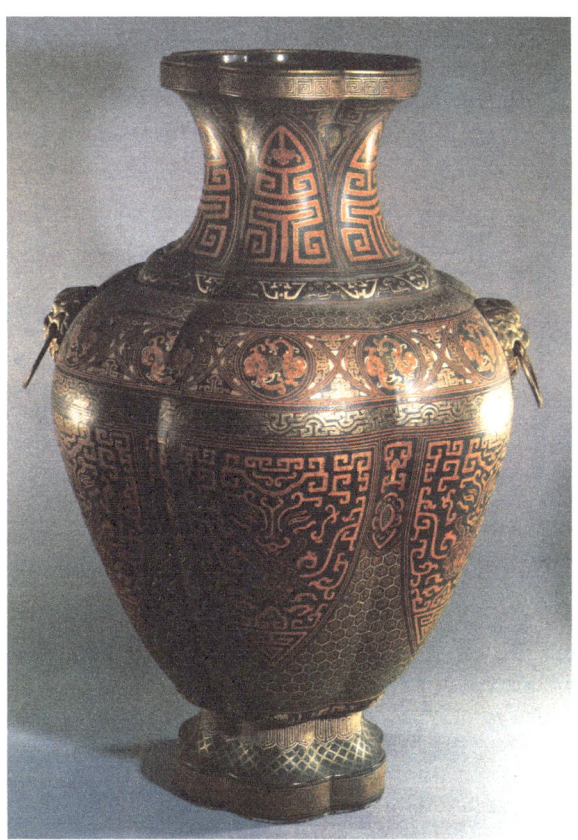

Figure 15.1 [Qing] *Louqian Tianqi* Large Vase, collection of the Palace Museum, Beijing, from *Zhongguo Gudai Qiqi* (*Ancient Chinese Lacquerware*) by Wang Shixiang

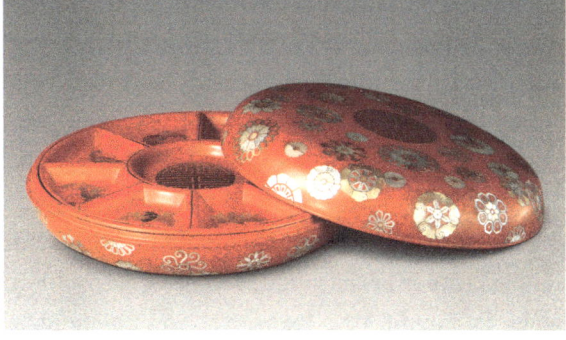

Figure 15.2 [Qing] Red Lacquer Inlaid with Hard Seashell Pattern Gathered Box, from *Gugong Bowuyuancang Wenwu Zhenpin Daxi: Qingdai Qiqi* (*Treasures of the Palace Museum's Collection: Qing Dynasty Lacquerware*) by Li Jiufang

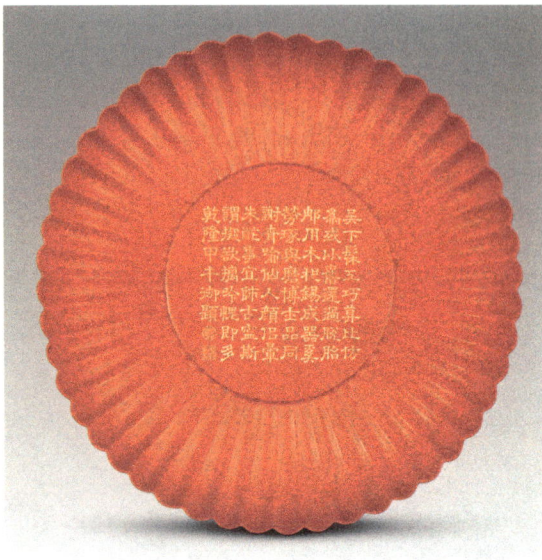

Figure 15.3 [Qing] Cinnabar Lacquer Plate in the Shape of Detached Lotus Petals, selected from *Gugong Bowuyuancang Wenwu Zhenpin Daxi: Qingdai Qiqi* (*Treasures of the Palace Museum's Collection: Qing Dynasty Lacquerware*) by Li Jiufang

Regarding lacquerware tribute to the Qing court from various regions, Suzhou can be considered the foremost in terms of quantity. During the Qianlong reign, Suzhou contributed a large number of cinnabar lacquerware, including dishes, bowls, and boxes in the form of lotus petals. The "Cinnabar Lacquer Plate in the Shape of Detached Lotus Petals" (Figure 15.3) is lightweight, with well-arranged petals, and the cinnabar lacquer is warm and rich. In the center of the plate is a dense golden inscription of a poem composed by Emperor Qianlong: "The lacquer artisans in Wu below are unparalleled in skill, surpassing even the imitation of old works. Detached from nature, there is no need for wood or tin; why bother with carving and polishing to create an artifact ..." This poem is repeatedly inscribed in thick gold on the cinnabar lacquer plates and bowls in the form of detached lotus petals, which Suzhou offered as tributes to the imperial court.

Regarding lacquerware furniture tributes from various regions, Yangzhou and the Salt Administration in the two Huai regions can be considered the foremost in quantity. In the mid-Qing period, luxurious varieties emerged in Jiangsu's imperial tributes, which combined jade inlay with carved lacquer. The Palace Museum in Beijing houses a set of seven pieces, including the "Carved Lacquer Inlaid with Jade Landscape Screen" from the Qianlong era (Figure 15.4). Standing 8 feet tall, the screen features a grand scene with white jade, green jade, and ivory inlaid on a yellow lacquer background, depicting carved lotus flowers and flying swallows. The scene is magnificent, luxurious, and splendid, with all seven pieces adorned with red-carved lacquer. Qing Dynasty archives record tributes such as "A Pair of Bonsai Landscapes Depicting Prosperous Wheat Fields in Jiagu,"[2] presented by the Governor of Jiangsu, and the "Two Pairs of Four-Season Carved Lacquer Flower Bowls,"[3] offered by the Chief Supervisor of the Huai'an Canal Transport (Figure 15.5). These records indicate that the combination of jade inlay and carved lacquer bonsai was a notable contribution from Jiangsu.

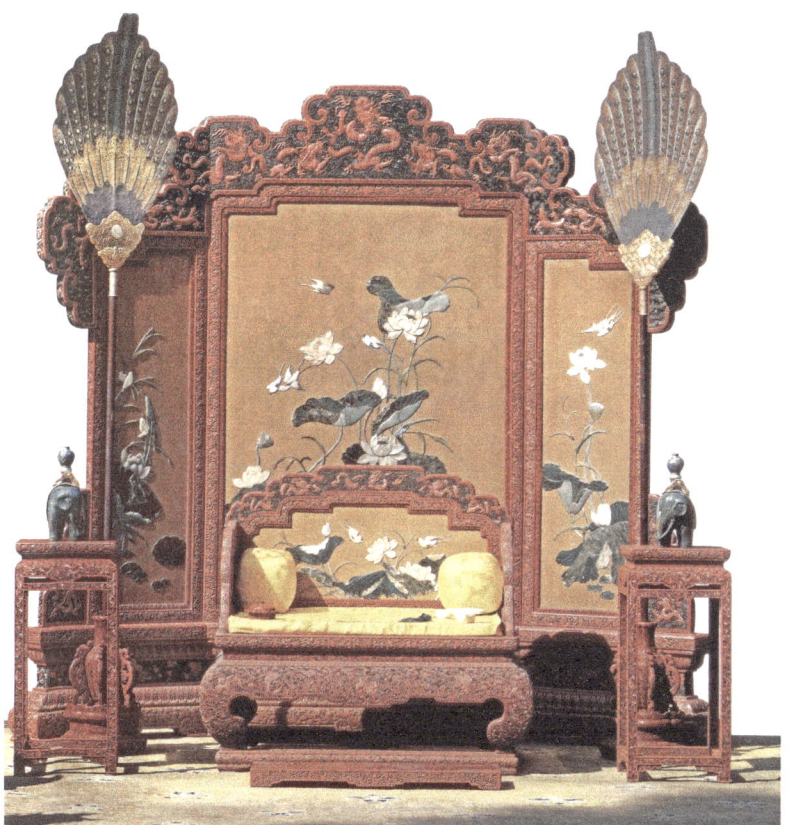

Figure 15.4 [Qing] A Set of Seven Carved Lacquer Inlaid with Jade Landscape Screen, selected from *Gugong Jingdian: Mingqing Gongting Jiaju* (*Classics of the Forbidden City: Ming and Qing Dynasty Court Furniture*) by Hu Desheng

---

2. The First Historical Archives of China and the Chinese University of Hong Kong Museum, eds., "Tribute Files," in vol. 55 of *Qinggong Neiwufu Zaobanchu Dangan Huizong* (*Comprehensive Archives of the Imperial Household Department's Construction Office*) (People's Publishing House, 2005), 744.

3. Ibid., 766.

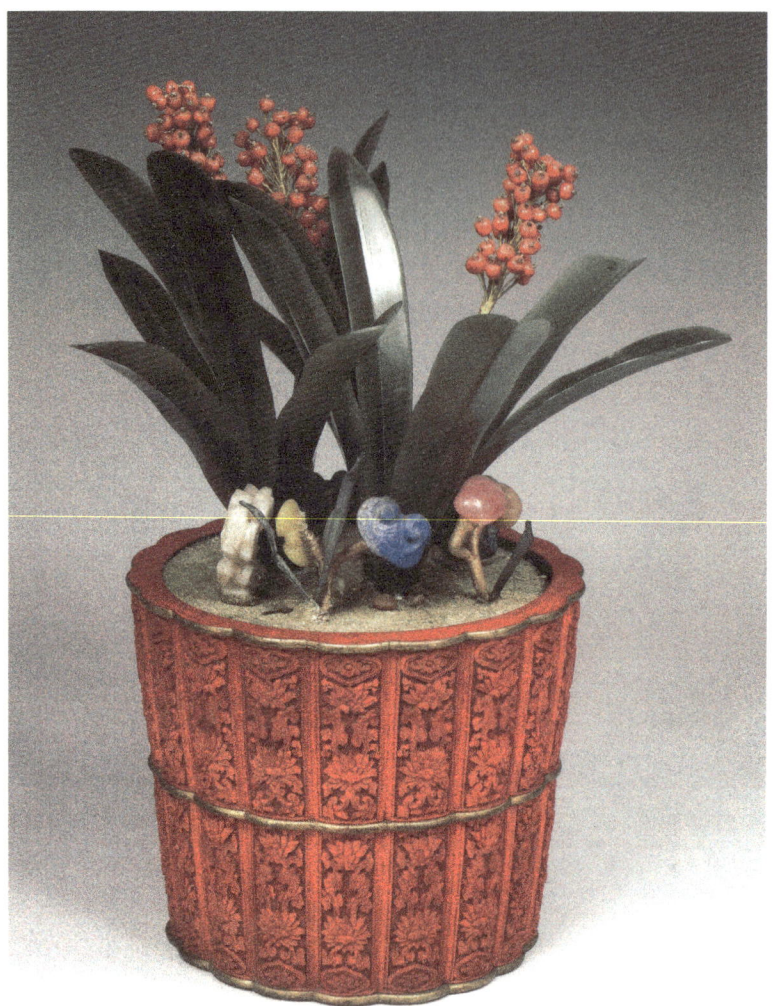

Figure 15.5 [Qing] Jade-Inlaid Red Lacquer Flower Pot with Gold-Plated Copper Buckle and Carved Patterns, selected from *Heguang Ticai—Gugong Cangqi (Radiance and Refinement—Lacquerware in the Collection of the National Palace Museum, Taipei)*

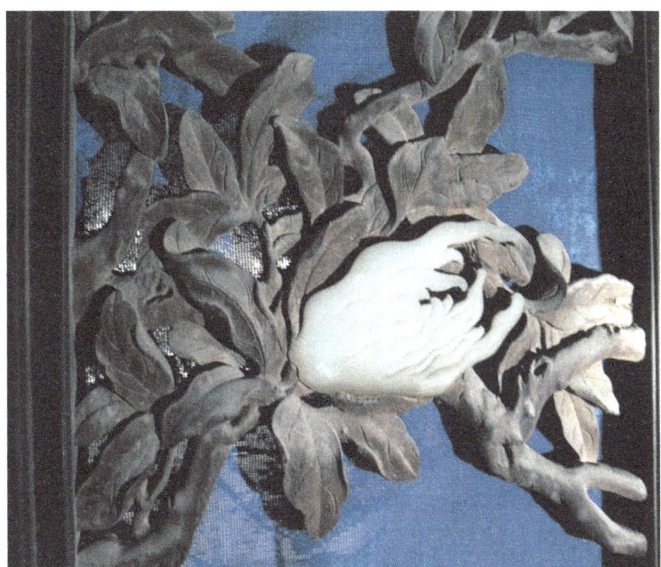

Figure 15.6 [Qianlong period] Wood Carving with Inlaid White Jade Buddha's Hand Surrounded by Carved Flowers and Leaves, photographed by the author at the Palace Museum, Beijing, in the Fuwang Pavilion

produced in Yangzhou. Upon examining the Fuwang Pavilion in the Ningshou Palace Garden of the Palace Museum in Beijing, which has not been restored by modern hands, it is observed that window lattices and partitions are adorned with a variety of craftsmanship, including inlaying with jade, cloisonné, mother-of-pearl, carved lacquer, red lacquer, wood carving, bronze chiseling, double-sided embroidery, and bamboo thread inlay. The diversity of categories, the high-quality materials, and the precision of craftsmanship are astonishing! The jade-inlaid "tieluo" (paste fallen)[4] of the emerald gauze cupboard uses green jade and white jade to create a folded branch floral and bird scene. The surrounding boards of the floor are entirely decorated with inlaid mother-of-pearl and gold pieces to create a brocade-patterned ground. On the brocade ground, equidistantly inlaid are diamond-shaped red lacquer patterns. The lattice hearts of the partition doors are carved and inlaid with white jade and green jade (Figure 15.6). Count the amount of mutton-fat white jade inlaid on the Fuwang Pavilion, you will understand how rapidly Hetian mutton-fat white jade was depleted!

During the Qing Dynasty, everyday items were adorned with natural lacquer. In the folk construction of houses, large wood surfaces were coated with a mixture of three hemp and two cloth layers, seven layers of rough oil, padding oil, gloss oil, and vermilion oil decoration. For the slightly lesser quality, two hemp and one cloth layer,

---

4. "Tieluo" refers to the decorative part of the building's bichrome cabinet, which extends from the front horizontal eyebrow to the top board.

seven layers of rough oil, padding oil, gloss oil, and vermilion oil decoration were used. Other methods included two hemp and five gray, one hemp and four gray, three coats of gray, and two coats of gray.[5] The craftsmanship of natural *xiushi* during the Qing Dynasty resulted in a diverse range of items resembling a myriad of blooming flowers, each region forming a distinctive local style. The traditional use of natural lacquer to decorate everyday objects in Chinese folk culture persisted until the late 20th century, before the Industrial Revolution wave.

---

5. [Qing] Li Dou, *Gongduan Yingzao Lu* (*Craftsmanship Construction Record*), vol. 17 of *Yangzhou Huafang Lu* (*Record of the Yangzhou Art Boat*) (Jiangsu Guangling Ancient Book Printing Society, 1984), 393.

CHAPTER XVI

Literary Collectibles of the Lu Family

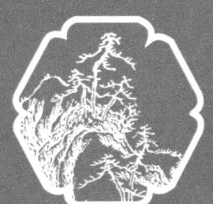

I n the late Qing Dynasty, while *xiushi* craftsmanship in China was declining, Lu's lacquer workshop in Yangzhou emerged as a unique producer of lacquer literary artifacts. Records of this phenomenon can be found in various works such as *Xiaocangshanfang Wenji* (*Collected Works of Xiaocangshan Hall*) of Yuan Mei, *Hualin Xinyong* (*New Odes of Hualin*) of Chen Wenshu, *Sishi Zhaiji* (*Collected Works of Sishi Studio*) of Gu Guangqi, and *Lüyuan Conghua* (*Miscellaneous Talks from the Lüyuan Garden*) of Qian Yong, among others.

The Lu family, renowned for lacquer craftsmanship, began manufacturing and marketing lacquerware during the Qing Dynasty, reaching its peak during the reign of Lu Ying's grandson, Kuisheng, in the Daoguang era. Various museums, such as the Palace Museum in Beijing, the National Museum of China, the Shanghai Museum, the Nanjing Museum, the Yangzhou Museum, the Suzhou Museum, and the Tianjin Art Museum hold more than 50 pieces of lacquerware bearing the mark of Lu Kuisheng. Their lacquer ink boxes, teapots, letter boxes, armrests, flowerpots, and flower stands embody a blend of simplicity and elegance, often featuring dark lacquer tones with minimal polychromatic decorations. Their specialty lies in shallow engravings or inlays of mother-of-pearl on dark lacquer bases, occasionally incorporating bone or ivory without intricate hollow carvings, solely focusing on embellishing colors. Thus, they created products characterized by a subtle, graceful, and refined spirit that resonated with the literati.

Lu Kuisheng's lacquerware is best known for its lacquer ink box sets. During a visit to Mr. Li Yimang's residence, the author observed their collection of "Lu Kuisheng-Marked Black Lacquer Rectangular Stationery Set Box" (see Figure 16.1), which has a wooden frame coated with dark ocher lacquer. The box lid is adorned with inlaid ivory and mother-of-pearl, depicting the painting *Shuangjun Tu* (*Twin Steeds*) by Hua Yan. Upon opening the lid, the lacquer cover reveals intricately carved and engraved landscapes and figures by the renowned painter Chen Nong, with

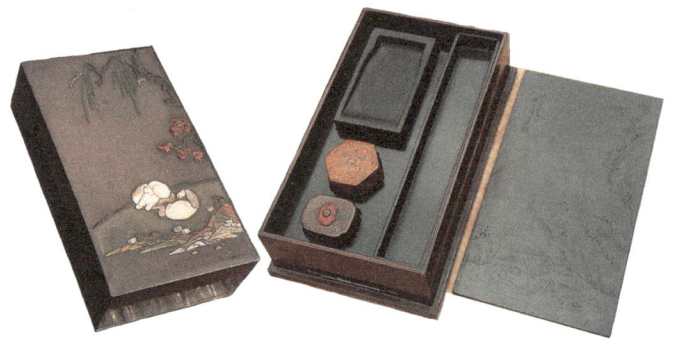

Figure 16.1 [Late Qing] Lu Kuisheng-Marked Black Lacquer Rectangular Stationery Set Box, photographed by the author at the residence of Li Yimang in Beijing

Chen Nong's cursive signature, "Spring Day of the Year Jiaxu," inscribed in the upper left corner and his square seal inscribed with the character "Chen" below. Lifting the hanging board reveals another lacquer panel lying flat at the bottom of the box, with a rectangular, hexagonal, and crab-apple-shaped groove carved on the left half, accommodating a lacquer inkstone, a copper-based ink paste box with gold-plated fine hooks, and a copper-based dark ocher lacquer water dish with silver embellishments. A long lacquer box for holding brushes is placed on the right side, while the crab-apple-shaped water dish features a small hole on top for inserting a water ladle. Once the copper ladle is inserted into the water dish, the round knob on the ladle handle serves as a cover for the water dish. The box's middle layer contains a hidden drawer for storing documents and letters. This lacquer ink box, adorned with various *xiushi* techniques and exuding a scholarly aura, showcases exquisite craftsmanship without appearing excessive. Achieving harmony among multiple crafts in a single piece and attaining artistic coherence requires a high level of aesthetic sensibility, holistic design concepts, and proficiency in various *xiushi* techniques.

Imitation purple clay lacquer teapots and green sinking lacquer teapots are also distinctive among Lu Kuisheng's lacquerware. They come in both square and round shapes, with the round ones resembling the styles of Qin Quan and Jing Lan. During the Daoguang period, when Lu Kuisheng was active, the reputation of Man Sheng teapots had already spread throughout Jiangnan. Therefore, Lu Kuisheng produced lacquer teapots imitating Chen Mansheng's purple clay teapots. During a visit to the Shanghai Museum, the author encountered a "Lu Kuisheng-Marked Tin-Core Imitation of Mansheng's Purple Clay Lacquer Teapot" (see Figure 16.2). It has a diameter of 8.7 centimeters, a base diameter of 14.2 centimeters, and a total height of 8.5 centimeters, including the lid. It is cylindrical in shape, with one side featuring a spout and the other side a curved handle with a cylindrical knob on the top. On one side of the outer wall, there are 51 Chinese characters engraved in regular script with the inscription "In the sixth year of the Yuanhe reign of the Tang Dynasty, on the fifteenth day of the fifth month of the year Xinmao, Shamen Chengguan built a permanent stone well and basin for the Lingling Temple, for perpetual offering. The master craftsmen Chu Qing and Guo Tong composed a verse praising it." On the other side, there are 40 Chinese characters engraved with a verse stating, "This is the southern mountain stone, to be made into a well curb in the future. Passed down for thousands of generations, each forming a bond with the Buddha. Devote oneself to cultivate merit and virtue; there shall be no years of decay. Those who share the blessings will surpass Maitreya." The engraved seal script inscription consists of 18 Chinese characters, which is completely consistent with the design of the teapot, the

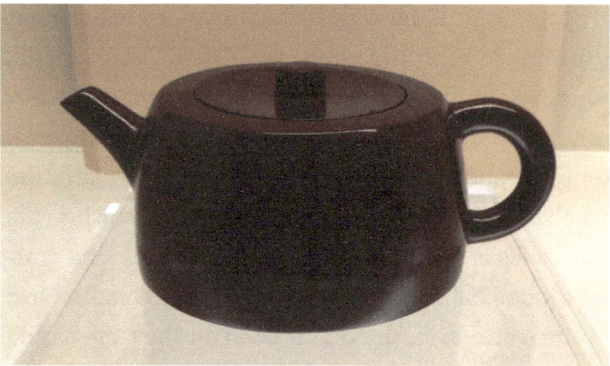

Figure 16.2 [Late Qing] Lu Kuisheng-Marked Tin-Core Imitation of Mansheng's Purple Clay Lacquer Teapot, photographed by the author at the Shanghai Museum

inscription of the stone well curb, and the verse found on the "Jing Lan-style pottery teapot" designed by Chen Mansheng and made by Yang Pengnian in the collection of the Nanjing Museum. The only difference is that the engraved seal script inscription "Mansheng made this tea set for Lingling Temple's Tang well" has been changed to "in the sixth month of the year Wushen, Kuisheng made this tea set for Lingling Temple's Tang well," followed by the engraved rectangular seal script characters "Dongyin." The engraving is square, thick, well-proportioned, with a strict and richly textured knife technique. "Wushen" refers to the year 1848, indicating that this teapot was made two years before the death of Lu Kuisheng.

The achievements of the Lu family's lacquer literary artifacts are inseparable from the extensive interactions between Lu Kuisheng and the literati of the time, as well as his own understanding of calligraphy and painting. Their lacquer boxes, teapots, and armrests often incorporate the sketches of Hua Yan, Chen Nong, and Wang Shishen, as well as the calligraphy of Jin Nong, Qian Daxin, and others, shallowly engraved onto the lacquer surface. These lacquer literary artifacts became a place where literati could express themselves, combining poetry, calligraphy, painting, and seals into one, complementing each other with exquisite craftsmanship and artistic charm.[1] During the Jiaqing period, the calligrapher Gu Guangqi wrote *Qishayan Ji* (*Records of Lacquer Inkstones*) to praise Lu Ying for reviving the craft of lacquer inkstones. He praised Lu

---

1. The mentioned calligraphers and painters: Hua Yan, courtesy name Qiuyue, sobriquets Xinluo Shanren; Wang Shishen, courtesy name Jinren, sobriquets Chaolin; Jin Nong, courtesy name Shoumen, sobriquets Dongxin Xiansheng. They, along with Zheng Xie, Huang Shen, and others, are listed as the "Eight Eccentrics of Yangzhou." Chen Nong: A Qing Dynasty painter from Yangzhou. Qian Daxin: A Qing Dynasty historian who made significant contributions to historiography, classical studies, epigraphy, and philology, excelling in calligraphy and painting with voluminous works.

Kuisheng for his mastery of the six methods, superior quality, and interactions with many literary figures. Gu Guangqi predicted that Lu Kuisheng would eventually be esteemed as highly as "Mi Fu or Sun Guoting, whether in history or on paper, leaving a lasting legacy in the world."[2] Mr. Li Yimang privately owned a scroll of *Lu Kuisheng Shese Sanshui Hua* (*Lu Kuisheng's Landscape Painting*), with a small seal reading "Ancient Elm Study" at the beginning and the inscription "Corrected by Mr. Yunqiao in the summer of 1823, Lu Dong's seal" at the end, along with the collector's seal "Ma Qianli from Hebei." Though not comparable to works by renowned artists, it still reflects meticulous skill and depth.[3] The Nanjing Museum holds Lu Kuisheng's painting *Shankou Daidu Tu* (*Crossing the Mountain Pass*), while the Yangzhou Museum has two pieces of Lu Kuisheng's landscape fan paintings, showcasing his accomplishments in both calligraphy and painting.

As the reputation of the Lu family's lacquer literary artifacts spread, various workshops began producing imitations. Lu Kuisheng had to insert imitation inkstones into his inkstone cases, condemning the imitators for their lack of authenticity. This indicates that there are counterfeits among the extant lacquerware bearing Lu Kuisheng's mark. During the Qing Dynasty, Lu Zishou was acclaimed as follows: "Lu Dong, a native of Yangzhou, excelled in lacquer art. Most of Lady Gu's inkstone boxes are handmade, and those coated with vermilion lacquer are especially exquisite. The engravings of branches, flowers, birds, animals, insects, and fish on them were beyond the skill of ordinary painters. Co-artists only began to carve their names; otherwise, they only used Lu Kuisheng's small seal."[4] This passage provides the following information: the inkstones in Lu Kuisheng's lacquer inkstone cases were made by Gu Erniang; lacquerware bearing the inscription "Made by Lu Kuisheng" were acknowledged by Lu Kuisheng, while those with only inscriptions like "Kuisheng" or "Made by Kuisheng" were typical workshop productions. Based on the comparison of observed Lu Kuisheng lacquerware, those with the square seal inscription "Made by Lu Kuisheng" in vermilion lacquer on the bottom center inside or outside of the box, on

2. [Qing] Gu Guangqi, *Qishaiyan Ji* (*Records of Lacquer Inkstones*), vol. 5 of *Sishi Zhaiji* (*Collected Works of Sishi Studio*), housed in the Ancient Books Department of the Yangzhou Library, from a Qing Dynasty engraved edition, 15.

3. Li Yimang, "Ba Lu Kuisheng Shanshui Huajuan (Postscript to Lu Kuisheng's Landscape Painting)," *Cultural Relics*, no. 7 (1988).

4. [Qing] Lu Zishou, *Luochuang Xiaodu* (*Small Letters from the Louvered Window*), original text not found, quoted from Wang Shixiang and Yuan Quanyou, "Yangzhou Mingqigong Lu Kuisheng He Tade Yixie Zuopin (Yangzhou Lacquer Artist Lu Kuisheng and Some of His Works)," *Cultural Relics Reference Materials*, no. 7 (1957).

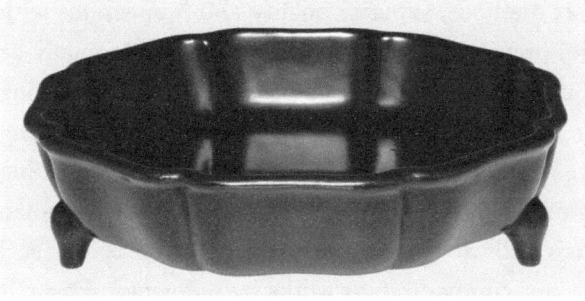

Figure 16.3 [Late Qing] Three-Footed Brown Lacquer Kui Mouth Plate supervised by Lu Kuisheng, from the collection of the Museum of Lacquer Art, Münster, Germany, provided by Dr. Monika Kopplin

the reverse side of the compartment, or on the bottom of the inkstone, were generally high-quality products. The vermilion seal was bright red, neat, and beautiful, with consistent specifications and sizes, mostly exquisite pieces. Those with subsequent inscriptions such as "Kuisheng" or "Made by Kuisheng" in running script, "Kuisheng Engraved" in clerical script, or "Kuisheng" with the addition of "Dong" character seal were often imbued with scholarly air. Those with inscriptions like "Supervised by Kuisheng" or "Supervised by Lu Kuisheng from Jiangdu" on the side of the inkstone, vermilion inscriptions on the wall of the inkstone, or inscriptions like "Made by Kuisheng" in square seal characters, "Dong," or "Supervised by Kuisheng" combined with "Kuisheng" small seal, were often mediocre. Lu Kuisheng was likely a workshop owner proficient in lacquer art and design, with high artistic accomplishment. He frequented literary circles, occasionally participating in production during gatherings, while most works were overseen rather than crafted by him directly.

The Lu family's lacquer literary artifacts delicately embody techniques of inlaying, carving, engraving, hooking, and drawing, representing the aesthetic taste of Jiangnan literati in the late Qing Dynasty and directly advancing the literary refinement of lacquerware in Yangzhou. In the late Edo period of Japan, there was a trend of using sets of lacquer-decorated writing instrument boxes. Renowned artists such as Ogata Kōrin, Ogawa Haritsu, and Hon'ami Kōetsu became famous for manufacturing lacquer-decorated inkstone boxes and inkstones during the Edo period, some of whom imitated the style and decoration of Lu Kuisheng's lacquer literary instrument boxes. Lu Kuisheng's lacquerware even made its way to the West. For example, the Münster Museum of Lacquer Art in Germany holds a "Three-Footed Brown Lacquer Kui Mouth Plate" (Figure 16.3), which is elegant and dignified. The bottom of the plate bears a circle of vermilion lacquer inscription, "Supervised by Lu Kuisheng of the Ancient Elm Study in the spring month of the Bingwu year of the Daoguang era." Lu Kuisheng became a key figure in the history of lacquerware in Yangzhou.

CHAPTER XVII

Shen Family in the South and Liang Family in the North

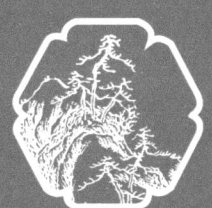

I n the long history of China's agrarian economy, besides state-owned workshops, rural households engaged in handicrafts during agricultural downtime and halted during busy seasons. During the Song Dynasty, citizen workshops emerged with the rise of urban markets. In the Yuan and early Ming dynasties, state-owned handicrafts were once again strengthened. In the late Ming Dynasty, citizen culture flourished in Jiangnan, and the market economy thrived unprecedentedly, making citizen workshops the main form of operation in the handicraft industry. It wasn't until the collapse of imperial power that China's handicraft industry truly bid farewell to state-owned workshops, replaced by a myriad of citizen workshops. In the late Qing Dynasty and into the modern era, the workshops of Shen Shao'an in Fuzhou and Liang Fusheng in Yangzhou enjoyed considerable fame for a time.

Shen Shao'an (1767–1835), a native of Fuzhou, founded a lacquerware workshop near Shuangpao Bridge on Yangqiao Road during the Qianlong period of the Qing Dynasty. The business lasted for five generations, with each generation prefixing "Shen Shao'an" before the shop's name. The successor of the first generation, Shen Chuzhu, seized the commercial opportunities presented by Fuzhou's opening to the outside world, producing lacquerware imitating Western goods such as tea sets, smoking accessories, and coffee sets. This initiative opened up an export channel for Fuzhou lacquerware. The successor of the second generation, Shen Zuolin, excelled in making imitation antique bronze lacquerware. Among the successors of the third generation, Shen Yunzhong inherited the family business, Shen Yunji excelled in gold-painted lacquer painting, Shen Yunqin specialized in lacquer color matching, and Shen Yunhua was skilled in copper nail decoration. Among the successors of the fourth generation, Shen Zhenggao, as the eldest grandson of the main branch, took over the old shop named "Shen Shao'an Zhengji," also known as "Gaoji"; Shen Zhengxun opened a business in Gongxiang and named it "Shen Shao'an Xunji"; Shen Youlan opened a business in Cangqianshan and named it "Shen Shao'an Lanji"; Shen Zhengkai, Shen Zhengyu, and Shen Zhengxi respectively opened shops named "Shen Shao'an Kaiji," "Shen Shao'an Yuji," and "Shen Shao'an Xiji." In 1887, local officials in Fujian purchased lacquerware from Gaoji and Kaiji and presented them to Empress Dowager Cixi as tribute. As a result, Empress Dowager Cixi conferred the fourth-rank commercial honor and fifth-rank headgear upon the brothers Shen Zhenggao and Shen Zhengxun, leading to the mention of Shen Shao'an in the *Minhou County Annals* and the reputation of the Shen family's lacquerware soared. In contemporary times, Shen Yuan, the sixth-generation descendant of Shen Shao'an, transitioned to a career in aerodynamics research, thus ending the family's tradition of craftsmanship.

The outstanding contribution of the Shen lacquerware workshop lies in its adoption of the "detachable fabric" lacquer technique, where fine summer cloth or silk is coated with lacquer to create hollow figures, birds, flowers, and animals. These lacquerware pieces are sturdy yet lightweight, intricately detailed, lifelike, and flexible, giving rise to the renowned Fuzhou detachable fabric lacquerware. "Detachability" refers to the silk fabric being removed from the clay mold. Their descendants improved upon the single-use clay molds, introducing a single mold for multiple detachments. Shen Zhenggao and Shen Zhengxun, the fourth-generation successors, pioneered the use of gold and silver clay in lacquerware, creating "thin lacquer" by lightly patting the lacquer surface with their palms. Compared to traditional thick lacquer application, the use of thin lacquer greatly saved lacquer usage. It also introduced brilliant colors containing gold and silver, giving lacquerware a subtle and not overly ostentatious glow. This innovation stands as one of the most outstanding

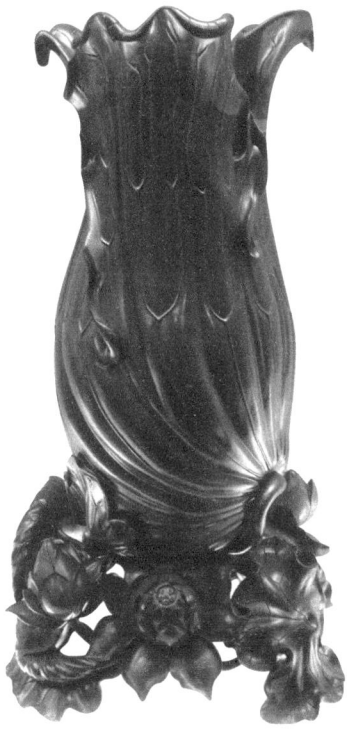

Figure 17.1 [Late Qing] Thin Lacquer Lotus Leaf Vase, made by Shen Zhenggao, photographed by the author at Fujian Museum

achievements in the late Qing Dynasty's lacquer decorative arts history (Figure 17.1). As a result, Fuzhou detachable-fabric lacquerware came to feature a wide array of colors, including delicate yellows and soft greens, forming a local characteristic known for its wide variety of shapes, sturdy yet lightweight construction, bright and vibrant appearance, and the ability to reflect light. The widespread use of thin lacquer patting became common in Fuzhou lacquerware decoration (Figure 17.2).

The rise of Shen lacquerware's reputation coincided with the emergence of international expositions. Starting from 1898, when Shen Zhenggao created the "Lotus Box" and "Tea Box" and won gold medals at the Paris Exposition, Shen lacquerware began to receive numerous accolades at international expositions. For instance, they won the first-class gold medal at the 1904 Saint Louis World's Fair, the first-class commercial honor gold medal at the 1910 Nanyang Industrial Exposition, and numerous awards at exhibitions such as the 1915 Panama–Pacific International Exposition in San Francisco, the 1926 Sesquicentennial Exposition in Philadelphia,

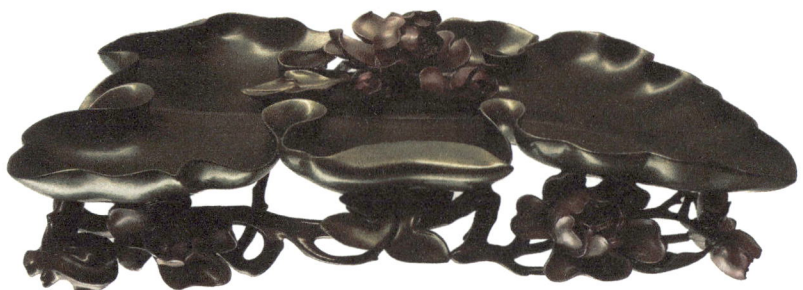

Figure 17.2 [Modern] Thin Lacquer Lotus Leaf Plate with Autumnal Leaves, made by Shen Zhenggao, photographed by the author at the Shanghai Museum

the 1928 Chinese Products Exhibition, the 1929 West Lake Expo, and the 1933 Century of Progress International Exposition in Chicago. As a result, over 40 counterfeit shops emerged in Fuzhou, with names like "Sheng Shao'an," "Xin Shao'an," "Zhen Shao'an," and "Jin Shao'an."

Compared to Shen Shao'an lacquerware, the "Liang Fusheng Lacquerware Works," founded by Yangzhou native Liang Youshan, emerged more recently, spanning four generations. In the seventh year of Tongzhi (1868), they established their business at the Yuanmen Bridge in Yangzhou. The eaves of their store were adorned with a lacquered gold-filled horizontal plaque inscribed with "Liang Fusheng Imitation Antique Lacquerware," indicating their adherence to the traditional lacquerware craftsmanship of Yangzhou. According to the *Minguo Jiangduxian Xuzhi* (*Continued Annals of Jiangdu County of the Republic of China*), "Lacquerware has been a Yangzhou specialty since Lu Kuisheng, with extensive sales. Among the best imitators is Liang Fusheng. The sales of silver coins in various stores in the county amount to about thirty thousand annually, with Liang Fusheng accounting for half of them."[1] Additionally, "Jade-inlaid plaques in various bird and flower shapes are embedded for display, and lacquer boxes adorned with beautiful shells are also available ..."[2] Furthermore, "Lacquered chests are gold-plated or lightly engraved after lacquering, often using wooden molds with fine tile powder work. Lacquer stationery varies in

1. *Shiye Kao* (*Industrial Examination*), vol. 6 of *Minguo Jiangduxian Xuzhi* (*Continuation of Records of Jiangdu County in the Republic of China*), a 1921 edition kept in the Ancient Books Department of the Yangzhou Library, 3.
2. *Wuchan Kao Xia: Xiuwu Zhishu* (*Compendium of Material Resources: Classification of Lacquered Objects*), vol. 7 of *Minguo Jiangduxian Xuzhi* (*Continuation of Records of Jiangdu County in the Republic of China*), a 1921 edition kept in the Ancient Books Department of the Yangzhou Library, 34.

style ... Lacquer tea trays come in various round shapes, including magnolia flower designs, while lacquer table boxes are either round or shaped. Lacquer-inlaid plaques are lacquered or engraved with green landscapes for display ... Liang Fusheng's products have won awards in competitions."[3]

During the Guangxu period, Liang Fusheng lacquerware primarily targeted the domestic market with items such as flowerpots, fruit trays, hat boxes, pen holders, inkstone cases, letter boxes, presentation boxes (see Figure 17.3), assorted carrying cases, and others. A small quantity was presented to the Qing court, with an annual output of around ten thousand pieces. From the early 20th century to the 1930s, during the reign of the third-generation Liang Ticai, the Liang Fusheng brand reached its peak. With the Tianjin-Pukou Railway's opening and the Shanghai port's rise, the products shifted towards export. The range expanded to include carved lacquer, inlaid mother-of-pearl, and treasure-embedded screens. Employing over 200 workers, they shipped out a cargo of lacquer screens every ten days to two weeks, with an annual export volume of 20,000 to 30,000 pieces. Their carved lacquer screens became the main product, often featuring famous calligraphy and paintings as references, with carved patterns, exposed lacquer dust, and sprinkled with shell sand, presenting a refined and elegant simplicity (Figure 17.4).

Liang Fusheng lacquerware capitalized on the opening of the Shanghai port to establish its export channels and gained considerable recognition through participation in exhibitions. Their lacquerware products received numerous awards, including the Gold Medal and Excellence Certificate at the 1910 Nanyang Industrial Exposition, the Second Prize at the 1914 Jiangsu Panama-Pacific International Exposition, the Third Prize at the 1915 Ministry of Agriculture and Commerce National Commodity Exhibition, the First Silver Medal at the 1915 Panama-Pacific International Exposition in San Francisco, the First Prize and Certificate of Excellence at the Jiangsu Provincial Local Cultural Relics Exhibition, and the Third Prize Certificate, among others. However, with the onset of wars, Liang Fusheng Lacquerware faced bankruptcy, and the fifth-generation Liang Shang'an switched to the education sector, ultimately closing the business in 1948.

If Shen Shao'an lacquerware is mostly utilitarian with a touch of civic artistry, Yangzhou's Liang Fusheng lacquerware expanded its products to include exported furniture and garden decorations, thus continuing the literati characteristics of Yangzhou lacquerware. At the 1915 Panama-Pacific International Exposition in San Francisco, two Chinese lacquerware pieces stood out. One was the "Lacquered Water

---

3. Ibid., 37–38.

Buffalo" by Shen Shao'an's Gaoji, a huge creature weighing just two kilograms, easily lifted above the head with one hand, much to the audience's surprise. The other was the "Jade-Embedded Flower Lacquer Bonsai" by Yangzhou's Liang Fusheng, featuring a red lacquer basin adorned with gold, planted with lucky grass in jade and evergreen in jade, radiating with lush greenery and shimmering brightness, with the coral jade fruits shining brilliantly. Both Shen and Liang families' lacquerware was awarded the First Silver Medal. From then on, the legend of "Shen Family in the South and Liang Family in the North" began to spread.

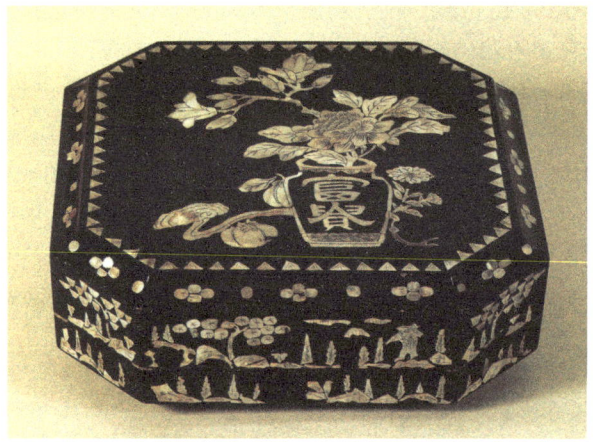

Figure 17.3 [Late Qing] Black Lacquer Inlaid with Mother-of-Pearl Auspicious Octagonal Box, crafted by Liang Fusheng, selected from *Zhongguo Qiqi Quanji: Qing* (*Complete Collection of Chinese Lacquerware: Qing Dynasty*)

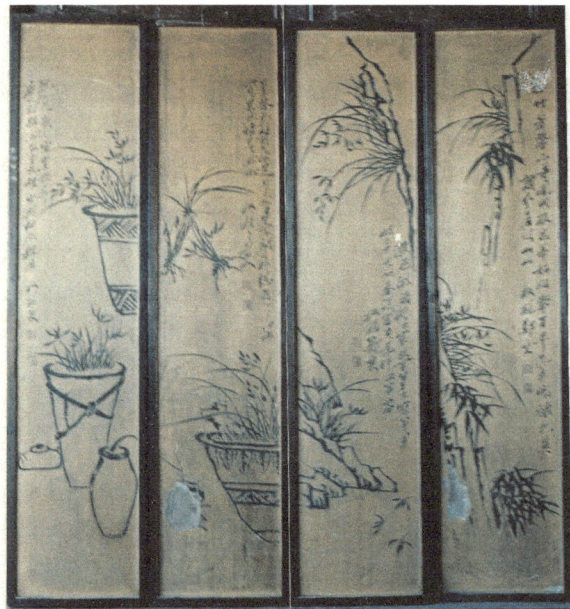

Figure 17.4 [Modern] Painting of Orchids and Bamboo Carved Lacquer Hanging Screen by Zheng Banqiao, selected from *Yangzhou Qiqi Shi* (*History of Yangzhou Lacquerware*) by the author

CHAPTER XVIII

Towards Modernity

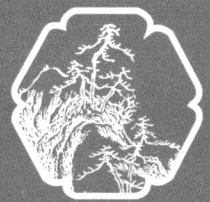

I n modern times, two gentlemen, Mr. Li Zhiqing and Mr. Shen Fuwen, emerged in the Chinese lacquer industry. With modern concepts infused into the lacquer art, they pioneered a craft language capable of depicting contemporary life and conveying modern ideas. They laid the foundation for the transformation of lacquer art into a pure form of artistic expression, both in terms of concept and craftsmanship, leaving behind a lasting legacy that continues to be revered.

Mr. Li Zhiqing (1894–1976) from Fuzhou began his apprenticeship in lacquer art at the Fuzhou Lacquer Art Training Institute during his youth, studying under Lin Hongzeng, a Chinese craftsman, and Harada, a Japanese artisan. In 1924, he followed Harada to continue his studies at the Nagasaki School of Fine Arts and Crafts in Japan. Upon returning to China in 1926, he worked as a lacquer technician at the Hui'er Institute in Fuzhou and later at "Shen Shao'an Lanji." In 1934, his antique-style bronze lacquer pieces depicting "Confucius" and "Yue Fei" were selected to be exhibited and won awards at the Chicago World Expo. In the 1940s, Mr. Li Zhiqing established the Yong'an Overseas Chinese Lacquerware Cooperative. In 1956, he joined the Fuzhou Institute of Arts and Crafts and later became part of the Fuzhou Lacquerware Company (predecessor of the Fuzhou Second Lacquerware Factory). He continued working until his old age.

The main focus of Mr. Li Zhiqing was the traditional Chinese *xiushi* craft, which integrated Japanese lacquer techniques. He creatively explored and invented a series of *xiushi* techniques such as "taihua,"[1] "chenhua"[2] (Figure 18.1), "liuhua,"[3] "fuhua"[4] (Figure 18.2), and "miaohua,"[5] which were collectively referred to as the "Five Golden Flowers" of Fuzhou lacquerware industry. In essence, "taihua," "chenhua," and "fuhua" were derived from the inlay techniques dating back to the Tang Dynasty, while "fuhua" and "miaohua" were recorded in the *Xiushi Lu*. Mr. Li Zhiqing dared to break the

---

1. "Taihua" (台花): "台" or "刣" refers to tin foil peeling, derived from the traditional technique of peeling gold and silver foil. Tin foil is applied and carved on the surface, and after the lacquer solidifies, it is polished to reveal the pattern. Chengdu lacquer workers call it "silver foil carved lacquer."

2. "Chenhua" (沉花): Also known as "yinhua" or "anhua," it evolved from traditional *zhangxiu* and gilding techniques.

3. "Liuhua" (流花): Diluted colored lacquer is applied to wet lacquer, and different lacquer colors are manipulated to create patterns resembling Tang Sancai or Song Dynasty pottery.

4. "Fuhua" (浮花): Developed from the "pile color" technique recorded in *Xiushi Lu*, a mixture of raw lacquer, fish bladder glue, boiled tung oil, fragrant ash, and clam powder is prepared and pressed into molds. After drying, it is removed from the mold, revealing a relief pattern that is then applied to the lacquer surface.

5. "Miaohua" (描花): Derived from the "descriptive" technique recorded in *Xiushi Lu*.

traditional barriers of *xiushi* techniques, flexibly manipulating the crafts. For example, in traditional techniques, transparent lacquer is most susceptible to being worn out. Still, Mr. Li Zhiqing deliberately applied convex textures on the base, using foil powder to cover the transparent lacquer and deliberately wearing it out in certain areas. This technique created a contrast of light and dark in the lacquer surface, resulting in unpredictable texture changes beneath the lacquer, and the combination of gilding, transparent lacquer, and worn-out lacquer became widely used among Chinese lacquer painters. Furthermore, Mr. Li Zhiqing integrated traditional techniques like *zhangxiu* and *xipi* crafting, borrowing from Japanese varnishing techniques, and created a hundred lacquer art samples with intricate variations and unique pathways. These samples resembled the tranquility of a jade pool, the setting sun, mossy patches, crying blood azaleas, morning sun rays, and frosty leaves, displaying ingenious color

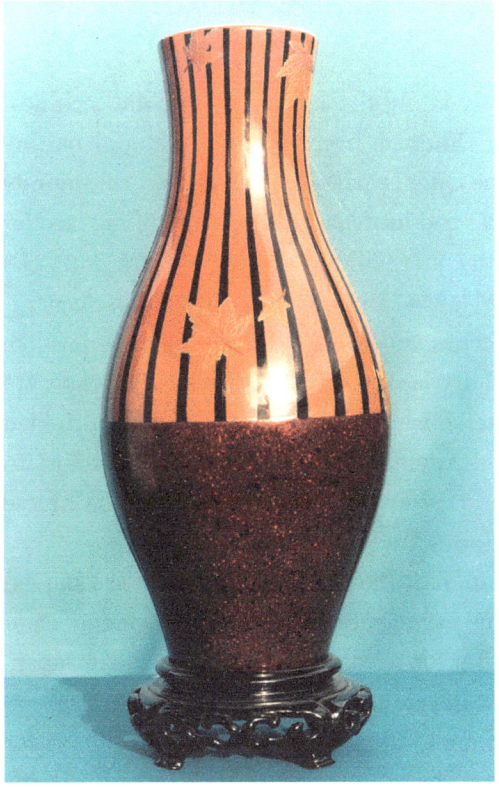

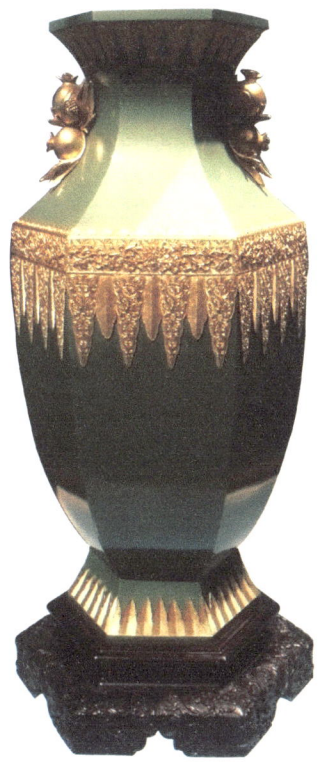

Figure 18.1 [Modern] Lacquer Vase with *Chenhua* Stripes by Mr. Li Zhiqing, provided by Mr. Lin Yinxuan

Figure 18.2 [Modern] Lacquer Vase with *Fuhua* Necklace Patterns by Mr. Li Zhiqing and Mr. Gao Xiuquan, photographed at the Fujian Museum by the author

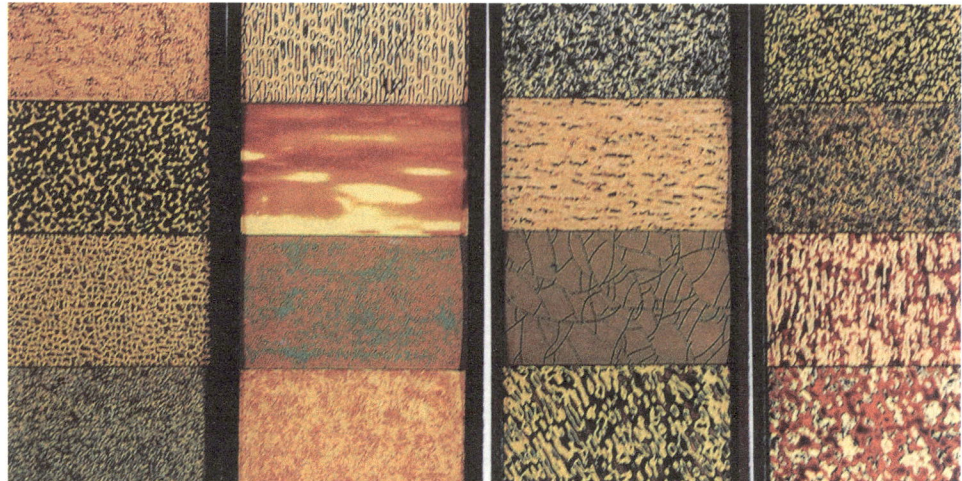

Figure 18.3 [Modern] One Hundred Samples of Thick Lacquer Filling and Inlay, by Mr. Li Zhiqing, selected from *Fujian Gongyi Meishu* (*Fujian Arts and Crafts*)

patterns and ever-changing variations, becoming the most fundamental technical vocabulary of modern lacquer painting. Different from the thin material patting technique created by Shen Zhenghao in the Qing Dynasty, the lacquer art community in Fuzhou refers to Mr. Li Zhiqing's flexible and intricate grinding and filling lacquer technique series as "houxiu tianqi" (thick lacquer filling and inlay) (Figure 18.3). His artworks, such as the "Gushan Landscape" (1956) and the "Wuyi Mountain Scenery" large screen (1959), drew from real-life scenes and were crafted using materials like mother-of-pearl, gold and silver foil, and dry lacquer powder. These artworks were either embedded under transparent lacquer, flush with the lacquer surface, sprinkled on the lacquer surface, or raised above it, demonstrating his conscious effort to transform traditional lacquer art into pure art, drawing inspiration from both Chinese and Japanese lacquer art and Western painting traditions.

Mr. Shen Fuwen (1909–2000), a Fujian native 15 years younger than Li Zhiqing, was expelled from the university due to his participation in student movements and subsequently arrested and imprisoned. After his release, he went into exile in Japan, where he studied lacquer art under the tutelage of the Japanese "Living National Treasure" Matsuda Gonroku. Upon returning to China, he traveled to Dunhuang for inspiration, using his skills in grinding and painting to depict Dunhuang patterns on lacquerware, creating over 100 pieces, including lacquer plates (Figure 18.4) and lacquer bottles. He organized the "Professor Shen Fuwen Dunhuang Pattern Lacquer

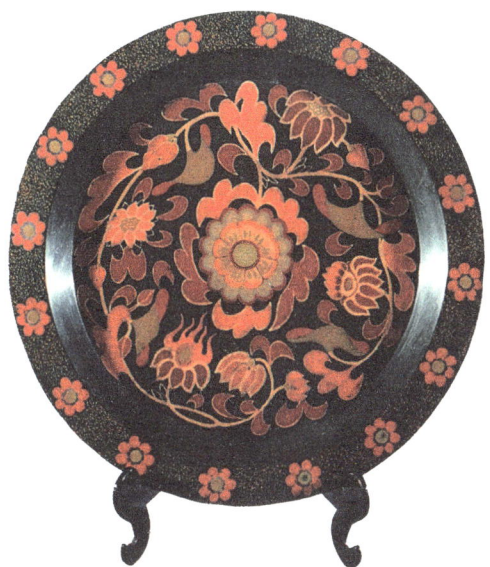

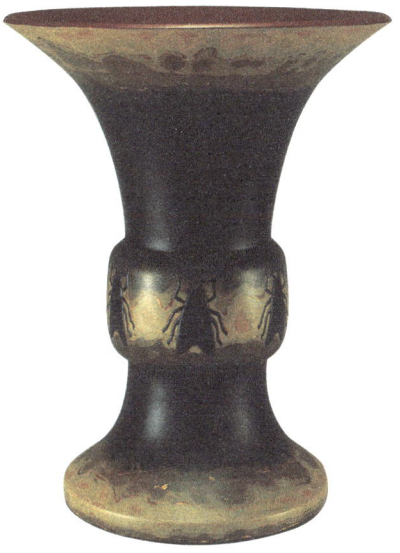

Figure 18.4 [Modern] Lacquered Plate with Painted Dunhuang Patterns Ground and Polished, by and provided by Mr. Shen Fuwen

Figure 18.5 [Modern] Green-Sunk Gold-Piled Lacquer Cicada-Patterned Vase, by and provided by Mr. Shen Fuwen

Art Exhibition," which was praised by prominent figures such as Xu Beihong. Within five years, Mr. Shen held six solo lacquer art exhibitions in Chengdu, Shanghai, Nanjing, Lanzhou, and other cities. In 1939, Mr. Shen participated in the establishment of Sichuan Provincial Art College and later served as the dean of Sichuan Fine Arts Academy. He integrated techniques such as *hira maki-e*, *taka maki-e*,[6] and *shishiai togidashi maki-e* learned in Japan with traditional Chinese *xiushi* crafts. His work "Green-Sunk Gold-Piled Lacquer Cicada-Patterned Vase" (Figure 18.5) featured gold foil sunken beneath green transparent lacquer, shimmering brightly. Using the *taka maki-e* technique he learned in Japan, he created cicada patterns involving over 100 processes, resulting in vibrant and elegant pieces collected by the Beijing Palace Museum. He also promoted the integration of Chinese and Japanese *xiushi* techniques in the academy and later in Sichuan lacquerware enterprises,

---

6. *Taka maki-e*: Using water-soluble polishing powder (similar to China's "floating brick powder") mixed with lacquer, images are gradually built up layer by layer, dried, finely polished, and finished with lacquer or polishing. It is known as "high-lacquer grinding and painting" in the Chongqing lacquer art community.

making lacquer-underneath grinding and painting,[7] flat grinding and painting,[8] and high-lacquer grinding and painting characteristic crafts of Sichuan. At the age of 81, Mr. Shen held a "Shen Fuwen Personal Works Exhibition" in Beijing. His lacquer-underneath grinding and painting "Morning Glow Lacquer Plate," depicting a red sun bursting with light, radiates vibrant hues and profound meanings, showcasing the lacquerware's magnificent and mystical beauty. The flat grinding and painting "Space Plate" depicts a Tai Chi diagram sprinkled with thin spiral sand particles, embodying simplicity and perpetual dynamism. The high-lacquer grinding and painting "Brocaded Carp" features fish scales protruding above the lacquer surface while the fish tail remains hidden beneath, shimmering with red scales.

Mr. Li Zhiqing's "houxiu tianqi" and Mr. Shen Fuwen's "grinding and painting" may be called by different regional names. Still, they both led to the "moxian tianqi" recorded in *Xiushi Lu* of the Ming Dynasty. *Xiushi Lu* mentions five methods of "moxian tianqi": *qiwen tianqi, zhangxiu,* and *xipi,* aiming at revealing the natural texture through polishing while inlaying with mother-of-pearl or gold and silver involving patterns.[9] In other words, in ancient times, the five methods of "moxian tianqi" did not specifically refer to painting. Mr. Li and Mr. Shen were the first to lead the traditional "moxian tianqi" technique towards painting creation. Since then, "moxian tianqi" has become the foundation of modern lacquer painting language. Future lacquer painting creations, when tracing their origins, generally lead to the "moxian tianqi" after the digestion, reference, and advancement by Li and Shen, following the path of traditional Chinese *xiushi* crafts. Mr. Li Zhiqing's "houxiu tianqi" and Mr. Shen Fuwen's "grinding and painting" have become eternal flags waving in the history of modern *xiushi* crafts.

---

7. Lacquer-underneath grinding and painting: Developed from the Ming Dynasty's "moxian Tianqi," it also borrows from Japan's polished painting technique. The difference lies in the application method: grinding and painting under lacquer involves burying the pattern with colored lacquer, waiting for it to dry, then polishing to reveal the pattern, while Japan's technique involves burying the pattern with coarse gold or silver powder, then polishing.

8. Flat grinding and painting: After drawing images on the lacquer surface and waiting for them to dry in a shady room, lacquer is not applied uniformly, nor is the grinding; only the images are polished, dried, dusted, and polished.

9. Chang Bei, *Xiushi Lu and East Asian Lacquer Art* (People's Fine Arts Publishing House, 2014), 126–146.

CHAPTER XIX

Glory of the Era

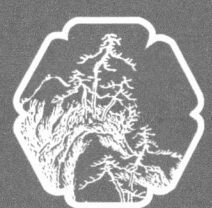

The art of lacquer painting has a long history in ancient China, with particularly imaginative examples found on lacquerware from the Warring States and Qin and Han dynasties. The fundamental difference between ancient and modern lacquer painting lies in the former's association with lacquerware, making it a form of applied art. At the same time, the latter stands as a pure art form independent of vessels. In the late Ming Dynasty, the Jiangnan region produced lacquer screens imitating calligraphy and painting techniques, emphasizing overall decorative effects rather than individual expression of spirit, thus still falling short of being classified as pure art (see Figure 19.1). Today, the distinction between lacquer painting as an applied art and lacquer painting as pure art is often blurred, making it difficult to differentiate between the two. The key difference lies in the purpose: the former is "for others" (manufacturing), while the latter is "for oneself" (personal expression); the former emphasizes material value, while the latter emphasizes spiritual value.

In modern and contemporary times, the influence of Japanese lacquer art, French easel painting, and its creative concepts, as well as Vietnamese lacquer painting techniques and artistic expressions, have all entered China in successive waves of foreign culture, creating external conditions for the birth of modern lacquer painting. However, looking at internal factors, the pioneering figures who led the conceptual breakthrough of lacquer painting from being an applied art to pure art were Mr. Lei Guiyuan and Mr. Pang Xunqin. As mentioned earlier, Mr. Li Zhiqing and Mr. Shen

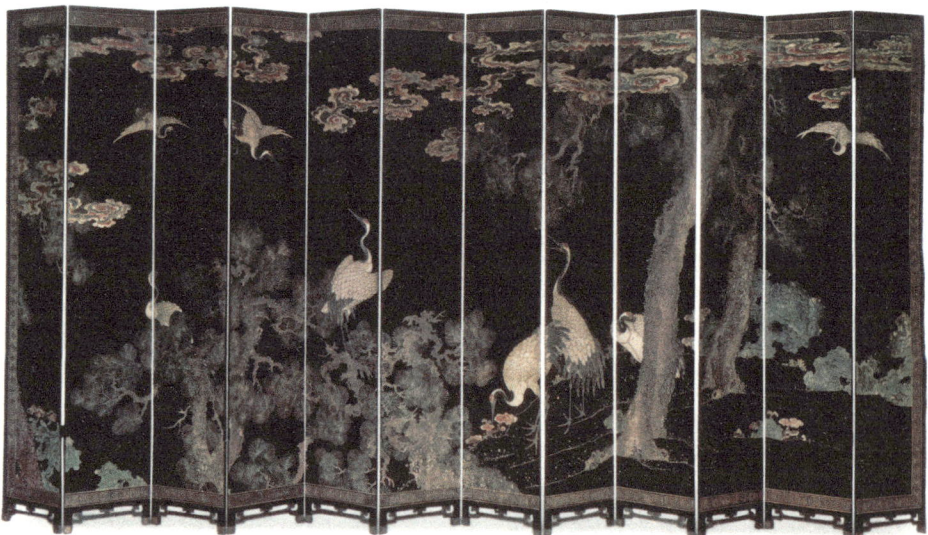

Figure 19.1 [Early Qing] Six-Fold Screen with Colorful "Pine and Crane" Pattern, collection of the Musée Guimet, Paris, provided by *Hushang Magazine*

Fuwen led the linguistic transformation. With the emergence of first-generation lacquer painters like Qiao Shiguang and Wang Heju, modern lacquer painting in China completed its transition to pure art, achieving both formal independence and the establishment of its own system. At the 6th National Art Exhibition in 1984, lacquer painting was recognized and established as an independent genre on par with "oil painting," "printmaking," and "traditional Chinese painting."

Fujian is the birthplace of the authentic method of lacquer painting known as "moxian tianqi." Wang Heju (1936–) came to Fujian after graduating from Sichuan Fine Arts Institute, where he perfectly inherited Shen Fuwen's technique of grinding and painting as well as Li Zhiqing's method of thick lacquer filling and inlaying. He has become the patriarch and benchmark of modern lacquer painting in Fujian.

Qiao Shiguang (1937–2022) from Beijing not only integrated tradition but also embraced diversity and innovation while keeping pace with the times. He conducted research on *xiushi* techniques originating from various regions across the country, consciously establishing a modern lacquer painting rooted in traditional language systems. He creatively invented the technique of covering with aluminum foil powder to create a matte painting surface, transforming black lacquer boards that could not be stained like Dao Lin paper into silver grain boards that could absorb color like Xuan paper. Depending on the powdering technique used, the surface could resemble raw Xuan paper or mature Xuan paper, allowing for versatile rendering and even producing effects similar to ink washes, greatly expanding the depth and space for portraying characters in lacquer painting. In works like *Dai Women Dressing Up* (Figure 19.2), the faces, hands, feet, and banana groves are all painted using lacquer on a rough aluminum powder surface, popularizing the technique of covering with aluminum powder and becoming a common vocabulary in modern lacquer painting. He utilized humble "eggshells" in lacquer painting, giving them the ability to create both real and abstract forms with light and shadow, as demonstrated in *Scenery of Suzhou* (Figure 19.3). He was the first to introduce abstract language into lacquer painting, using techniques like floating lacquer painting to create *Radiation* (1985) and eggshell inlay to create *Sky* (2009). After falling ill, he transitioned between sketches, ink washes, colored ink paintings, and calligraphy, imbuing each with a new "lacquer" style. Works like *Minjiang Colorful Boat* (2009) exhibit the transparency of watercolor, while *Remembering Jiangnan* (2008) portrays sketches on an aluminum powder surface, perfectly capturing the light and breezy atmosphere described in Bai Juyi's *Yi Jiangnan* (*Remembering Jiangnan*). Qiao Shiguang became the most prominent figure and contributor to China's modern lacquer painting scene.

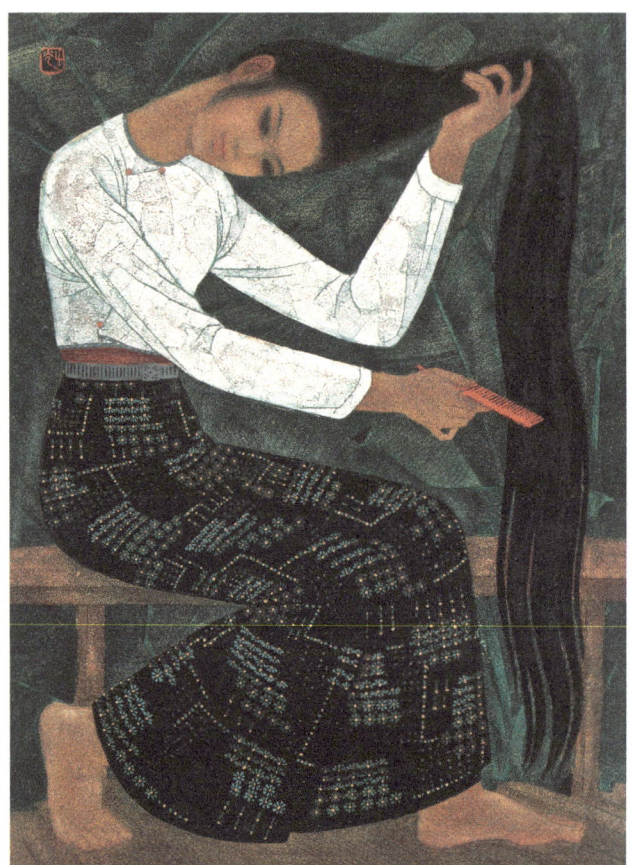

Figure 19.2 [Modern] Lacquer painting *Dai Women Dressing Up* (1978), with Coarse Aluminum Powder Ground, by and provided by Qiao Shiguang

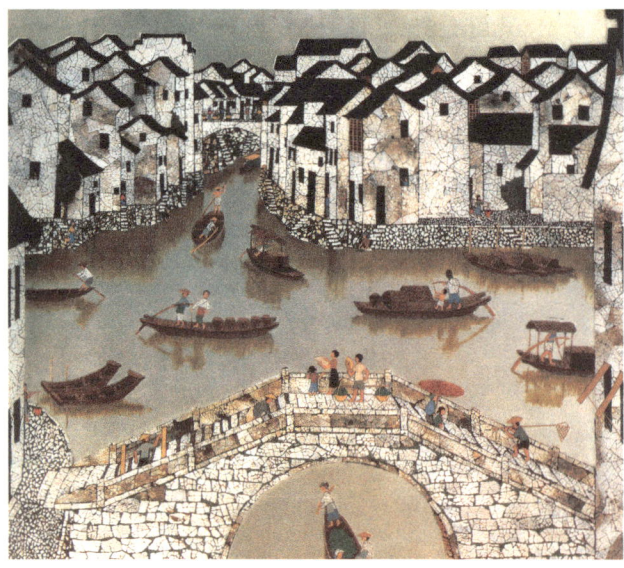

Figure 19.3 [Modern] Lacquer painting *Scenery of Suzhou* (1963), with Inlaid Eggshell, by and provided by Qiao Shiguang

Quanzhou's Chen Lide (1948–) originally started as an oil painter. In the early 1970s, he accidentally encountered lacquer painting and was immediately captivated. As a second-generation lacquer painter, he consciously chose deep realism, making painting a matter of creative awareness and standing out amidst a sea of decorative styles. At the 7th National Art Exhibition in 1989, Chen Lide's *Bright Moon and Red Candles* (Figure 19.4) depicted overseas Chinese elders returning home and reuniting with their families, portraying a world of mixed emotions. This work won him the first national gold medal for lacquer painting at the National Art Exhibition,

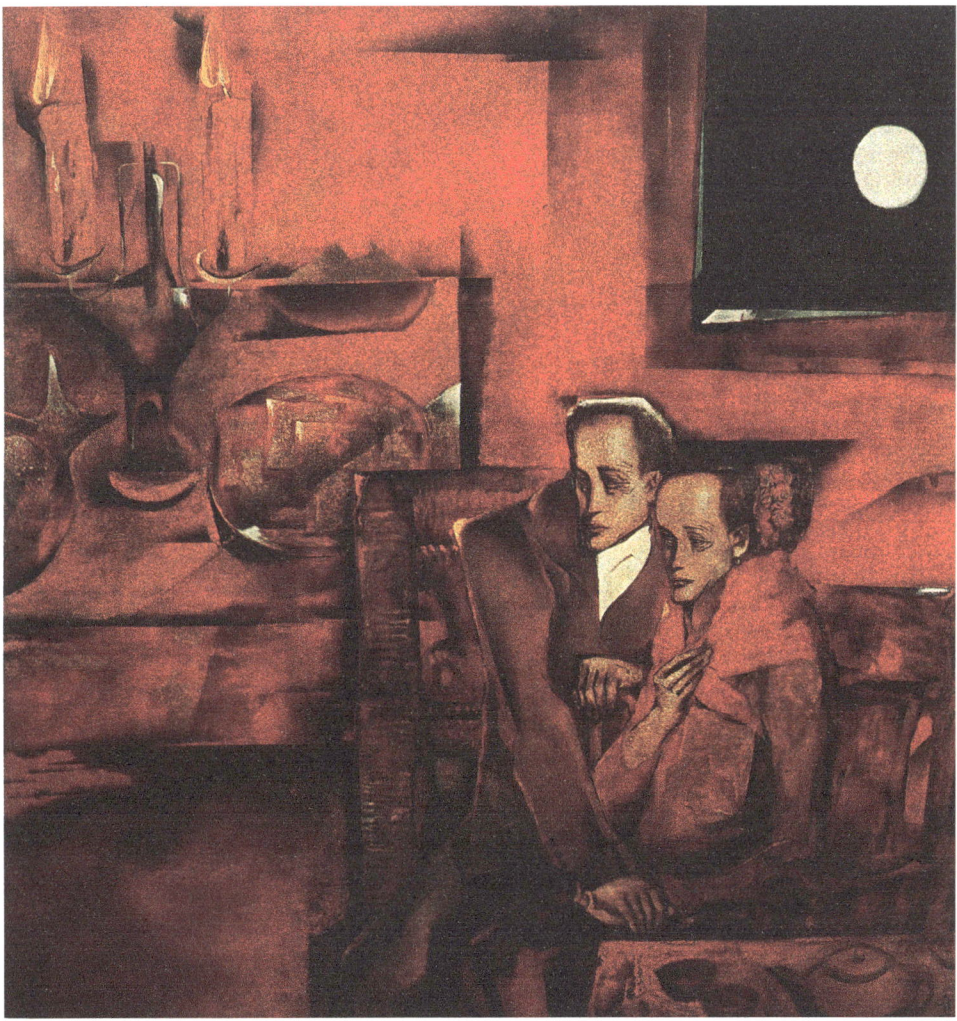

Figure 19.4 [Modern] Lacquer painting *Bright Moon and Red Candles* (1989), by and provided by Chen Lide

setting a precedent for future gold awards at national exhibitions. Despite living in a small town, he excelled at adapting, precisely balancing techniques, and using them appropriately. His *Travel Notes* series depicted his unique visual experiences traveling in Western Europe. In *Travel Notes: Twin Churches* (2011), the subtle gray tones reveal the brushstrokes and light-shadow effects reminiscent of oil painting, while *Travel Notes: Golden Autumn Park* (2011) employs strong contrasts between black and gold to create a magnificent oil-painting-like scene with concise character depictions reminiscent of prints. Leveraging his profound skills in oil painting and immersed in the rich atmosphere of Quanzhou's lacquer craftsmanship, Chen Lide emerged as the most innovative thinker, widest path creator, most outstanding painter, and master of both skilled and restrained lacquer techniques among second-generation lacquer painters.

Fuzhou's Shen Kelong (1964–), as a third-generation lacquer painter, epitomizes the style of a master craftsman in his works—not in terms of physical volume, but in terms of visual intensity. He initially held a solo lacquer painting exhibition titled "Contemplation and Meditation," featuring pieces like *Birth of Buddha* (2012) and the *Avalokitesvara* series (Figure 19.5), which skillfully balanced between presence and absence, perfectly capturing the mysterious and ethereal historical ambiance of the grottoes. Shen Kelong, who is widely traveled and well-read, took another significant stride in 2017 with his exhibition titled "Meteorology" in Beijing. His works featured subdued matte finishes, uneven protrusions, overlapping obstructions, and layers of mist and clouds, evoking a sense of vastness and mystery within the cosmos, embodying the circulation of "*yin* and *yang* energies." Clearly, the themes of Shen Kelong's second solo exhibition have transcended earthly realms, drawing influences not only from Western abstract painting but also from the deep-rooted cosmic consciousness found in traditional Chinese art. In his lacquer painting *Cutting Shadows*, deliberately hung at an angle with nails scattered across the panel, the white wall becomes integrated into the flat segmentation of the artwork, with wall projections becoming part of the composition. Similarly, in *Observing the Wall*, lacquer panels of varying sizes are arranged horizontally and vertically, overlaid and staggered, unfolding like flowing clouds, exuding both brilliance and tranquility. Shen Kelong's creations uphold the tradition of lacquer art while embracing avant-garde aesthetics, drawing insights and reflections from traditional lacquer craftsmanship, yet remaining distinct from the works of both ancient and contemporary artists. Fearlessly delving into the visual impact of materials buried within lacquer artifacts for millennia, he transforms rigid crafting procedures into

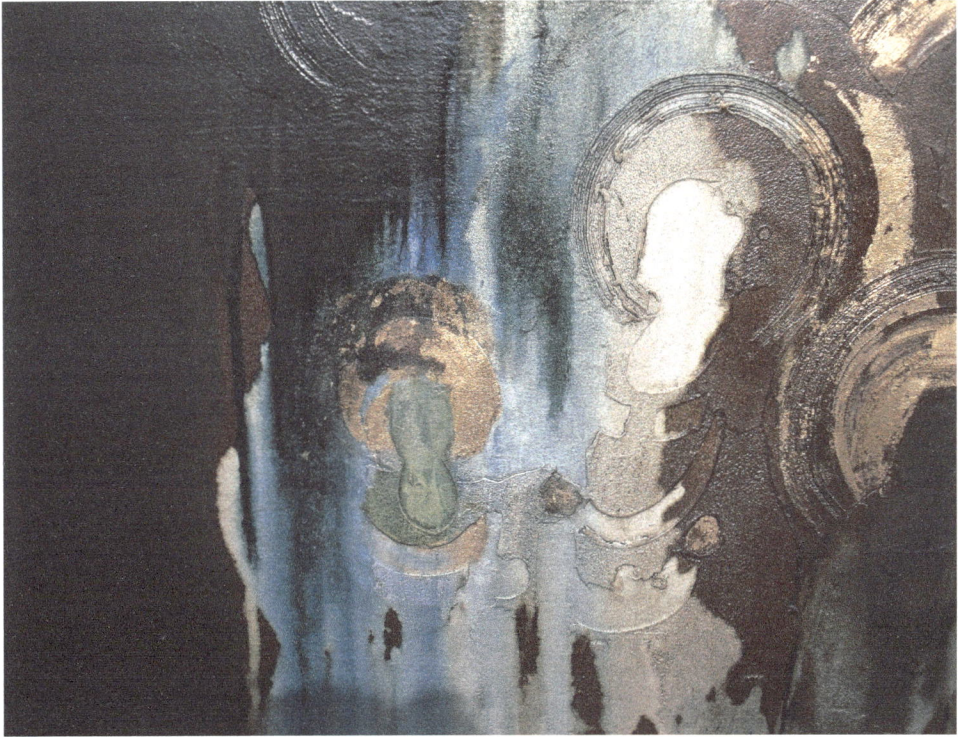

Figure 19.5 [Modern] One of the lacquer painting *Avalokitesvara* series (2012), by and provided by Shen Kelong

dynamic expressions of personality, using the rawest and most authentic natural materials to convey elegance, tranquility, subtlety, and dignity in his art.

Looking back globally, Japan did not develop lacquer painting into an independent art form because the Japanese culture tends to prioritize rationality over sensibility, and the meticulous nature of lacquer painting techniques does not favor the free expression of subjective emotions. Although Vietnamese lacquer painting emerged independently before Chinese lacquer painting, its foundation is relatively shallow, often drawing inspiration from oil painting. In contrast, China's modern lacquer painting possesses a rich indigenous tradition, distinctive national characteristics, and extraordinary inclusiveness and self-renewal capabilities. In terms of depicting depth in social life, conveying subjective emotions, delving into technical connotations, and generating visual impact, lacquer paintings from East Asian countries cannot rival even a fraction of China's modern lacquer paintings. Former President of the Central Academy of Fine Arts, Mr. Zhang Ding, remarked, "Lacquer painting is an art native to the nation, and it is the most gratifying achievement of applying ancient methods to modern aesthetics."[1] As a shining beacon of contemporary Chinese art, China's modern lacquer painting has already illuminated the Chinese art scene and is destined to shine brightly on the world stage.

---

1. Chang Bei, "Xinxin De Huazhong: Qihua (An Emerging Art Form: Lacquer Painting)," *Artist*, no. 9 (1993).

CHAPTER XX

Adhering to Tradition and Innovating

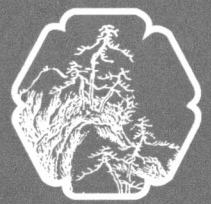

The profound and rich craft system of natural *xiushi* in China has gradually been created and accumulated throughout the long agricultural society. On the one hand, the rapid pace of life in industrial society has led to the rapid disappearance of handcrafted skills characteristic of a slower society; on the other hand, human intellect is always evolving, materials and tools are constantly being updated, and inventions and creations are boundless. With the advancement of the times, some contemporary lacquer artists have skillfully integrated the intelligence and capabilities of the craft, far surpassing the ancients.

For example, as previously mentioned, in traditional Chinese gilt lacquerware, the metal foil powder floating on the surface is not durable, and over time, the patterns become blurred. Since the mid-Ming Dynasty, the technique of "piaoxia," which combines Chinese and Japanese *xiushi* techniques, has been used to create simple symbolic patterns rather than elaborate designs. In contemporary times, Zheng Yikun (1936–) of Fuzhou pioneered the use of metal foil powder covered with transparent lacquer. Mr. Zheng's specialty is painting goldfish. There are numerous lacquer artists who paint goldfish, but Zheng's goldfish are exceptional (Figure 20.1). When painting the goldfish, he layers gold, silver, and aluminum foil powder on the partially dried lacquer, covers it with transparent lacquer, and repeats this process to expand the painting area. After finishing the goldfish and allowing the foil powder to dry, he applies transparent lacquer in layers, waits for it to dry, and finally performs the last polishing. The fish's dorsal fin is visible near the water surface;

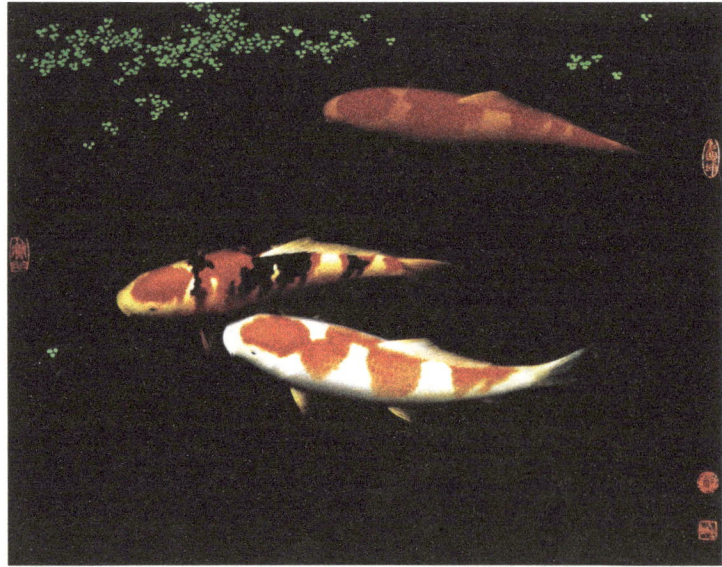

Figure 20.1 [Modern] Lacquer painting *Joyful Fish in Water*, with foil powder ground and polished, by and provided by Zheng Yikun

its gold and silver foil powder should be bright. When starting to paint the fish's dorsal fin, it should be raised and thickened. The fish's belly is hidden deep in the water; the gold and silver foil powder on it should be concealed beneath transparent lacquer. It should be done thinly when starting to paint the fish's belly. The thickness of the fish's dorsal fin, fins, belly, and tail varies. Gradually build up the layers when painting, using overlapping gold and silver foil powder and transparent lacquer. The foil powder includes gold and silver, while the lacquer varies in thickness. Due to the semi-transparency of the lacquer, repeatedly paint, apply foil powder, cover with lacquer, and polish repeatedly. Some foil powder may be exposed, while some may be hidden beneath the lacquer. Finally, polish to achieve the desired sheen. Under the lacquer, there may be red, yellow, white gold, and silver. The fish may be submerged in the "water" or partially exposed on the surface, with its tail or eyes visible. This technique vividly captures the profound imagery of fish swimming in clear water. Upon seeing Zheng Yikun's fish paintings, Mr. Wang Chaowen remarked that Zheng Yikun's fish, hidden under the lacquer, are not immediately visible, jokingly suggesting they are capable of "scaring cats to death." Since then, the elegant title of "Golden Fish Kun" has spread far and wide. Mr. Zheng's mastery lies in the innovative integration of traditional gilt lacquer and traditional inlay techniques in the contemporary era, which is not merely a replication of the Japanese technique. The Japanese technique of shell inlay is expensive, precise, and lacks variation. However, Mr. Zheng, using the wisdom of the Chinese, flexibly employs metal foil powder to create a visual beauty far superior to that of Japanese gold pellet inlay. Before the birth of aluminum foil powder and a wide variety of artificial grinding stones, it was extremely difficult for Chinese craftsmen to create such high-level techniques that repeatedly use metal foil powder, repeat the application of transparent lacquer, and flexibly grind with multiple layers.

Another innovative lacquer artist who successfully integrates traditional crafts is Mr. Cai Shuikuang from Xiamen (1939–2021). As mentioned earlier, during the Song Dynasty, lacquer craftsmen invented the technique of recognizing characters and depicting gold. In the Qing Dynasty, lacquer craftsmen in Fujian and Taiwan used lacquer dough[1] to twist into long threads, which were then wound around Buddha statues as clothing or arranged as sun-pattern designs on vessels. In modern times, lacquer craftsmen in southern Fujian combined the winding lacquer threads with engraving and molding, giving the lacquer sun patterns a sense of "carving,"

---

1. Lacquer dough: A finely textured and malleable mixture of refined lacquer, clear oil, and powdered shells, it is used to build up relief designs or bas-relief images.

becoming a combination of "recognizing characters"[2] and "building up"[3] known as "lacquer thread carving." The 11th-generation descendant of the Cai family of lacquer craftsmen in southern Fujian, Cai Wenpei, relocated the workshop to Xiamen. The 12th-generation descendant, Mr. Cai Shuikuang, was a national-level intangible cultural heritage inheritor. In Mr. Cai Shuikuang's hands, lacquer threads are used in double or single winding; he employs tools such as "dragon scale stamps," "flower bud stamps," and "leaf-shaped stamps" to engrave and mold dragon heads, lion heads, flower petals, and leaves into high relief shapes. Then, lacquer threads are wound around the edges of the high-relief shapes to form dragon scales, floral veins, and leaf veins. Cai Shuikuang also creatively adds gold-colored shadow patterns to the relief patterns using relief engraving. His methods for creating shadow patterns include the "zhengba" (positive method), which involves carving color lacquer on gold foil, and the "jiaba" (negative method), which uses a brush to draw patterns on gold foil, leaving some areas blank to reveal the gold thread underneath, as recorded in *Xiushi Lu · Miaoshi* (*Record of Xiushi: Description of Depiction*). Mr. Cai Wenpei's work "Zheng Chenggong Recaptures Taiwan" features swirling cloud dragon patterns on fluttering flags, which are intricately detailed and breathtaking. Mr. Cai Shuikuang's work "Portrait of Zheng Chenggong" depicts cloud dragon patterns on armor (Figure 20.2), with background clouds as delicate as hair strands and the dragon's eyes and mane bold and powerful. It is evident that the Cai family has integrated various traditional crafts such as "recognizing characters," "building up," "embroidery molding," "chasing gold," and "description" to create the distinctive characteristics of their own works.

Another successful lacquer artist who integrates traditional techniques is Mr. Li Guangzhao (1941–) from Ningbo. The craft of Ningbo, "mud-gold colored lacquer," was recorded in the Ming Dynasty in *Zhejiang Tongzhi* (*Comprehensive Gazetteer of Zhejiang Province*). Dowry items such as lacquer buckets and lacquer baskets were decorated with "recognizing characters and depicting gold" and "hidden gold" techniques, known locally as "fuhua." In modern times, Ningbo mud-gold colored lacquer has been recognized as a "national-level intangible cultural heritage." Li Guangzhao and his predecessors, such as He Yuegui, have derived "stacked lacquer mud-gold and silver colored painting" from Ningbo's "mud-gold colored lacquer." The technique involves using lacquer dough to pile up paintings on lacquer boards

---

2. Recognizing characters: *Yangwen* (positive relief decoration). *Tongya* states, "The inscription is the concave character, and the recognition is the protruding positive relief."

3. Building up: A separate chapter in *Xiushi Lu* refers to building up volumetrically shaped pictures.

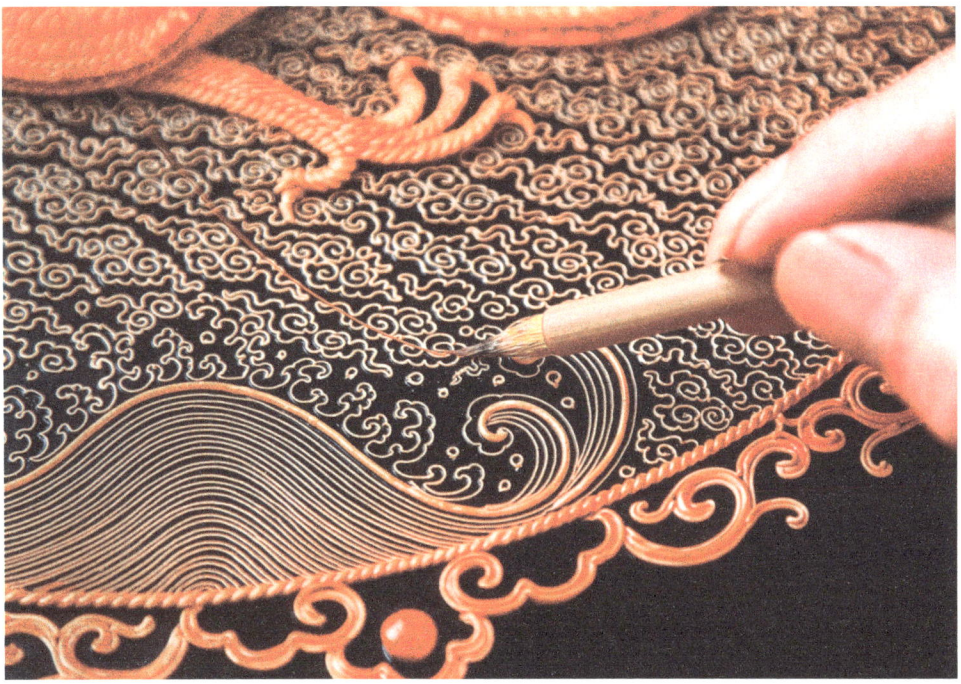

Figure 20.2 [Modern] Cloud dragon pattern on armor in *Portrait of Zheng Chenggong*, by and provided by Cai Shuikuang

that have been completed in the middle. Red and yellow gold foil is ground into gold mud, which is then patted onto the piled-up images with the thumb. Fine lines are brushed in with a wolf hair brush, and after the mud-gold and silver images are completely dry, they are repeatedly carved with a stylus and supplemented with gold. Transparent colors are repeatedly applied to make the gold and silver appear from under the colors. A large hanging screen of stacked lacquer mud-gold and silver-colored paintings requires four people to work for over six months. Traditional mud-gold colored lacquer mostly piled up recognizing characters on utensils, while stacked lacquer mud-gold and silver colored painting piles up images on screens. Traditional mud-gold colored lacquer features rich decoration in red, green, blue, and gold, while stacked lacquer mud-gold and silver colored painting is realistic yet decorative. Traditional mud-gold colored lacquer rarely involves carving, while stacked lacquer mud-gold and silver-colored painting excels in relief carving, adding fine lines and wrinkles to the gold and silver images. Traditional mud-gold colored lacquer is rich in folk flavor. In contrast, stacked lacquer mud-gold and silver colored painting uses "mud gold," "carved gold," "convex-concave gold," and transparent

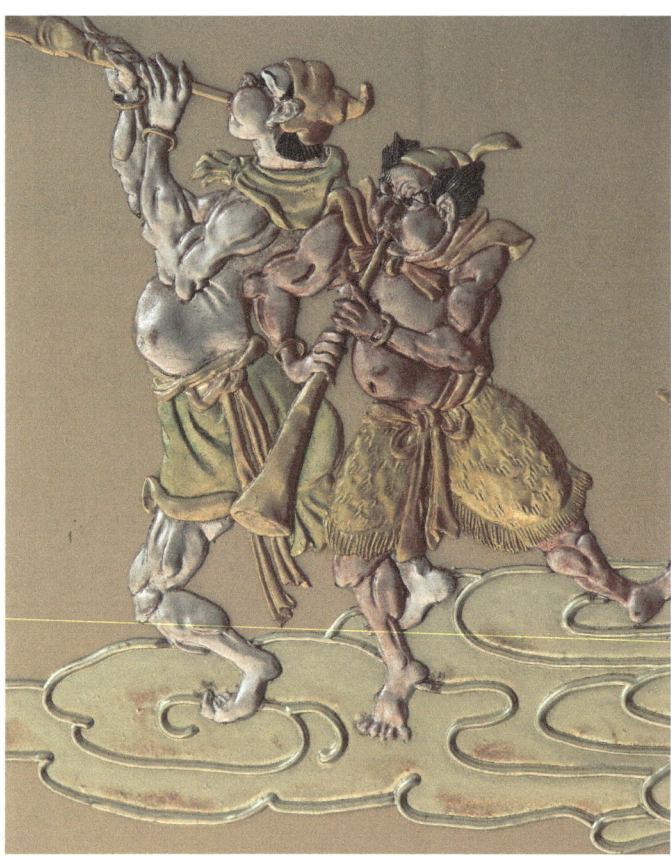

Figure 20.3 [Modern] Partial view of lacquered mud gold and silver painted ground screen *Zhong Kui Marrying off His Sister*, by and provided by Li Guangzhao

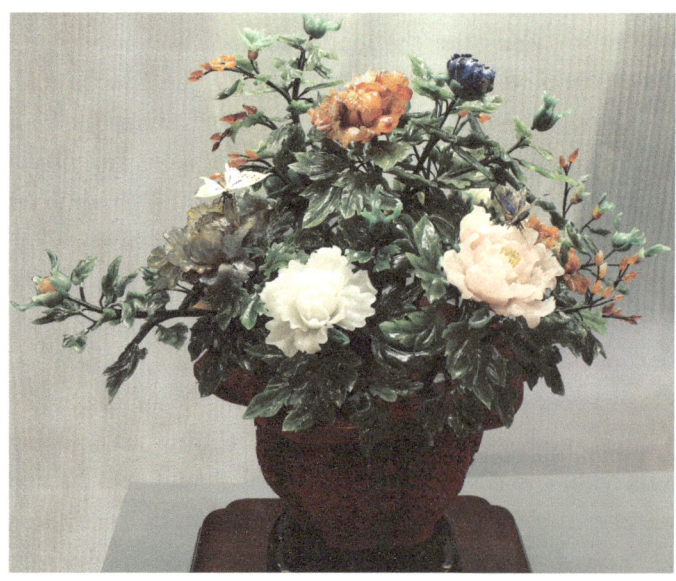

Figure 20.4 [Modern] Jade-wrapped flower carved lacquer bonsai "Splendor among Flowers," by and provided by Kan Fengxiang

colors to create a soft and beautiful scene, greatly expanding the artistic expression capabilities of traditional *xiushi* techniques. Li Guangzhao's hanging screen *Group of Immortals Celebrating Longevity* vividly depicts the characters with the essence of Chen Laolian's brushwork, while the ground screen *Zhong Kui Marrying off His Sister* (Figure 20.3) portrays lively and vivid spirits, eliciting uncontrollable laughter.

Yangzhou's Kan Fengxiang, hailed as a rising star (1959–), is renowned for his active mind and penchant for innovation. Although considered a latecomer, he has been in the art field for over forty years. In ancient times, "jade-wrapped flower lacquer bonsai" involved drilling holes in jade petals and threading them with copper wire, resulting in stiff flower shapes and obvious traces of manual bundling. Kan Fengxiang challenged tradition and sought to surpass it by planning and leading the production of several jade-wrapped flower-carved lacquer bonsai (Figure 20.4): using diamond powder tools to first carve out three-dimensional peony flower cores, followed by carving out gracefully curling petals, with each petal's back leaving a stub to be inserted into the outer layer of petals, allowing each petal to fit closely together. He successfully overcame the difficulties of ancient jade-wrapped flower lacquer bonsai, where jade petals were thick, flower shapes were difficult to fill out, and bundling petals together was challenging. The jade peony branches are full, the flowers delicate, and the leaves lifelike, far surpassing the traditional aesthetic height of jade-wrapped flower-carved lacquer bonsai, earning him awards such as the Golden Award for Lacquer Flower Cup Chinese Lacquer Art Boutique Exhibition. Kan Fengxiang has been honored as a National Master of Arts and Crafts. Without the inspiration from ancient "jade-wrapped flower lacquer bonsai" and the modern updating of tools, Kan Fengxiang's innovative mind would have been at a loss.

The innovators mentioned above have been lifelong adherents to traditional craftsmanship, familiar with the various processes of traditional techniques. They understand both its strengths and weaknesses, thus integrating tradition, transforming it into something new, and highlighting their own creative personalities. It can be seen that the true path of innovation is not to discard tradition as sewage and start anew but to draw from the living waters of tradition. The author refers to such innovation as "upholding tradition and innovating," which is also emphasized in *Xiushi Lu* as "gaining new insights through reviewing old material." Tradition is an ever-flowing river, providing lacquer artists with eternal inspiration for innovation. The new generation should strive to learn from tradition, promote their creative personalities, and adhere to tradition while innovating. Modern people with modern thoughts and intelligence will undoubtedly propel China's modern lacquer art forward in step with the world, ushering in new generations of creativity.

CHAPTER XXI

Return to Green

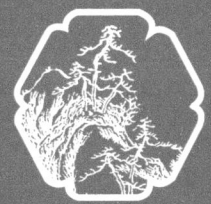

After China's economic transition, people gradually have disposable income, and there has been a resurgence in the love for handicrafts. The domestic art market is more active than at any other time in history. However, it is undeniable that materialism has made people restless, and artisans find it difficult to focus on honing their craft. With the opening of the country's borders, chemical coatings have entered the domestic market, making natural lacquer-coated products increasingly rare. The craft of natural lacquer coating has been pushed to the margins.

China's handicrafts have weathered many storms and finally encountered unprecedented opportunities. In 1997, the UNESCO General Conference adopted the resolution on the *Representative List of the Intangible Cultural Heritage of Humanity*; in 2003, the UNESCO General Conference adopted the *Convention for the Safeguarding of the Intangible Cultural Heritage*. A wave of enthusiasm for protecting intangible cultural heritage has swept across China, with various original lacquer coating crafts entering various levels of the "Intangible Cultural Heritage Protection Lists." The social status of artisans has been greatly improved, and their creative enthusiasm has been unprecedentedly stimulated. People from all walks of life have joined the trend of protecting handicrafts, with various lacquer art training classes being held across the country. The skill of natural lacquer coating has been widely disseminated and deeply rooted in people's hearts, with some techniques becoming more popular than ever before.

Given the precarious foundation of craftsmanship and the unprecedented opportunities in the sales market, the author has long advocated the concept of "green lacquer art," calling on the Chinese people to return to natural materials and handmade crafts consciously and deliberately.[1] Green lacquer art, which encompasses the craft of lacquer coating, represents the true essence of lacquer art. Returning to green lacquer art is not about retrogression but signifies humanity's transition from industrial civilization to a new era of ecological civilization in decorative arts. In the current context, where environmental protection has become a new focus, lacquer artists from various origins are embracing green lacquer art, while chemical lacquer makers are shifting their focus towards learning about it. China's modern lacquer art is returning to a "green" approach from a higher starting point, achieving extraordinary accomplishments that transcend tradition.

The island of Taiwan has prioritized the preservation and innovation of traditional crafts ahead of mainland China. The Taiwan Cultural Heritage Administration has

---

1. Chang Bei, "Lüse Qiyi—Zhongguo Qiyi De Shouwang (Green Lacquer Art—Guardian of Chinese Lacquer Art)," *Art Observation*, no. 11 (2008).

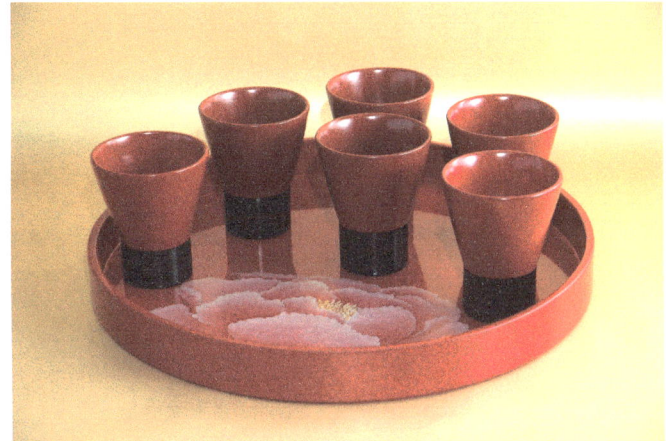

Figure 21.1 [Modern] Red lacquerware tea set for wedding, decorated with powdered gold and painted designs, by and provided by Huang Lishu

appointed only two traditional craft technicians in the lacquerware category: Mr. Wang Qingshuang, who is over a hundred years old (1922–), and Ms. Huang Lishu, who is in her seventies (1949–). Mr. Wang Qingshuang traveled to Japan several times in his early years to study painting and lacquer art. He is renowned for his skill in creating lacquerware and received the Taiwan Crafts Achievement Award in 2007. Ms. Huang Lishu graduated from the Taiwan Arts Specialized School (now Taiwan University of the Arts) in 1972 with a major in arts and crafts. She has visited Japan to study lacquer art more than ten times and conducted research trips to lacquerware companies in Fuzhou, Yangzhou, Chengdu, Beijing, and other places more than ten times. In 1997, she went to the Tokyo National Institute for Cultural Properties to study *maki-e* under Nakasato Toshikatsu. In 1998, she went to the Okinawa Craft Research Institute in Japan to study pile embroidery. Her studies in Japanese and mainland Chinese lacquer art have greatly enriched her skills. She flexibly applies various *xiushi* techniques from China and Japan to create multiple lacquer paintings. She has held several personal exhibitions in Taiwan and exhibited her works worldwide. While pushing her own craftsmanship to high levels, she has also devoted herself to popularizing *xiushi* techniques and integrating lacquerware into modern life (Figure 21.1). She has organized five craft workshop sessions commissioned by the Taiwan Cultural Affairs Department with about fifty to sixty students. Including workshops held before her retirement, she has taught over a hundred students.

As a region with a deep-rooted tradition in lacquerware production, Chengdu in Sichuan Province has a history of *xiushi* craftsmanship spanning over two thousand years. While lacquerware in various original production areas succumbed to the dominance of chemical coatings, the Chengdu Lacquerware Factory continued to

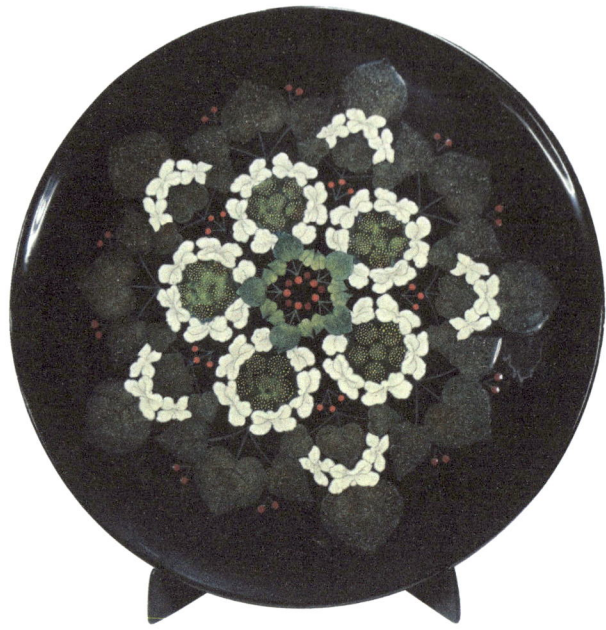

Figure 21.2 [Modern] Black Lacquer Plate with Eggshell Inlay and Powder Sprinkling and Hand-Painted Qionghua Pattern, photographed by the author at Chengdu Lacquerware Factory

use natural lacquer for lacquer decoration and remained committed to local traditional craftsmanship. "Adherence" here refers to the commitment to local traditional craftsmanship and the use of natural materials rather than adherence to outdated functions or aesthetic tastes. Yin Liping (1953–), a representative inheritor of Chengdu lacquer art, designated as a national-level intangible cultural heritage, embodies this commitment. She began her apprenticeship at the Chengdu Lacquerware Factory in 1975. She pursued further studies in lacquerware design at the Sichuan Fine Arts Institute in 1980 and 1984, as well as in decorative painting at the Central Academy of Arts and Crafts. With 47 years of experience in the field, her works, such as "Zhu Lacquer Box with Relief Plum Blossom and Bamboo Leaf Pattern with Tin Plate," "Zhu Lacquer Cong-Shaped Vase with Relief Plum Blossom Pattern with Tin Plate," and "Black Lacquer Plate with Eggshell Inlay and Powder Sprinkling and Hand-Painted Qionghua Pattern" (Figure 21.2), skillfully employ Chengdu's local characteristic *xiushi* techniques. Many of her pieces are housed in the Treasure Hall of the China Arts and Crafts Museum. Recognized as an advanced individual in the national intangible cultural heritage protection, she has been sent to France, Turkey, South Korea, Japan, and other countries for cultural exchanges. Upon her return, she incorporated techniques such as *maki-e* and variable coating into her creations. Her new work, the "Portable Lacquer Tea Set 'Qingfeng'" consisting of eight pieces, including an outer box, teacups, kung fu cups, tea tray, and teapot, features tin-plated leaves gently diffused with transparent lacquer, partially adorned with gold powder and inlaid with mother-of-pearl, highlighting the cool atmosphere of tea leaves floating in the water.

Pingyao in Shanxi is also a region in China with its own rich lacquerware heritage. Xue Xiaodong (1962–), a lacquer artist, is the eldest son of the Chinese master craftsman Xue Shengjin. He graduated from the Fujian College of Arts and Crafts in 1987 and pursued further studies in the art specialty at the Central Academy of Arts and Crafts. Subsequently, he conducted investigations in various domestic and foreign locations, returning to Pingyao in 2001 to oversee the Xue Shengjin Studio. In contrast to the older generation's emphasis on traditional skills, Xue Xiaodong places greater importance on openness and integration. He recognized the former renown of Pingyao's dry-color lacquerware, now obscured in modern times, and dedicated himself to restoring traditional craftsmanship. His work "Dry-Color Lacquer Box with *Maki-e*" (Figure 21.3) features bird feathers crafted in dry-color technique, with small sections of the box lid carved out to apply gold powder *maki-e*, echoing the gold powder lacquer painting on the peacock feathers. The use of black, white, and gold creates a simple and lively aesthetic imbued with a modern sensibility and forward-thinking consciousness. His lacquer painting "Homeland" exhibits the beauty of printmaking with black lacquer and white eggshells, selected for the Ninth National Art Exhibition. The lacquer box "Soaring" is housed in the National Museum. Xue Xiaodong has become a young master of arts and crafts in China, continuing the family legacy of excellence, with two generations of masters becoming a celebrated story within the industry.

Times are always moving forward. Nowadays, masters and inheritors are often no longer content with simply inheriting their family trade. They are no longer willing to adhere to what *Xiushi Lu* criticizes as "keeping one's skill to oneself," which refers to the arrogance of keeping one's expertise secret and not passing it on to others. Instead, they are rooted in research institutions or enterprises, attending professional training, expanding their horizons within and outside their provinces, and even beyond their countries' borders. As a result, they can truly understand, respect, and creatively utilize tradition, drawing nourishment from it to shape their own creative personalities. With people's growing ecological awareness, more and more individuals realize that natural lacquerware can last for centuries, while chemical coatings pose risks to both practitioners and users. Consequently, they

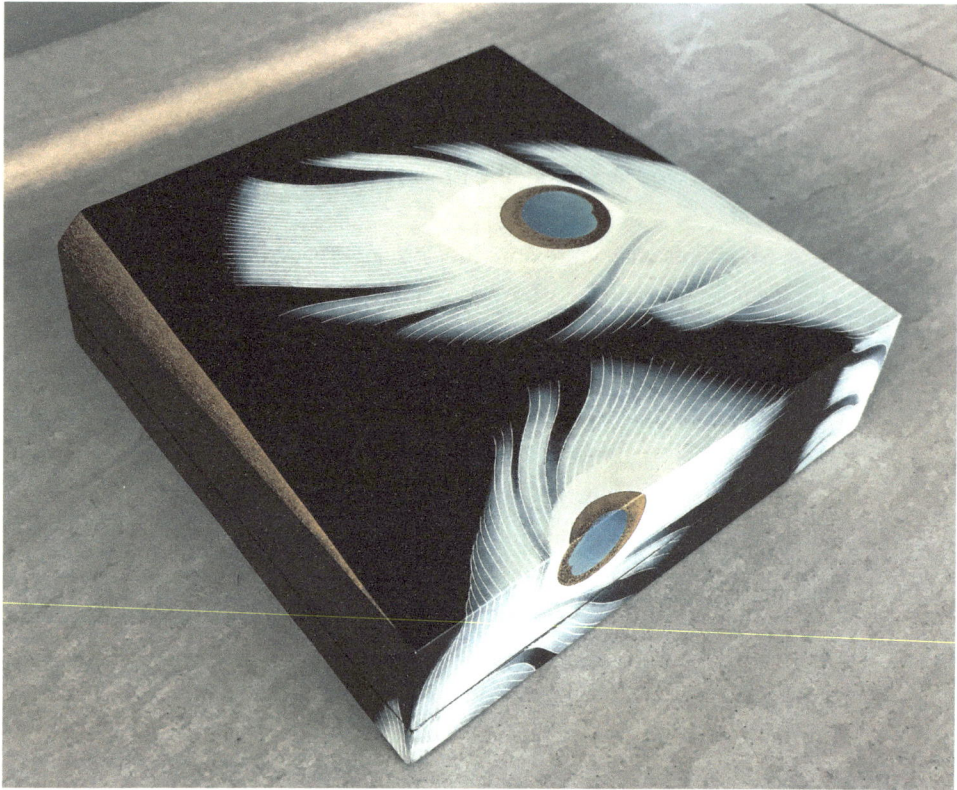

Figure 21.3 [Modern] Dry-Color Lacquer Box with *Maki-e*, by and provided by Xue Xiaodong

consciously choose natural lacquer artworks and distance themselves from mass-produced chemical coatings. China's natural *xiushi* craft doesn't necessarily have to adhere strictly to ancient traditions. Influences from the East and the West have nurtured individuals who contribute to the evolution of China's natural *xiushi* craft.

The Beauty of *Xiushi*

In the brief span of the preceding text, the author and readers have traversed the eight-millennia journey of Chinese *xiushi* craftsmanship together. In the long agricultural era, ancient Chinese, guided by poetry and education, delved deeply into the art of *xiushi*—a quiet, intricate, and emotionally rich art form. They harmonized with the natural elements, utilized natural materials, employed skilled craftsmanship, and fully maximized the decorative potential of natural lacquer. As a result, lacquerware adorned with natural lacquer exudes unparalleled inclusiveness and expressive power. The lacquered wares, with their modest yet warm beauty and reserved yet mysterious aura, symbolize the gentle and sincere temperament of ancient Chinese. The profound and dignified color tones and the refined aesthetic tastes of Chinese lacquerware have profoundly influenced the formation of solemn, profound, and reserved color tones and the refined aesthetic taste emphasizing careful examination and appreciation, not only in the East but also in the West. The influence of Chinese lacquerware decoration styles can be observed in Western Baroque and Rococo furniture and interior wall decorations from the late 17th to the 18th century, where extensive use of *xiushi* techniques was evident, showcasing the impact of late Ming and early Qing Chinese lacquerware decorative styles.

Through a simple tour of the history of Chinese *xiushi* craftsmanship, one can see that the understanding and mastery of natural lacquer by the ancient Chinese were gradual processes. It was during the deepening understanding of natural lacquer and the continual discovery and invention of new materials and tools that the craft of natural *xiushi* underwent constant renewal and innovation. The innovation and creation seen worldwide serve as external forces driving the continual renewal of Chinese *xiushi* craftsmanship, while the improvement of artisan cultural cultivation and the broadening of artistic perspectives serve as internal forces propelling its continual renewal. Chinese *xiushi* craftsmanship is still in the process of continuous renewal.

Since the Industrial Revolution, despite the convenience and expediency of chemical coatings, the aesthetic appeal of natural *xiushi* remains beyond the reach of chemical coatings. Chemical coatings are mostly used for protective purposes, while natural lacquer is predominantly employed in the adornment of artistic pieces. In modern times, apart from its traditional uses in lacquerware, lacquer painting, and the restoration of ancient buildings, natural lacquer is also utilized in cutting-edge scientific research endeavors such as transportation and national defense due to its impact resistance, resistance to certain levels of illumination, anti-corrosion properties, insulation capabilities, anti-marine biofouling, and resistance to atomic radiation. The future of natural *xiushi* craftsmanship is promising. There is reason to believe that the Chinese people, driven by a desire to cherish life and protect the environment, will value and develop lacquer resources, prioritize and cherish natural lacquer artworks, and collectively advance *xiushi* craftsmanship towards a return to green craftsmanship. Chinese *xiushi* craftsmanship will bring new glory to China and serve as a benchmark for traditional crafts to enter modern life and convey modern aesthetics.

Bibliography

Art Museum, Chinese University of Hong Kong. *Two Thousand Years of Chinese Lacquer Art*. Hong Kong: Chinese University of Hong Kong Gallery, 1993.

Beijing Palace Museum. *Carved Lacquerware in the Palace Museum*. Beijing: Cultural Relics Publishing House, 1985.

Chang, Bei. *Analysis of Xiushi Lu*. Nanjing: Jiangsu Phoenix Fine Arts Publishing House, 2017.

———. *Chang Bei's Lacquer Art Notes*. Nanjing: Jiangsu Phoenix Fine Arts Publishing House, 2018.

———. *Chinese Handicrafts: Lacquer Art*. Zhengzhou: Elephant Publishing House, 2010.

———. *Collection of Traditional Chinese Crafts: Natural Lacquer Decoration Volume*. Beijing: China Science and Technology Publishing House, 2018.

———. *Complete Collection of Chinese Arts and Crafts: Jiangsu Volume—Lacquer Art*. Beijing: People's Fine Arts Publishing House, 2020.

———. *History of Yangzhou Lacquerware*. Rev. ed. Nanjing: Jiangsu People's Publishing House, 2017.

———. "The Historical Progress and Current Dilemmas of Modern Chinese Lacquer Painting." *Art*, no. 4 (2017).

———. *Illustrations and Discussions on Xiushi Lu*. Rev. ed. Jinan: Shandong Pictorial Publishing House, 2021.

———. *Xiushi Lu and East Asian Lacquer Art: A Study on Traditional Lacquer Decoration Craft System*. Beijing: People's Fine Arts Publishing House, 2014.

Editorial Committee. *Chinese Art and Craftsmanship through the Ages*. Beijing: Cultural Relics Publishing House, 1994.

———. *Complete Collection of Chinese Art: Complete Collection of Chinese Lacquerware*. Fuzhou: Fujian Fine Arts Publishing House, 1993–1998.

———. *Complete Collection of Modern Chinese Art: Lacquerware*. Shijiazhuang: Hebei Fine Arts Publishing House, 1998.

Lee, Jonghyun. *The Beauty of Chinese Lacquerware*. Seoul: Bukchon Museum of Art, 2007.

———. *East Asian Lacquer Art*. Seoul: Bukchon Museum of Art, 2008.

Li, Jiufang. *Treasures of the Palace Museum's Collection: Qing Dynasty Lacquerware*. Shanghai: Shanghai Science and Technology Press, 2006.

National Palace Museum. *Overseas Treasures: Lacquerware*. Taipei: National Palace Museum, 1987.

———. *Radiance and Refinement—Lacquerware in the Collection of the National Palace Museum, Taipei*. Taipei: National Palace Museum, 2008.

Nezu Museum. *Beauty of the Song and Yuan Dynasties: Focusing on Transmitted Lacquerware*. Tokyo: Nezu Museum, 2004.

Qu, Zhiren. *East Asian Lacquerware*. New York: Metropolitan Museum of Art, 1991.

Shen, Fuwen. *History of Chinese Lacquer Art*. Beijing: People's Fine Arts Publishing House, 1992.

Shoto Museum of Art. *Chinese Lacquer Art*. Tokyo: Shoto Museum of Art, 1991.

Suo, Yuming. *A Collection of Five Thousand Years of Chinese Cultural Relics: Lacquerware*. Taipei: National Palace Museum, 1984.

———. *Research Collection on Chinese Lacquer Art*. Taipei: National Palace Museum, 1977.

Wang, Shixiang. *Ancient Chinese Lacquerware*. Beijing: Cultural Relics Publishing House, 1987.

Xia, Gengqi. *Treasures of the Palace Museum's Collection: Yuan and Ming Lacquerware*. Shanghai: Shanghai Science and Technology Press, 2006.

Zhang, Yan. "Lacquer Art in Twentieth-Century China." *Literature and Art Studies*, no. 3 (1997).

———. "Spring and Autumn of Lacquer Art." In *Miscellaneous Discussions on Chinese Culture: Art and Culture Volume*, edited by Gu Yun and Teng Zhencai, 207–230. Beijing: Beijing Yanshan Publishing House, 1997.

HUA JUEMING, a researcher and former associate director of the Institute for the History of Natural Sciences at the Chinese Academy of Sciences, is a renowned expert in the history of science and technology in China. His main research areas include ancient bronze metallurgy, steel technology, the history of machinery, and the philosophy of technology. In recent years, he has been devoted to the research and preservation of traditional crafts. He is the author of several works, including *Essays on the History of Chinese Metallurgy, Ancient Chinese Metal Technology, Five Thousand Years of Chinese Science and Technology,* and *Ancient Chinese Metal Technology.*

FENG LISHENG, a researcher and director of the Institute for the History of Science and Ancient Documents at Tsinghua University, is mainly engaged in research on the history of mathematics in China and abroad, the history of Chinese machinery, the history of metrology, the history of physics, and the history of science and technology among Chinese ethnic minorities. He is the author of works such as *The History of Ancient Chinese Surveying* and *The History of Sino-Japanese Mathematical Relations.*

ABOUT THE AUTHOR

CHANG BEI, originally named Zhang Yan, was born in 1944 in Yangzhou. She is a professor at the School of Art, Southeast University, holding a master's degree in literature. Her research focuses on art history and aesthetics, with a particular focus on folk art and crafts. She has published several monographs, including *Outline of Chinese Art History, Chinese Handicrafts: Art of Lacquer, Chinese Lacquerware* (Korean edition), and *A History of Yangzhou Lacquerware*, among others.

ABOUT THE TRANSLATORS

CHEN WEI: PhD, English professor of Jiangnan University, Wuxi, Jiangsu Province, PRC.

PAN MENGJIE: MA candidate of Jiangnan University, Wuxi, Jiangsu Province, PRC.